Stepping Up to ISO 9004:2000

Also Available from Paton Press LLC

The Corrective Action Handbook
Denise Robitaille

Customer Satisfaction: Tools, Techniques, and Formulas for Success
Craig Cochran

How to Audit ISO 9001:2000: A Handbook for Auditors
Chad Kymal

Internal Quality Auditing: Meeting the Challenges of ISO 9000:2000
William A. Stimson

ISO 9000:2000 In a Nutshell, Second Edition
Jeanne Ketola and Kathy Roberts

ISO 9001:2000 Management Responsibility In a Nutshell
Jeanne Ketola and Kathy Roberts

The Management Review Handbook
Denise Robitaille

The Preventive Action Handbook
Denise Robitaille

To request a free catalog of Paton Press LLC publications or to order any of our titles, call
(530) 342-5480 or visit *www.patonpress.com.*

Stepping Up to ISO 9004:2000

A Practical Guide for Creating a World-Class Organization

Russell T. Westcott

Paton Press LLC
Chico, California

Most Paton Press LLC books are available at quantity discounts when purchased in bulk. For more information, contact:
Paton Press LLC
PO Box 44
Chico, CA 95927-0044
Telephone: (530) 342-5480
Fax: (530) 342-5471
E-mail: *books@patonpress.com*
Web: *www.patonpress.com*

07 06 05 04 03   5 4 3 2 1

ISBN 0-9713231-7-8

CONTENTS

LIST OF FIGURES AND TABLES

ACKNOWLEDGMENTS

I thank Jim Mroz, senior editor of *The Informed Outlook*, for his many helpful suggestions and careful editing of much of the material contained in this book.

Thanks also to my fellow volunteers on the PSI ISO 9004 subteam No. 6 for their continuing insights as we work toward increasing the usage of ISO 9004.*

Further, I'd like to acknowledge the inspiration, guidance, and continual improvement suggestions provided by my colleague, co-editor (on another book project), business mentor, and good friend, Duke Okes.

My special thanks to Jeanne Westcott, my wife and chief supporter for 54 years, for putting up with my work schedule and behavior as deadlines approach.

*The U.S. Technical Advisory Group (TAG) to ISO Technical Committee (TC) 176 established a Product Support Initiative (PSI) task group as a means of obtaining feedback from users of the ISO 9000 series standards. This initiative is to provide guidance for future revisions of ISO 9001 and also factual information to assist organizations implementing the ISO 9001:2000 and ISO 9004:2000 standards.

The PSI ISO 9004 subteam No. 6 is responsible for establishing communication channels and products for feedback and awareness of the ANSI/ISO/ASQ Q9004-2000. The committee is responsible for ensuring that standard users and potential users are aware of the advantages and uses of ISO 9004 and for soliciting input for continual improvement. As of January 2003, this subcommittee consists of the following volunteer members: Art Gold; Joseph Green; Karen Hitchcock; Sandford Liebesman, Ph.D.; Robert Peach; Art Ramos; J.P. Russell; Russ Westcott; and Larry Wilson.

NOTE TO READERS

The chapters in this book can be read in any sequence; however, there's a logical reason for the lineup, so you might want to scan them in the order presented, and then decide which chapters to read in depth and in which order.

Many of the topics presented here have been addressed in other books and magazine articles. This book is intended to summarize those topics and stimulate the reader to do additional research.

ISO 9004:2000 contains much information and guidance on the topics it covers. For this reason, you'll find instances in this book where a number and title appear in brackets; they refer to a clause or subclause of ISO 9004 that's the source of discussion. Readers are encouraged to keep a copy of *ISO 9004:2000, Quality management systems—Guidelines for performance improvements* close at hand and refer to it while considering the concepts in the following chapters.

Many of the chapters' contents have been adapted from articles published in *The Informed Outlook*[1] from December 1999 to early 2003, as well as from white papers prepared by the author for his clients.

I offer no apology for using the term "Total Quality Management." Despite hundreds of articles, and even some books, taking aim at TQM as a failure, the fact remains: If TQM is done right, it works!

H. James Harrington titled a brief article, "If TQM is Dead, Its Blood Stains the Hands of Those Who Implemented It Poorly."[2]

Scott Paton, in an address at the Connecticut Quality Council's October 1994 conference, reiterated his reminder from his April 1994 *Quality Digest* article that "TQM is a philosophy, not a science."[3]

More recently, Richard J. Schonberger stated that TQM "is a way of thinking about how you run your business."[4] He affirms that TQM's primary emphasis on taking care of the customer, striving to continually improve quality, using statistically based analyses of processes, and working in collaborative, multiskilled teams is completely valid.

I think I'm in good company in perpetuating the TQM philosophy, regardless of what name it's called or what the critics write. TQM was never intended to be a static approach, although some purveyors of the lore would have you believe it comprises a given set of techniques and tools. Like it or not, TQM remains in my quality management kit.

1. *The Informed Outlook* is co-published monthly by the American Society for Quality and INFORM
2. Harrington, H. James. "If TQM is Dead…" *Quality Digest*, September 1999, p. 18.
3. Paton, Scott M. "Is TQM Dead?," *Quality Digest*, April 1994, pp. 24-30.
4. Schonberger, Richard J. *Let's Fix It: Overcoming the Crisis in Manufacturing*. New York: The Free Press, 2001.

PREFACE

This book is intended to stimulate those organizations where management hasn't yet taken advantage of the benefits derived from developing and implementing an ISO 9001/9004-based quality management system.

Reportedly, more than 500,000 ISO 9001/2/3:1994 and ISO 9001:2000 certificates exist in the business world today. These quality management systems (QMSs) range from minimalist systems that barely satisfy the standard's requirements to comprehensive systems that treat every organizational activity as a quality process. For those organizations that view upgrading their quality systems or implementing brand-new QMSs simply as a means of conforming with *ISO 9001:2000, Quality management systems—Requirements* read no further. Note, however, that these companies shouldn't expect to get their money's worth from their QMSs or registrations.

Granted, ISO 9001:2000 requires an organization to have a QMS rather than a simple quality assurance system. It also requires management to take greater responsibility for, and play a more active role in, the QMS. Nevertheless, ISO 9001:2000 remains a set of minimal, generic requirements that any organization should be able to satisfy. Not every organization has jumped at the opportunity to implement an ISO 9001/9004-based QMS, and those that haven't are missing some powerful benefits.

In today's competitive marketplace, "quality management" means the set of concepts, techniques, and tools that any organization can apply to its processes to better satisfy the customer, reduce waste and nonconforming product, and improve its operations. A truly comprehensive and effective QMS allows an organization to work more efficiently and will lead to actual improvements in its products and services. In a very real sense, a good QMS makes everyone, even employees, more satisfied customers of the organization. Your organization can accomplish this while satisfying ISO 9001:2000 requirements.

You might ask, "Where will my organization get the guidance it needs to pursue a comprehensive QMS that goes above and beyond the basic requirements of ISO 9001:2000?" After all, your organization is like no other and therefore can only benefit from a QMS that suits its particular operations, activities, and response to satisfying customer requirements. *ISO 9004:2000, Quality management systems—Guidelines for performance improvements* is an excellent guide. It can assist your organization in considering which elements your QMS should contain and which should be implemented to support your processes and organizational culture. Understanding what ISO 9004 contains and how it can be used will enhance the value it can provide.

It's unlikely that many—or perhaps any—organizations will implement a QMS that satisfies every suggestion in ISO 9004, nor should they. But by exploring new key concepts and describing techniques for stepping up to ISO 9004, this book will outline the means by which your organization can build toward excellence.

Remember: ISO 9004:2000 isn't a guideline for implementing ISO 9001:2000, although it can—and should—be used to implement a QMS that will satisfy ISO 9001 requirements. ISO 9004 has far more to offer organizations that already have functioning QMSs and want to improve system performance.

Although the information in these chapters is useful for any organization, it's written for quality professionals whose companies have an ISO 9001/2/3:1994- or ISO 9001:2000-conforming or registered QMS in place (or are well on the way to meeting ISO 9001:2000 requirements). This book focuses on raising an organization's business processes from minimum-requirements to best-practices level—and ultimately to world-class status—rather than on addressing deficiencies in meeting basic requirements. This approach can bring your organization closer to the Malcolm Baldrige National Quality Award criteria, which determines success in terms of results achieved.

Although this book encourages you to adopt ISO 9004's guidelines when implementing or enhancing your QMS, no attempt is made to consider every suggestion contained within those guidelines. Instead, some of the more useful tools and techniques are addressed as well as a few ideas drawn from implementation experiences.

Opportunity knocks; just open the door and come on in.

—*Russ Westcott*
June 1, 2003

CHAPTER 1

Setting Strategic Direction
and Implementing Action Plans

Strategic direction and plans are critical to your QMS

ESTABLISHING AND DEPLOYING THE STRATEGIC DIRECTION

A concept at the heart of the quality of management—note the placement of these words—is that senior leaders, based on the vision they have, establish or guide their organization's strategic direction [5.1.1, Management responsibility—General guidance, introduction]. A vision statement explains what the organization wants to become and hopes to achieve. Management, through a strategic planning process similar to the one depicted in figure 1.1, establishes strategic goals, a mission statement, values, principles, and policies. These policies include an overall quality policy that's deployed throughout the organization, enabling the relevant personnel to generate action plans [5.3, Quality policy]. Table 1.1 provides two examples of how this process plays out.

Strategic planning is the process by which an organization sets its long-range goals and identifies the actions needed to reach them. Everything an organization does should link to the strategic plans. Therefore, if no strategic plans are in place, developing a strategic planning process is one of the first activities an organization's management should undertake before commencing a companywide improvement initiative. Implementing a brand-new quality management system (QMS) or revising an existing system to move beyond baseline quality assurance and quality management is a major change effort. It will likely take a substantial amount of time to accomplish.

In relation to strategic planning and the QMS, the term "process" refers to an activity or group of activities that take an input, add value to it, and provide an output to an internal or external customer. Thus, a process is a planned and repetitive sequence of steps by which a defined product or service is delivered—including strategic plans.

Integral to these strategic plans are long-range goals and shorter-range organizational objectives. When pursuing QMS performance improvements, an organization must define an objective as a quantitative statement of future expectations and indicate when they should be achieved. Management must understand that each objective, whether a quality or other business goal, ultimately flows from strategic goals and clarifies what the organization and its employees must accomplish.

Figure 1.1

OVERVIEW OF THE STRATEGIC PLANNING PROCESS

(Traditional)

Plan for Planning

Conduct Environmental Scans

Visualize the Future

Develop Mission Statement

Establish Future Goals

Set Measurable Objectives

Deploy Strategic Plans

Implement Action Plans

Track & Measure Progress

Evaluate Results

Feedback Loops

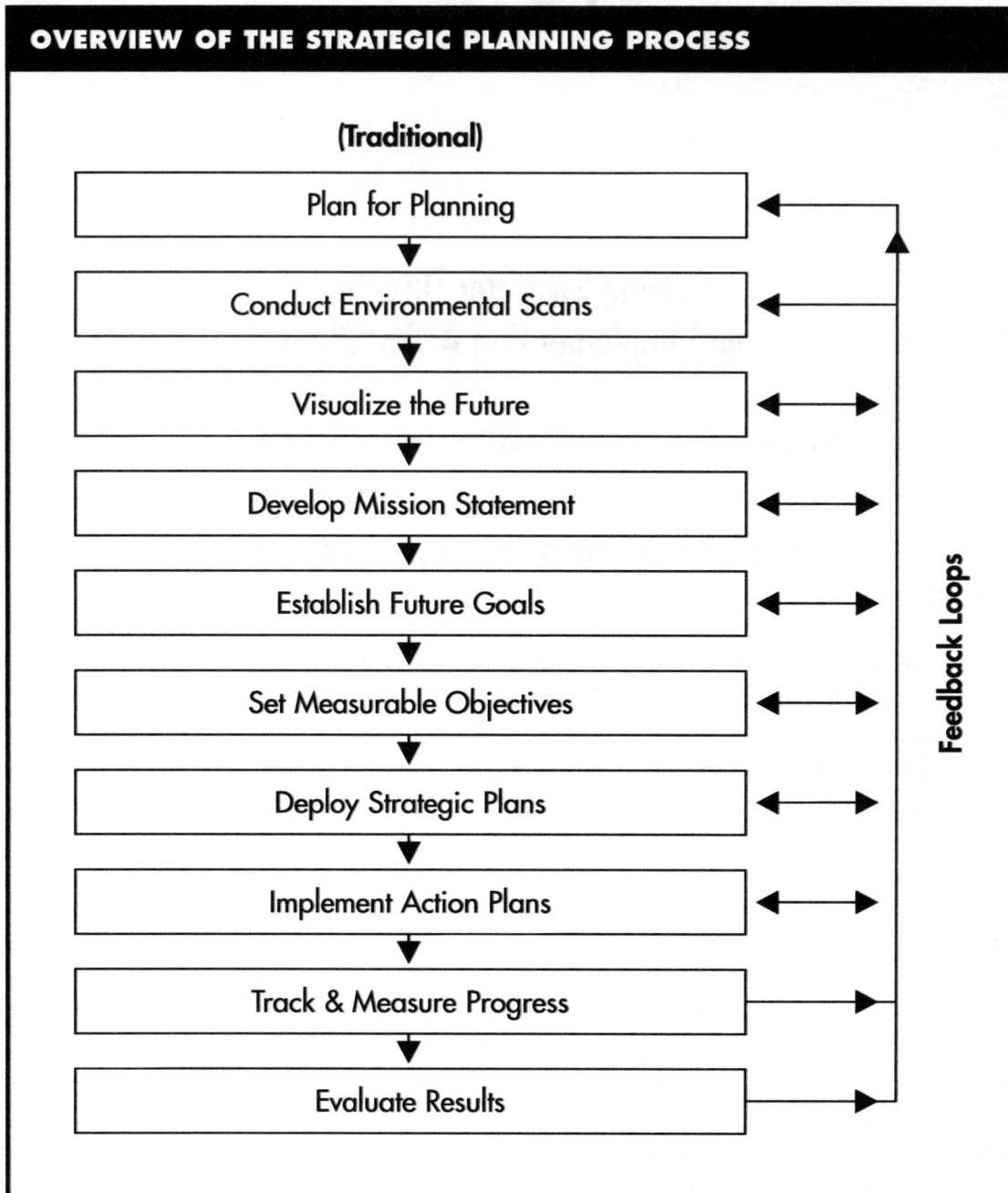

As top management's quality plans cascade through the organization, functional goals and objectives—both those relating to a QMS and to other business—must be set to support the strategic plans. At the functional level, measurable quality objectives for each function's performance must be selected and implemented through action plans to ensure the strategic plans are fulfilled. Action plans typically indicate persons responsible, steps to be taken, timelines, resources required, and relevant measurement criteria. An action plan is a simpler form of a project plan.

Table 1.1—Page 1

EXAMPLE OF STRATEGIC PLANNING PROCESS FOR TWO TYPES OF ORGANIZATIONS (PARTIAL)

Question	Vehicle	Not-for-Profit Organization	Manufacturing Organization
What is the organization striving to become?	Vision	Build A Life (BAL) will become the most respected privately funded charitable organization in the United States for the high percentage of its funds that directly reach its constituency through its programs and services.	Erving Spring Inc. (ESI) will become the preferred supplier of springs to the aerospace industry.
What does the organization intend to achieve?	Strategic Goals	BAL will reach the level where 96 cents out of every dollar of its funds directly benefit its constituency.	ESI will increase its share of the aerospace market to 65 percent.
What does the organization intend to deliver?	Mission Statement	BAL's mission is to devise and deliver programs and services to the needy. These programs and services not only will provide stop-gap relief when needed, but also educate and train the recipients in developing the behavior that will help them to build and sustain a life that is healthy and productive.	Through the provision of innovative solutions, the highest quality spring products, superior customer service and satisfaction and the fielding of a highly competent workforce, ESI will become the supplier of choice for customers within the aerospace industry worldwide.
How will the organization act in achieving its mission?	Values, Principles, Policies	BAL will conduct its activities to the highest known ethical and quality standards. BAL will assess its practices, processes, products and services annually to ensure its high standards are maintained.	ESI will build and stake its reputation on its responsiveness to customers' needs, production and delivery of defect-free products, its strict adherence to the highest ethical standards, and maintenance of an unconditional guarantee.
How will the organization's personnel know what direction to take?	Deployment Process	BAL management will deploy the vision, mission, values/principles, and strategic objectives at every organizational level. Responsible management at each level will develop functional objectives and action plans to address each strategic objective for which they have a pertinent linkage.	The management of ESI will deploy the vision, mission, values/principles, and strategic objectives to every organizational level. Responsible management at each level will develop functional objectives and action plans to address each strategic objective for which they have a pertinent linkage.
What will the organization's personnel do to meet the strategic objectives?	Action Plans/Project Plans	As an example, the action plans from the Community Services Enhancement Program (CSEP), one of BAL's functional organizations, include the following steps:	An example is the action plan for the ISO 9001 project within production, one of ESI's functional organization. Commencing May 2003, production will:

Table 1.1—Page 2

EXAMPLE OF STRATEGIC PLANNING PROCESS FOR TWO TYPES OF ORGANIZATIONS (PARTIAL)

Question	Vehicle	Not-for-Profit Organization	Manufacturing Organization
		■ Starting May 2003, design and implement a "funds flow-through" tracking, measuring, and reporting system, to be implemented by October 1, 2003. ■ Starting May 2003, assess existing services and initiate changes or new services that will yield increases in funds flow-through to meet or exceed 90 percent by July 1, 2004. ■ By August 2003, CSEP will initiate a waste-assessment and reduction process aimed at reducing nonvalue-added practices and processes. Target is 20-percent reduction by November 2003 and an additional 10 percent by July 1, 2004.	■ Form a cross-functional steering committee to guide the ISO 9001 project. ■ Appoint the management representative. ■ Conduct gap analysis of existing QMS (ISO 9001:1994-registered) against ISO 9001:2000 and ISO 9004:2000. ■ Institute project management of ISO 9001 project, including return-on-investment (ROI) measurements of improvements. ■ Add to or modify the quality manual, procedures, and work instructions. ■ Re-train personnel and implement new and changed procedures. ■ Re-train internal auditors. ■ Have registrar conduct ISO 9001:2000 pre-assessment; target October 2002. ■ Implement corrective actions for nonconformances found in pre-assessment. ■ Have registrar conduct ISO 9001:2000 registration assessment by registrar; target December 2002.
How will the organization know how effective it is in meeting its objectives?	**Project Management and Results Evaluation**	1. CSEP's "funds flow-through" system will be modified as needed and implemented throughout the organization. Action plans/project plans will be continuously monitored throughout the year, adjustments being made as necessary to achieve the objectives. 2. Results of all actions are summarized and flowed upward to aid in evaluating the overall results, the extent to which the strategic goals and objectives were met and the effectiveness of the strategic planning process.	1. ESI's ISO 9001 enhancement project will be closely monitored and modified as needed to achieve the registration target. 2. Progress will be reported at weekly top management staff meetings. 3. Detailed review of the progress and ROI results will be reviewed at the quarterly QMS review meetings. 4. Present and potential customers will be informed of ESI's successful registration upgrade.

STRATEGIC PLANNING

Top management is responsible for strategic planning. Clearly, planning from an ISO 9004:2000 perspective involves deciding, defining, and communicating:

- What the organization is striving to become (vision)
- What the organization intends to achieve (goals)
- What the organization intends to deliver and/or achieve (mission)
- How the organization intends to act in achieving its mission (values/principles)
- How the organization intends to meet its goals and mission (objectives)
- How the organization's personnel will know what direction to take (deployment)
- What personnel will do to meet the organization's strategic objectives (action/project plans and management)
- How the organization will determine how effective it is in meeting its objectives (measurement and evaluation)

Strategic plans that delineate and deploy the strategic direction guide the organization toward achieving its ultimate vision. Strategic planning typically occurs annually within organizations in a stable environment but might be undertaken more frequently and informally—for instance, at emerging high-tech or dotcom enterprises. In any case, the organization's stakeholders (i.e., customers, employees, investors, local and other communities, owners, suppliers, and top management) must know where the organization is headed. In particular, employees must understand their roles in the overall scheme.

Much has been written about the practicality of strategic planning. In today's fast-track economy, plans can become obsolete before they're executed. Granted, the window for planning might be very small for an emerging dotcom business, where products, services, and the processes used can change radically in a few months or days, particularly when compared to the planning cycle needed for, say, a public utility that continues to provide the same product and services as in the past with only gradual changes to some processes.

However, whether the life cycles of your organization's products and services, or the processes used to develop, produce, and provide them, are very short or very long, navigating without a strategic plan means bouncing wildly about without direction. Although some meaningful enterprises and their product or services have emerged from brainstorms hatched in a college dormitory or garage, even those needed direction, structure, and resources to become viable, sustainable, and profitable entities.

Among fast-track organizations, unfortunately, visionary leaders often move far in front of those they lead, leaving their staff members to guess at what they must do to fulfill the organization's mission and prepare for what will come next. This results in unnecessary waste and causes employees to make costly mistakes, leave customers dissatisfied, delay product offerings, and lower employee morale. Waste and missteps can deplete resources and create crises, sometimes even crippling the organization permanently. Planning and deploying strategic objectives effectively throughout an organization might prevent its demise.

Even among successful and well-managed companies such as Microsoft, sometimes it's apparent to customers that the vision held by its leaders isn't completely and efficiently reflected in the products and/or services delivered. This causes such companies and their customers to expend energy and resources to correct or eliminate the nonconformances.

Strategic plans, and the delegation of actions needed to implement them, aren't and shouldn't be cast in concrete. Deployment is the process of cascading strategic plans throughout an organization, to all levels. The organization's monitoring, measuring, and reporting systems must enable management to assess ongoing progress and make course corrections as necessary. Although it occurs faster in some industries than in others, change is inevitable and always a factor for which an organization should be prepared. Major economic upsets could conceivably result in postponements or redrafting of a strategic plan.

However, understanding what's involved in developing the plan also allows management to assess more accurately the risk in changing or abandoning it. Without the planning process, risk assessment, establishing goals, and directing personnel so that they pursue the goals and objectives effectively would be a guessing game. Most importantly, strategic plans move the entire organization in a commonly understood direction with clear milestones— i.e., points in time when a critical event is to occur—for measuring achievement along the way. To paraphrase a famous baseball player, "If you don't know where you're going, you're liable to end up somewhere else."

ISO 9004:2000 is designed to serve as a guide for QMS implementation, maintenance, and enhancement in any type of organization and is clearly oriented toward directing top management to accept responsibility for QMS performance improvement. (It devotes substantial attention to clause 5.4, Management responsibility—planning.) An organization that hasn't implemented a strategic planning process or that finds its process ineffectual, should consider strategic planning as a first breakthrough to improvement.

Implementing an effective strategic planning process is neither easy nor inexpensive. Many organizations find it takes up to three years to effectively assimilate strategic planning. It represents a cultural change for many organizations, especially fast-trackers that may view the time taken for planning as an impediment to progress.

For this reason, if your organization hasn't already implemented a strategic planning process or at least begun the effort, you must convince top management to get the process underway.

ESTABLISHING STRATEGIC OBJECTIVES

Everything an organization does should be linked to its strategic plans, for which its long-range goals and shorter-range organizational objectives are critical [5.4.1, Planning, quality objectives]. When pursuing QMS performance improvements, an organization must define an objective as a quantitative statement of future expectations and indicate when the expectations should be achieved. Management must understand that each objective ultimately flows from strategic goals and clarifies what the organization and its personnel must accomplish.

As top management's quality plans cascade through the organization, functional goals and objectives must be set to support the strategic plans. At the function-level, measurable quality objectives for each function's performance must be selected and implemented through action plans to fulfill the strategic plan.

ISO 9004 CITES QUALITY AND PERFORMANCE OBJECTIVES

ISO 9000:2000, Quality management systems—Fundamentals and vocabulary defines a "quality objective" [3.2.5] as "something sought, or aimed for, related to quality." ISO

Table 1.2

WHERE QUALITY AND PERFORMANCE OBJECTIVES ARE CITED IN ISO 9004:2000		
Reference	Title	Top Management/The Organization Should...
5.4.1	Planning—Quality objectives	Provide a framework for setting measurable quality objectives and defining responsibility for deployment
5.6.3	Management review—Review output	Establish performance objectives for products and processes as part of the outputs of reviews
6.2.2.2	Competence, awareness, and training—Awareness and training	Support the organization's objectives when planning for education and training, and include training on the objectives
6.3	Resource management—Infrastructure	Provide an infrastructure that's defined by the organization's objectives
6.5	Information	Use data, information, and knowledge to set and meet the organization's objectives
7.1.3.2	Product realization—Process inputs, outputs, and review	Review the consistency of product realization process inputs and outputs with planned performance objectives
8.5.4	Improvement—Continual improvement of the organization	Set objectives for people, projects, and the organization so as to involve people in identifying performance improvement opportunities

9004:2000 indicates that a performance objective relates to improving a specific performance, whether of a system, machinery and equipment, or a human being, that relates to organizational QMS performance.

Quality and performance objectives clearly are important in ISO 9004:2000, particularly when you examine the seven instances where guidance related to these objectives appears in the clauses, sub-clauses, and elements of ISO 9004. Table 1.2 lists the seven instances.

SETTING OBJECTIVES THE SMART WAY

The following eight-step process, called the "SMART WAY," serves as a guide to setting objectives for improving organizational performance.

S—Focus on *specific* needs and opportunities. From your organization's quality policy and plan, select specific opportunities for your improvement efforts. Draft an objective for each opportunity but don't combine opportunities. For example, given the plant's current workload level, increase customer satisfaction by improving on-time delivery (OTD) of customer orders.

M—Make each objective *measurable*. The measurement can be in dollars, percentages, quantities, or, if the objective is a onetime event, simply "achieved." Wherever applicable, the objective should include the baseline, which is your organization's present level of performance. Redraft the following example: Given the plant's current workload level, improve delivery performance for all future customer orders from 35 percent OTD to 90 percent OTD.

A—Structure objectives to be challenging but *achievable*. This stimulates achievement and creates a feeling of accomplishment when goals are reached.

R—Set stretching but also *realistic* objectives. A quality or performance objective that's physically, economically, legally, or ethically impossible to achieve is inappropriate to any organization. It won't motivate people and could cause customer dissatisfaction.

T—Ensure that every objective has a clearly indicated *time frame*. Expanding upon the objective example in M: The OTDs will reach 75 percent by February 28, 2004; 85 percent by May 31, 2004; and 90 percent by July 31, 2004.

W—Check to be sure every objective is *worth* doing.

A—*Assign* responsibility for each objective.

Y—Ensure that all objectives are structured to *yield* the desired results.

Suggested objectives for your organization to consider setting the SMART WAY include:
- Routine, ongoing work (e.g., preparing quotations for customers)
- Special assignments or projects (e.g., reengineering the product design process)
- Growth/expansion of the organization (e.g., increase customer base)
- Employee development (e.g., provide quality training for all employees on a yearly basis)

Additional guidelines for preparing objectives are:
- Specify a single outcome and any pertinent conditions. For example, given a project budget of $8,650, complete documentation of all procedures needed before the ISO 9001 audit on February 1, 2004.
- Select a quantifiable method for measurement (e.g., a percentage, dollar amount, volume or other number, or Y/N outcome). For example, a QMS documentation objective might be to document 25 percent of procedures by August 1, 2004; 50 percent by October 1, 2004; 75 percent by December 1, 2004; and 100 percent by January 15, 2005.
- Set an ambitious target.
- Determine if the objective is realistic. Do a reality check.
- Establish a deadline and any interim milestones needed. (For example, the percentage to be completed combined with milestones like those suggested in the last example.)
- Include a cost parameter if that's practical. Remember that every performance and quality objective should be completed within budget and achieve expected savings and/or revenue growth.
- Make objectives clear, brief, and easy to understand.
- Write objectives as action statements. Examples might include:
  - ☐ Reduce scrap rate from a 20-percent level as of June 1, 2004, to 12 percent by April 1, 2005.
  - ☐ Complete Project W by October 31, 2004, within its $8,650 budget.
  - ☐ Given the installation of a model Z ultrasound testing device, decrease defects detected at final inspection from six per 100 on November 1, 2004 to one per 1,000 by November 1, 2005.

- Collaborate with the personnel responsible for writing objectives and choosing measurements.
- Develop action (i.e., project) plans for meeting the objectives.

Figure 1.2 (Front)

ACTION PLAN		
Plan title:	Plan No.:	
	Date Initiated:	
Description:	Date Needed:	
	Approval:	
	Team Leader:	
	Team Members:	

Linked to what overall strategic objective:

Linked to what corrective or preventive action:

Major outcomes/objectives desired/required:

Scope (Where will the solution/implementation be applied? What limitations?):

By what criteria/measures will completion and success of project be measured?

Assumptions made that might affect project (resources, circumstances outside this project):

Describe the overall approach to be taken:

When should the project be started to meet the date needed/wanted?

Estimate the resources required (time and money):

Estimate the benefits vs. costs value:

Outline the proposed major steps to be taken, a projected start and completion date for each step, and the person responsible for each step. Use the back to detail your timeline. Attach any backup data.

Figure 1.2 (Back)

ACTION PLAN IMPLEMENTATION SCHEDULE					
					Plan No.
Step No.	Activity/Event Description	Depends on Step	Start Date	Finish Date	Person Responsible

- Establish a tracking and reporting system and document the procedures.
- Determine an interim progress review and course correction dates (i.e., milestones).
- Identify the consequences for achievement (and/or failure).
- Ensure that the quality/performance objectives support the organization's strategic goals and objectives.
- Determine the criteria by which the plans for achieving the objectives will be evaluated.
- Develop the action plans needed to implement the objectives.

USING ACTION PLANS HELPS ACHIEVE MOST OBJECTIVES

Action plans are, in actuality, mini-project plans. On those occasions when a quality or performance objective indicates that the resulting initiative will be very extensive, complex, and/or long-lasting, then more extensive and formal project planning tools and techniques might be required. Such is the case with initiatives that will lead to permanent corporate culture changes (e.g., implementing a Six Sigma initiative). However, most quality/performance objectives involve short-term design, implementation, and execution stages, and involve mostly one work unit. In such cases an action plan usually is sufficient. Figure 1.2 shows a sample action plan form that any organization could use in planning a typical quality or performance objective.

Among its advantages, an action plan form:

- Ensures that the implementation process has been carefully thought through, thereby lessening the potential for failure
- Scrutinizes the feasibility of the course of action under consideration. The form forces planners to answer the following questions:
  - ☐ Are there sufficient resources available in the time frame specified?
  - ☐ Is the organization competent and capable of achieving the objective?
  - ☐ Will achieving the objective further the organization's overall strategic objectives?

- Is logged and the progress is tracked, offering greater assurance that objectives won't be sidetracked by intervening pressures
- Leads to documentation of the action's progress and results, making objective evidence of continual improvement available for the internal audits and management reviews
- Provides a before-and-after measurement of the action's effectiveness when coupled with a benefits-cost analysis
- Can be retained along with accompanying documentation as part of a knowledge base of lessons learned. This "project history" can then be accessed when similar objectives must be met in the future.
- Contributes to a knowledge base from which examples can be drawn for training employees in planning and implementing objectives

By using action plans, your organization can pursue measurable objectives in a process-oriented way that will avoid inefficiencies and errors. It's important to keep in mind, however, that differences exist between quality and performance objectives and how they're measured.

For example, determining if quality objectives are effectively achieved might require measurements to verify if the organization meets or exceeds:

- External customers' requirements, including interested parties (e.g., regulatory bodies or industry good-manufacturing practices) that must be satisfied
- Internal customer requirements
- Internal process and product standards, such as workmanship and product finish standards

Performance objectives, which can overlap with quality objectives, include meeting or exceeding internal targets for:
- Facility usage and maintenance
- Equipment usage and maintenance
- Tools usage and maintenance
- Raw materials usage and storage
- Finished goods warehousing
- Delivery fleet usage and maintenance
- Acceptable productivity levels
- Procedural documentation and maintenance, including forms (i.e., are documented procedures maintained and used to improve performance, and are required documentation and records maintained and/or completed to measure performance improvements?)
- Computer-based operations planning, scheduling, production, and delivery-systems use and maintenance, including backup
- Clerical and computer-assisted order-entry, purchasing, and control systems use and maintenance
- Acceptable human behavior vis-à-vis customers, other employees, and the public
- Training, education, and development of personnel resources
- Partnering with suppliers to achieve mutually improved process inputs and outputs.

Although the lists of quality and performance objective measures are not intended to be all-inclusive, they should convey what types of continual improvement objectives can be established. Each of the entries relates to potential performance objectives, and each is measurable in a way that will give management (and the organization as a whole) feedback on the QMS. These measurements show where improvement is occurring and how much.

When internal or external audits uncover a nonconformance, the action plan can be used to develop and implement those corrective actions that involve a number of people and cross-functional lines. Preventive actions arising from audits or management reviews also will be better enabled if action planning is used. In any case, there should still be a discernible link between the actions, the planning, and the organization's strategic objectives.

CLOSING THE GAP: TEN KEYS TO SUCCESS

Follow-through remains the failing of many strategic planning efforts. The process is a wasted effort if the planning hasn't been translated into action and tracked to ensure that the plans are fulfilled. Ten keys to ensure successfully implemented strategic plans are:
- Top management is visibly involved in supporting the strategic planning process, especially as it relates to scarce resources—i.e., time and money.

■ Top management ensures that the strategic plan, strategic goals, and strategic objectives are deployed throughout the organization.

■ Those responsible for the actions fully participate in preparing the action plans.

■ The action plans are realistic and validated against the strategic plan (i.e., the action plans are linked, by means of the organization's strategy, through all organizational levels).

■ A system exists for tracking, measuring, and reporting on the action plans' fulfillment.

■ A system exists for recognizing and rewarding achievements relating to action plans.

■ A knowledge management system exists to capture and transform data into a resource for decision making, guidance for future projects, and training purposes.

■ Management commits to keeping people throughout the organization informed of progress made toward achieving the strategic plans.

■ The strategic planning process itself is continually improved.

■ Management's commitment and actions ensures the strategic planning process is both effective and efficient.

A top priority of the strategic planning process is building and improving customer satisfaction. Chapter two focuses on this vital necessity.

CHAPTER 2

Focusing on the Customer

The voice of the customer is critical to your QMS

What's an organization's true purpose, whether in broad business or only quality management system (QMS) terms? *ISO 9004:2000, Quality management systems—Guidelines for performance improvements* indicates that an organization has two purposes [clause 0.1, Introduction—General]:

■ To identify and meet its customers' needs and expectations—to achieve competitive advantage and do this in an effective and efficient manner
■ To achieve, maintain, and improve overall organizational performance and capabilities

In emphasizing that you should go beyond a baseline ISO 9001:2000 QMS and pursue total quality management, this chapter uses examples to describe how an organization can focus on its customers [clause 4.1, Quality management system—Managing systems and processes]. These include:

■ Defining and promoting processes that lead to improved organizational performance
■ Acquiring and using process data and information on a continuing basis
■ Directing progress toward continual improvement
■ Using suitable methods to evaluate process improvement, such as self-assessments and management review

"THE CUSTOMER IS ALWAYS RIGHT!"

For years, you've heard exhortations to pay attention to the customer. Yet, organizations that sought to satisfy only the minimal requirements of ISO 9001/2/3:1994 gave little effort to proactively learning more about customer wants and needs. Unless these organizations experienced product returns or customer complaints, they assumed their customers were satisfied and that customer satisfaction efforts were unnecessary.

However, the American Customer Satisfaction Index (ACSI)[1], a quarterly index that provides composite scores of customer satisfaction in the United States, shows few if any signs of improvement. The ACSI average score stood at 74.2 (out of 100) when it was launched during the fourth quarter of 1994, reached a low of 70.7 during the first quarter of 1997 and stood at 73 during the third quarter of 2002. It's obvious there is work to be done!

To step up to ISO 9004:2000, organizations must understand the needs of their customers, both existing and potential. An organization must also reach out to customers to learn more about their expectations and future plans. Organizations must answer strategic quality questions, such as:

- What will the customer's expectations be for the existing and/or for a contemplated product?
- What will the marketplace be like for our organization and its competitors a year from now or three years from now?
- Where will the business opportunities be in the future, and what can we do to take advantage of them?
- What strengths does our organization have that can be exploited to achieve a favorable position in the marketplace?
- What are the real and potential weaknesses of, and threats to, our organization?
- What are our employees' needs and expectations?

Common sense dictates that if an organization's employees buy its products and are satisfied by them, they treat customers more positively. Technically, if employees buy the organization's products, they are customers and deserve the same attention as other customers. Yet, how many organizations do you know of that ask employees for feedback about their products?

In many organizations, external customers are the stakeholders most often addressed publicly, while employees are noticed least. Yet, the investor-owner is the stakeholder whom most organizations make the most significant effort to satisfy. "Without the investor, there'd be no company" is top management's mantra in these organizations, and management views sales growth and profits as the best way to satisfy investors.

Top management should be encouraged to consider the organization chart as an inverted pyramid. As such, customers would appear at the top, employees in the middle, and management at the bottom. So far, this concept has been slow to catch on.

To develop an organizationwide management system that goes beyond an ISO 9001:2000-based QMS, appropriately balancing the needs of the company's many stakeholders must be emphasized. A critical early step up to ISO 9004:2000 is to look at what actions management should take to ensure the organization has a customer focus.

REACH OUT AND TOUCH ONE

How does an organization gain an inclusive view of customer expectations, needs, and requirements? Communication is the answer. Because communication is a multifaceted activity, many organizations wonder which approach or technique works best. Although many factors must be considered, usually no one approach or technique will create and sustain an ideal level of customer relationships. Reaching out to customers requires a combination of techniques and tools that will enable your organization to stay in touch with customers' expectations, needs, and requirements.

The goal of customer communication is for your organization to obtain and maintain a customer focus. Begin by asking the following questions of supervisors, middle management, and even top management. The answers you receive could provide a very meaningful assessment of how effective the QMS and its customer focus are.

■ Do you understand what customer focus means?

■ Do you know what the organization's goal is for customer focus?

■ How will you know when the function you are responsible for has achieved a customer focus?

■ How does achieving a customer focus translate to achieving internal customer satisfaction within the processes for which you are responsible?

■ What criteria and measurements make sense for improving internal customer satisfaction?

■ How can you link internal customer satisfaction within your sphere of influence with external customer satisfaction? How can you make this link clear to personnel within your sphere?

■ What techniques and tools are available to help personnel improve your department's and/or function's internal customer satisfaction levels and ultimately affect the whole organization's external customer satisfaction?

An organization attains a customer focus when all personnel know both the internal and external customers to whom they supply product. Further, all employees must know what they're responsible for supplying, how it's produced, and what customer requirements must be met to ensure that both internal and external customers are satisfied by what's delivered. (See appendix A for a discussion of NOAC, or "next operation as customer.")

Beyond proclaiming that the organization will achieve a customer focus, top management must help deploy this organizational goal so that functions at each organizational level can establish measurable objectives for how they're going to contribute. Cascading the goal and resulting objectives down through the organization helps educate all personnel about the meaning of customer focus.

Personnel who only work with internal customers should understand how their role affects external customers in the overall process. As each work unit and function measures its contributions to achieving its objective(s), its personnel will better understand the tie-in to the customer focus goal. Linking these organizational-level objectives to the organizational goal will allow each work unit and function to see its cumulative contributions to the overall goal.

TECHNIQUES AND TOOLS FOR CUSTOMER FOCUS

Some useful techniques and tools in achieving and sustaining a customer focus include:

■ Setting objectives the SMART WAY

■ Employing appropriate project management tools in managing improvement efforts

■ Using a focus group to gain a perspective on customer expectations

■ Keeping up with developing market trends through environmental scanning

■ Engaging in benchmarking to learn from the best practices of others

■ Applying quality function deployment to capture the voice of the customer

■ Gathering customer feedback through listening posts

■ Improving internal customer service through quality-level agreements

■ Assessing customer satisfaction with surveys

■ Conducting post-purchase follow-up to build good customer relations

■ Segmenting your customer base to determine how to best serve the best customers

The following summary of these techniques will provide you with insights on their function and how your organization can use them.

Set objectives the SMART WAY

Chapter one outlined eight attributes for setting meaningful objectives. Clearly stated objectives will establish the baseline for measuring the work to be done, assess the status of the work in progress, and evaluate the results. Interlocking objectives, from the lowest to highest organizational level, serve to keep everyone informed of his or her role in sustaining a customer focus.

Employ appropriate project management tools

Chapter nine discusses commonly used project planning and management tools. Changing the corporate culture and improving processes and product should be initiated either through action plans (i.e., mini-project plans) or full-scale project plans. Project planning and management not only provides structure and means for measuring progress but also signifies the organization's commitment to continually improving its processes and its focus on internal and external customers.

Use a focus group

A focus group is commonly used to gain customer views and insights about an existing product or service, or a proposed new one. It's a qualitative discussion group, usually composed of eight to ten participants invited from a segment of the (existing or potential) customer base.

Led by a skilled facilitator using predetermined questions, the group discusses an existing or planned product. The discussion can identify participant likes and dislikes, or potential requirements and/or improvement opportunities. Internal focus groups can furnish feedback to help improve processes and/or product.

Although focus groups don't represent a statistically sound sampling of the customer base, they do provide contact with a few customers in an environment in which open interaction is fostered. Feedback from a focus group can be used as a basis to structure other approaches for gathering feedback (e.g., questions for structuring customer surveys).

Keep up with developing market trends

Chapter one discusses the need for environmental scanning. On a daily basis, you hear and read about organizations that failed to see a trend developing and suffered—sometimes fatally—because of it. Using the Internet in purchasing decisions is significantly affecting industrial buying habits and altering how consumers shop. Businesses that are slow to respond are adversely affected.

What's happening technologically and globally affects your business and the marketplace. Will you recognize the next trend before it happens, or at least early enough to minimize any negative effects? Competition can be more than just another organization hitting the marketplace with a cheaper version of your product. Forces that can affect your organization include competitors with greater resources, a new product that makes yours obsolete, findings or hearsay (whether true or not) that your product is harmful, and changes in customer needs and wants.

Environmental scanning and analysis means monitoring factors from both inside and outside an organization that might affect its long-term viability. Market trends are one factor that might affect your organization's overall business, processes, and product.

A wealth of data about market trends is available in the business environment through a range of sources, including:

- General and business news sources, including industry-specific publications and the Web
- Customers and suppliers
- Field sales and service representatives and their communications
- Industry and/or trade association statistics and studies
- Advertisements, catalogs, and even "junk" mail

More data exist than your organization could feasibly digest and put to use. Scan what's available and select those sources that provide the most useful information, given the time and money available for data review. Not scanning the environment for market trends isn't a viable option in today's fast-paced, data-saturated marketplace.

Your organization must watch trends developing outside your industry. Remember, your customers might not always know what they want or need until your organization has the foresight to create a product that satisfies or creates that want or need. A risk remains, of course, that when your organization does foresee and create a needed product, a competitor will quickly copy it.

Maintaining a customer focus entails not only meeting customer requirements but also anticipating future customer needs and expectations. Environmental scanning is the most effective way to detect emerging trends, which you can translate into a product to address that developing need or want. With every organization now a part of the global village, being well-informed and responsive to change is crucial.

Engage in benchmarking

Chapter eight discusses benchmarking in more detail. This technique is an improvement process that compares an organization's operations, processes, and procedures against best-in-class organizations—or organizations that are good performers in other fields. Benchmarking helps to determine how the best-in-class achieved its performance levels and how to use that information to improve your organization's performance.

For example, a well-known retail and catalog sales enterprise achieved world-class status in its handling of all customer interactions and received extensive publicity as a result. Ultimately, it was deluged with requests from diverse organizations seeking to learn about the processes that contributed to its customer interaction success.

Benchmarking works best when an organization first cleans up its own processes and procedures. Most benchmarking partners would expect to have a meaningful dialog with your benchmarking team; they're interested in learning about new processes from your organization as part of the partnership. If you don't have something to share, you might have difficulty finding a partner.

To enhance your organization's approach to maintaining a customer focus, benchmark processes that directly affect your organization's customer relationships (e.g., delivery cycle time, billing procedures, customer representative training). As with any improvement effort, benchmarking is most effective as an ongoing activity. Serving on a benchmarking

Figure 2.1

```
QUALITY FUNCTION DEPLOYMENT MATRIX: "HOUSE OF QUALITY"
```

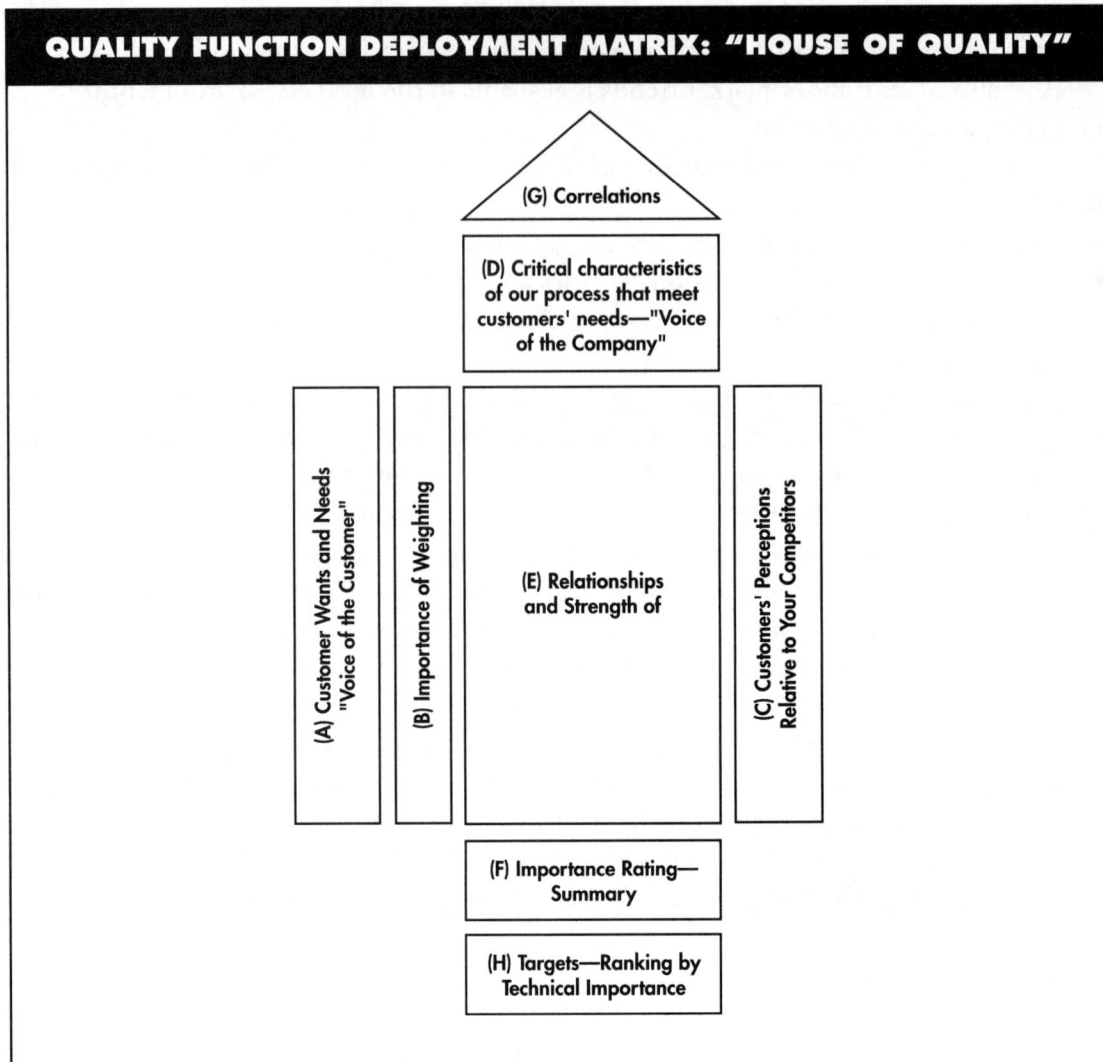

team and seeing how other organizations perform is a good way to motivate employees to think about and act in the customer's best interests.

Apply quality function deployment

QFD, also known as the "house of quality," is a structured method in which customer requirements are translated into appropriate technical requirements for each stage of product design, manufacture, and/or provision. Because it translates customer requirements into product requirements, the QFD process is often referred to as "capturing the voice of the customer." The term "house of quality" is derived from the appearance of the QFD matrix shown in figure 2.1, which resembles a house.

In its simplest form, the following steps are involved in generating an initial QFD matrix:

A. Identify and determine customer requirements (i.e., the voice of the customer)
B. Weigh the importance of the customer requirements
C. Rank the customer's perceptions of your organization's product vs. that of your competitor(s)

D. Identify the product characteristics needed to meet the customer requirements
E. Complete a matrix showing strength of the correlation between customer requirements for and the technical requirements of the product (with numeral nine designating "strongly related," three "moderately related," and one "slightly related")
F. Summarize the relative importance ratings—i.e., the sum of each importance weighting from step two times the corresponding strength of the correlation from step five
G. Weigh the correlation between customer requirements and product characteristics
H. Rank the relative importance of each technical characteristic (a high ranking equals a target for attention).

Since its first appearance in the automotive industry, QFD applications and use have spread to diverse situations and organizations. One example is the Connecticut Quality Council (CQC), a university-based coalition of organizations dedicated to quality. The CQC formed a team to develop a QFD matrix to determine where improvements could be made in the product (i.e., educational programs) and service (forums for sharing experiences) provided to CQC's members. A cross-organizational team, using QFD methodology, provided insights as to where the CQC should focus on its customers' needs, which led to improvements in CQC's product and service offerings.

In its extended form, figure 2.2, QFD cascades through an organization's functions. For example, the technical requirements from a higher-level organizational matrix replace the items in A in the QFD matrix in figure 2.1, while production characteristics replace the items in D. The relationships now relate to the importance of technical (design) requirements to the characteristics of how the product will be made. Additional matrices often are added to the right side of the "house" to show competitive ratings and other factors. QFD deploys the voice of the customer—i.e., the customer focus—throughout the organization.

Gather customer feedback

Most organizations lack a systematic way to listen actively to customers, record and analyze what's heard, then disseminate the information internally and act upon it. Using a methodology called "LCALI"[2] (listen, capture, analyze, learn, and improve), the many voices of the customer can be tapped.

LCALI is a process that allows employees to listen to the voice of the customer and capture, analyze, disseminate, and take action in response to it. If your organization isn't actively measuring how satisfied its customers are, it's left the door open to the competition. Be aware that investigating reasons for returned product is but a small part of the picture. Your customer's offhand remark to a salesperson or delivery person can appear insignificant by itself. However, when the remark is captured and properly evaluated, it can indicate a potential problem before it turns into a formal complaint.

Likewise, a clarification from a customer's engineer to your engineer can indicate existing or potential shortcomings in your organization's ability to identify customer requirements. Scattered remarks from a customer's personnel to personnel in your organization, although not appearing important individually, can, when collected and analyzed, reveal a pattern pointing to needed preventive action.

For example, a small engineering and consulting firm markets both structural design services along with field inspections of facilities and is organized on

Figure 2.2

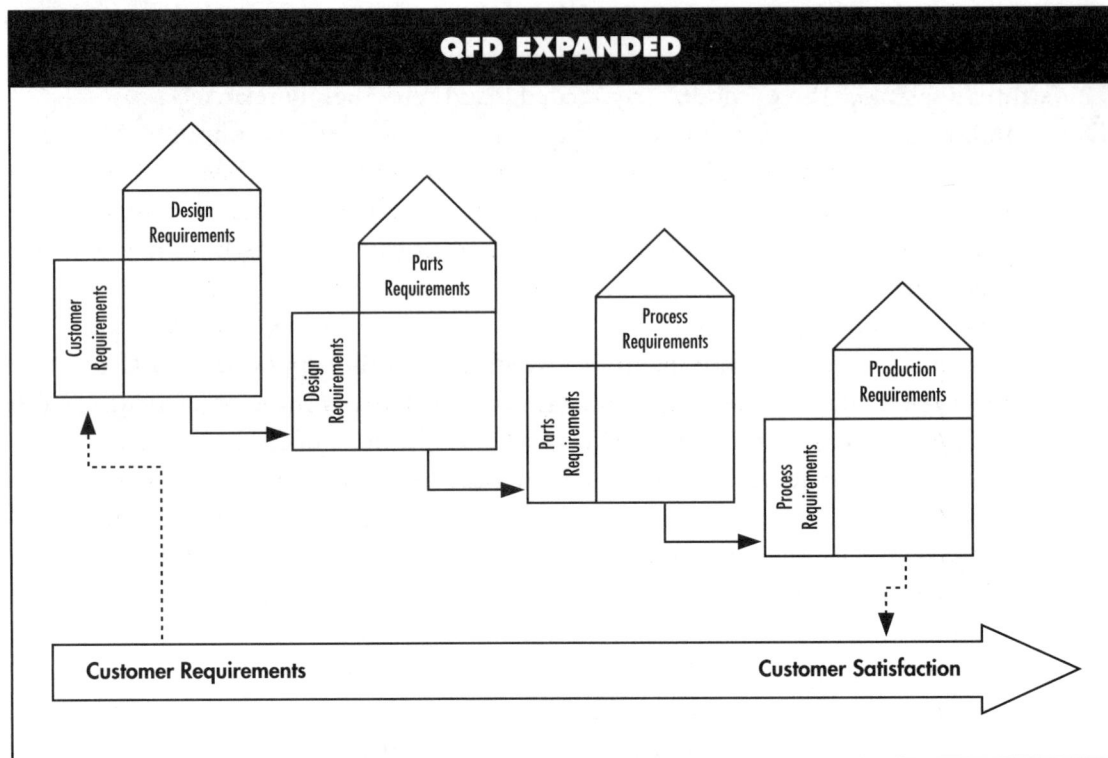

QFD EXPANDED

a project basis. Multiple projects are underway at any one time, each managed by a project manager, with the firm's engineering, legal, and administrative resources allocated according to project needs. Nearly everyone in the firm is, at one time or another, in contact with personnel in the clients' organizations.

Prior to implementing an ISO 9001 QMS, the firm had no formal process for gathering and evaluating client data from multiple sources to identify the need for preventive action—and the firm lost almost $1 million in revenue because data didn't reach management in time for action. This punctuated the need for the "listening post" concept. Now, each project manager in this firm serves as a listening post and provides a stream of input for management review, stimulates preventive action, and provides the basis for positive reinforcement for the personnel and teams responsible for customer satisfaction.

Established listening posts offer a link with nearly every customer—a true customer focus. (See appendix B for more detail.)

Improve internal customer service

A quality level agreement (QLA)—sometimes called a service level agreement—is a negotiated, documented agreement between an internal provider (i.e., supplier) and internal receiver (customer). The QLA represents the receiver's perspective and might include specifications for quality characteristics (e.g., quantity to be delivered, distribution schedule, accuracy and completeness of deliveries, product quality and/or usability), performance standards, and means for measuring actual vs. specified performance levels. (See appendix C for additional detail.)

An organization applying QLAs should expect to establish a tracking, measuring, and reporting system to maximize the agreements' benefits and to serve as a basis for continual improvement. QLAs don't replace necessary material or product inspections where there are key process handoffs. However, they do address the deliverables of the process itself. How do QLAs actually work?

At Mail-Order Outfitters Inc., cash payments must be deposited by 3:30 each business day to gain maximum interest, thus making it essential that mail processing picks up the mail from the post office early enough for accounting to process payments and prepare deposits for transport and deposit no later than 3:00 p.m. To ensure payments are deposited, the company established QLAs at the key handoffs: mail delivery to accounting, mail opening and sorting, payment processing, deposit preparation, deposit pickup, and delivery to bank.

Not only did the QLAs specify the schedules, accuracy, and completeness level required, but measurements were also established to evaluate QLA compliance (e.g., on-time delivery rates between key process steps, value of payments not processed or deposited on day received, customer complaints about misapplied payments, frequency with which 100-percent accuracy is achieved). Supervisors reviewed weekly performance data with their work units and took corrective action where needed. Management reviewed monthly summaries and initiated preventive action as appropriate. Any work unit meeting its QLA was recognized monthly.

In terms of customer focus, employees involved in the processes relating to payment deposits understood the relationship of the work they did relative to two strategic goals:

- Accurate, timely payment processing that affects external and internal customers
- Earning maximum interest on payments received, which affects internal customers and the bottom line

Assess customer satisfaction with surveys

Pursuing customer satisfaction is a requirement of ISO 9001:2000, but ISO 9004:2000 indicates that organizations should seek more. Clause 4.3, Quality management system—Use of quality management principles, states that an organization, "should understand current and future customer needs, should meet customer requirements and *strive to exceed customer expectations.*" (Emphasis added.) Such striving is likely to produce customer loyalty.

Thus, the primary objective of conducting any customer survey should be to obtain data to improve your organization's processes so it can strive to exceed customer expectations and increase customer retention. Wouldn't you rather know what you must improve to retain your customers, not just to meet their minimum requirements? After all, it costs substantially more in every industry to obtain new customers than to retain existing ones.

Before you even consider designing and conducting a survey, your organization will benefit by collecting some statistics about its past performance with customers—both those that came and went and those that have remained loyal. Determine a customer's value in dollars spent on your organization's product in a given month—compared with the average customer—and what it's worth to retain this customer for one, two, or three years.[3]

Compare these values with the average expenditures to secure a new customer that might not become a repeat, loyal buyer and ask yourself, "How many new customers would we have to acquire to equal the loss of one long-term customer?" As you begin to reflect on the relationship between customer satisfaction and customer retention, also consider the potential levels of satisfaction.

There are three basic ways to survey customers—written surveys (including e-mail and Web site), telephone surveys, and face-to-face interviews. Each method has it advantages and disadvantages, as shown in table 2.1.

Designing the survey process and constructing questions to produce the desired response rate might appear to be more art than science, but a poorly prepared and executed survey can do more harm than good. Three very important points must be considered:

■ Before launching your organization's survey: Have you sufficiently tested it on a small sample population to determine if the questions are clear and the content is understood?

■ Have you determined how and with what resources the responses will be processed? Scoring criteria must be developed for interpreting, categorizing, and tabulating qualitative data. If your organization wants many qualitative-type questions answered, you have much work ahead in interpreting responses.

■ Have you determined what your organization is going to do with the data? Have you informed the respondents how their responses will be used and why they're important?

■ Have you offered to provide feedback to the respondents? If so, that would require their responses to be identified. Note: There is nothing worse than responding to a survey where you're led to believe positive change will occur if you respond—this happens frequently—and then nothing changes. This doesn't build confidence or customer satisfaction.

Build good customer relations

Well-respected organizations conduct post-purchase follow-up all the time. Indeed, this is an excellent way to ensure the customer is satisfied with the product purchased, obtain feedback to improve your organization's product offerings, or identify potential customers for the same product and build customer loyalty.

Consider the following statement from the owner of a used car:

"I purchased a previously owned vehicle from a local car dealer and received a personalized letter within a week from the dealership owner. He wrote to tell me how pleased they were having me as a customer and asking if there was anything they could do to ensure my 100-percent satisfaction. A month later the sales manager wrote to ask how the car was working out for me and what the dealership could do to ensure a continuing relationship with me. He included a return postcard with three short questions. At the six-month point, I received a letter from the service manager inviting me to come in for a free diagnostic check with an enclosed return postcard for the diagnostic reservation that asked three new questions and thanked me for being their customer. This car is now over three years old, and yet they're staying in touch with me without pushing me to buy services I don't want. Any guess as to where I'll go when I eventually replace that car?"

Table 2.1

ADVANTAGES AND DISADVANTAGES OF SURVEY TYPES		
Survey Type	**Advantages**	**Disadvantages**
Mailed (paper and pencil)	■ Least obtrusive for respondent ■ Less expensive than telephone or personal interviews for organization ■ Most flexible to respondent's schedule ■ Allows respondent multiple readings before answering ■ Questions presented in unbiased manner to all recipients (a live survey-taker's word choice or tone might influence respondent's answer) ■ Can be designed for optical recognition of answers to multiple choice or ranking questions, thus saving tabulating time	■ Long cycle time ■ Qualitative data not as good as telephone or personal interviews ■ Surveys must be short and dedicated to a specific factor ■ Respondents not representative of full customer range (tend to be those most or least satisfied) ■ Response rates tend to be low
Web site	■ Inexpensive to conduct ■ Easy for respondent (just click responses and send back electronically) ■ Very easy to tabulate multiple choice and ranking questions ■ Unobtrusive for respondent ■ Easy to vary questions over time to collect a wide range of data and make it more interesting for repeat respondents ■ May be easier to obtain demographic data than with mailed survey	■ Respondent must seek out Web site ■ Respondents may be even less representative of customer range than with a mailed survey because of need to access Web site and confidentiality concerns with Web ■ Difficult to summarize qualitative responses
Telephone surveys	■ Good for obtaining answers to general questions about perception of the organization and performance relating to specific customer requirements ■ Response rates tend to be higher than for mailed surveys ■ Collecting qualitative data easier than mailed survey ■ Provides more flexibility for pursuing customers' perception in greater depth	■ Difficult to avoid bias due to interviewer word choice and speech patterns ■ Likely to be perceived as intrusive ■ Respondents might feel manipulated ■ Lack of visual props not good for evaluating complex concepts ■ Much more expensive than mailed surveys ■ Shorter duration required than with face-to-face interviews ■ Certain types of customers are unavailable by phone ■ Respondent may be embarrassed by language difficulty
Face-to-face interviews	■ Very helpful in determining what's important to customers before conducting written or telephone survey ■ When a sufficient number of respondents are interviewed, collective responses can provide valuable insights ■ One-on-one interviews avoid the influence of others that might be experienced in focus groups ■ Can usually engage a respondent's interest for a longer time period than with a telephone interview	■ Interviewer must be highly trained to be effective ■ Virtually impossible to obtain a statistically sound sampling due to format costs ■ Usually requires engaging interviewers from outside the organization to avoid bias ■ Virtually impossible to control potential bias of individual interviewers ■ Respondents might be embarrassed by language difficulty.

Follow-up should be done so as to make the customer feel in control of the situation, with your organization listening and responding while making it easy for the customer to make the first move. Your organization should strive to exceed the customer's expectations without pressuring the customer to buy something that isn't wanted—yet.

Conducting visits to customers can help many organizations build a solid relationship. Customer visits also expose your employees to the customers' environment and needs—a double value. (Appendix D provides additional detail.)

Segment your customer base

Your organization should consider segmenting its customer base when customers purchase product in varying volumes and they represent a mix of industries, economic strata, geographic locations, demographics, and/or corporate or consumer cultures. That is, your customers are in different market segments; you can't expect to satisfy the needs of diverse markets effectively with a single product, level of service, or marketing strategy.

Your organization must know the segments it's attempting to serve for several reasons:

■ Henry Ford's "any car, as long as it's black" days are over. Learning to serve the individual needs of each customer is now a desirable goal. (Actually, Ford made this decision because cars initially were painted using enamel paint, which took more than a month to dry, and black paint dried the fastest. This practice ended when DuPont invented lacquer paint, which dried in about two hours, regardless of the color.)

■ When you segment and then analyze your organization's performance, you might discover four facts about the customer segments:

  ☐ Some customers cost more to serve than others.

  ☐ Some no longer represent the marketplace in which your organization wants to compete.

  ☐ Some segments demand a disproportionate share of your organization's resources. Efforts to maintain and grow the customer base should consider excluding those segments.

  ☐ Your organization might be ineffectively structured to serve some segments.

■ Customer dissatisfaction and loss will rise if you try to treat all customers the same; large-volume purchasers really expect preferential treatment.

Before you can expect to understand and meet customer needs and wants, your organization must know more about its customers. Segmentation can determine how your organization directs its marketing efforts, designs activities, and handles customer service. It comes down to turning "different strokes for different folks" into a way to satisfy every customer you want to keep.

CUSTOMER RELATIONSHIP MANAGEMENT

Customer relationship management (CRM) is an intense effort to better know and understand your customers. Its fairly recent emergence is due to the growing need for organizations to bring their products and services to the marketplace at lightning speed while also offering individualized products and service. Technological advances have enabled the development of techniques and tools to assist your organization in differentiating itself from the masses.

Figure 2.3

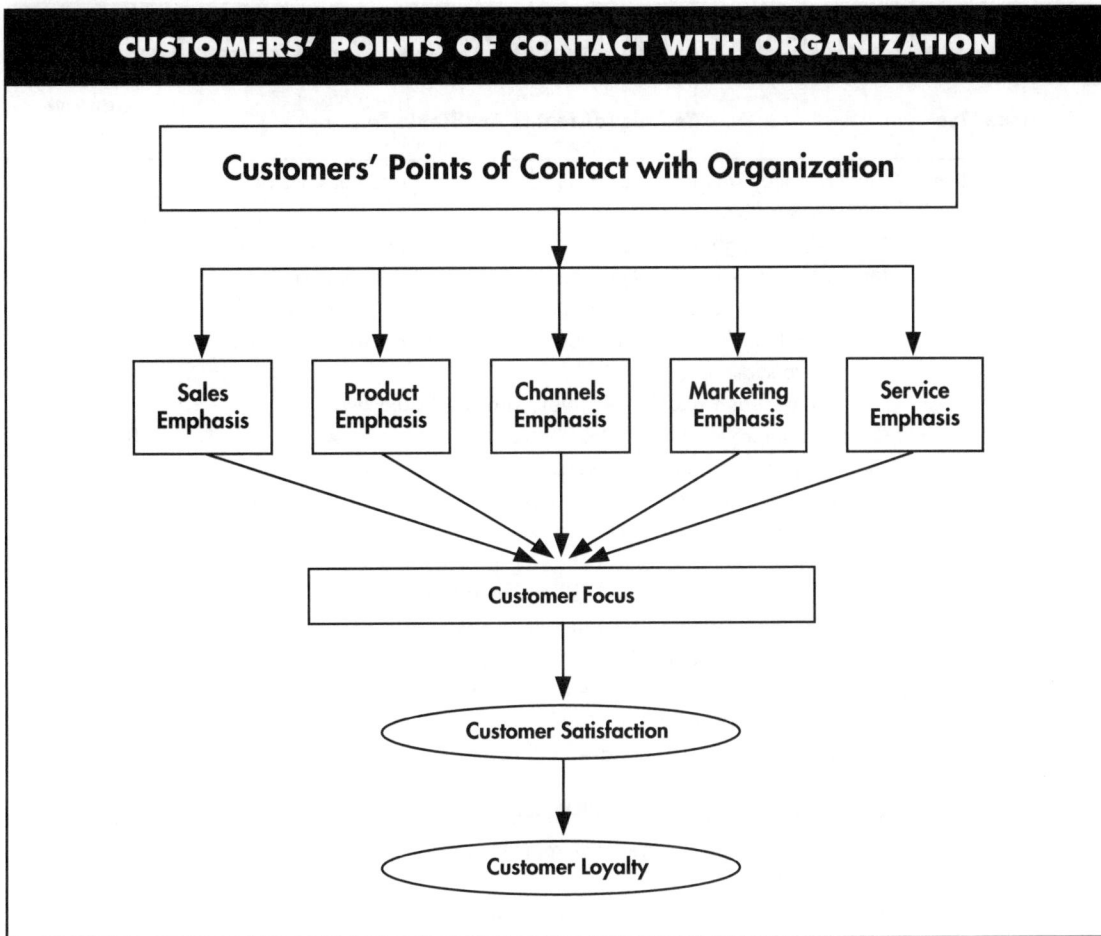

Figure 2.3 shows that customers, as they contact and interact with their provider, might encounter less than a total enterprise-oriented customer focus. Some providers might emphasize their sales force and sales activities, others might emphasize distribution channels, and so on. The provider's mind-set and activities must be integrated into a customer focus that permeates the entire organization.

CRM becomes the process, customer satisfaction becomes a key output, and customer loyalty is the outcome. CRM will affect:

■ Strategic plans, e.g., commitment to a customer focus for every facet of the organization
■ Organizational structure and culture, e.g., remaining flexible and adaptable to rapidly changing customer needs and wants
■ Managing style, e.g., encouraging greater employee empowerment
■ Key indicators, e.g., competitive differentiation
■ Metrics and decisions made there from, e.g., customer retention
■ Customer interactions, e.g., customer-friendly point-of-sale protocols
■ Business systems, e.g., systems to track customer contacts and relationships
■ Technology, e.g., data mining—examining multidimensional relationships and patterns

Table 2.2

USING TECHNIQUES AND TOOLS TO APPLY ISO 9004:2000		
Technique/Tool	**Technique/Tool Is Applicable To**	**ISO 9004 Clause/Subclause**
Setting objectives	Quality policy—expected or desired degree of customer satisfaction	5.3
	Quality objectives	5.4.1
	Quality planning inputs—defined customer needs and expectations	5.4.2
	Management review input—status and results of quality objectives	5.6.2
	People—individual and team objectives; facilitate involvement	6.2.1
	Design and/or development outputs—satisfaction of customer needs and expectations	7.3.3
	Measurement and analysis—achieving project objectives	8.1.1
	Continual improvement	8.5.4
Employing project management tools	Managing systems and processes	4.1
	Management responsibility—participating in improvement projects	5.1.1
	Resource management—project needs	6.1.2
	Measurement and analysis—achieving project objectives	8.1.1
	Planning for loss prevention—risk analysis; lessons learned	8.5.3
	Continual improvement—recognition and reward for improvement and breakthrough opportunities	8.5.4
Using focus groups	Management review input—feedback on satisfaction of interested parties	5.6.2
	Measurement and monitoring—feedback on aspects of product; focus groups	8.2.1.2
Deploying environmental scannings	Management review input—marketplace evaluation and strategies	5.6.2
	Market research—customer requirements; competitor analysis, benchmarking	7.2
	Measurement and monitoring—market needs; consumer organizations' reports; sector and industry studies	8.2.1.2
	Analyzing data—competitiveness	8.4
	Loss prevention—market analysis	8.5.3
Benchmarking	Management responsibility—methods	5.1.1
	Management review input—results from benchmarking activities	5.6.2
	Knowledge management—identification of information needs and sources	6.5
	Market research—customer requirements; competitor analysis, benchmarking	7.2
	Measurement and analysis—benchmarking individual processes	8.1.2
	Self-assessment—benchmarking	8.2.1.5
	Analysis of data—benchmarking processes	8.4
	Continual improvement—benchmarking competitor performance and best practices.	8.5.4
Applying QFD	Understanding current and future customer needs	4.3a
	Customer requirements	4.3a
	Customer expectations	4.3a
	Needs and expectations of present and potential customers	5.2.2
	Quality policy—expected or desired degree of customer satisfaction	5.3
	Quality planning—defined customer needs and expectations	5.4.2
	Market research—customer requirements; competitor analysis	7.2
	Measurement and monitoring—voice of the customer	8.2.1.2

Table 2.2—Continued

USING TECHNIQUES AND TOOLS TO APPLY ISO 9004:2000		
Technique/Tool	**Technique/Tool Is Applicable To**	**ISO 9004 Clause/Subclause**
Gathering cus-tomer feedback	Management review input—feedback on satisfaction of interested parties	5.6.2
	Effective communication with customers	7.2
	Measurement and monitoring—customers	8.2.1.2
	Continual improvement—customer complaints; recognition and reward for improvement	8.5.2
Improving internal customer service (QLAs)	Measurement and analysis—customer satisfaction	8.1.1
	Continual improvement—complaints, nonconformities, audits, measure-ments, etc.	8.5.2
	Continual improvement—recognition and reward for improvement	8.5.4
Assessing customer satisfaction with surveys	Management responsibility—assessment	5.1.1
	Quality planning inputs—defined customer needs and expectations	5.4.2
	Management review input—feedback on satisfaction of interested parties	5.6.2
	Measurement and analysis—customer satisfaction	8.1.1
	Measurement and analysis—measurements of customer satisfaction	8.1.2
	Measurement and monitoring—customer and user surveys	8.2.1.2
	Analysis of data—customer satisfaction	8.4
	Continual improvement—complaints, nonconformities, audits, measurements, etc.	8.5.2
	Loss prevention—satisfaction measurements	8.5.3
Post-purchase follow-up	Continual improvement—complaints, nonconformities, audits, measurements, etc.	8.5.2
	Loss prevention—customer needs and expectations	8.5.3
Segmenting the customer base	Needs and expectations of present and potential customers	5.1.2, 5.2.2
	Financial resources—waste reduction (unprofitable customer segments)	6.8
	Loss prevention—customer needs and expectations	8.5.3

FOCUS ON YOUR CUSTOMERS

In *The Agenda: What Every Business Must Do To Dominate the Decade,*[4] two of author Michael Hammer's nine management innovations focus on making your organization easy to do business with and adding more value. Establishing and sustaining a customer focus isn't just a matter of tracking customer returns and complaints or sending out perfunctory surveys. Building and keeping a customer focus must be a primary strategic goal for any organization that plans to survive and thrive. The sampling of techniques and tools presented in this chapter suggest ways to begin orienting your organization toward a customer focus.

However, one word of caution: No one technique or tool will achieve the goal. You must find the best combination of techniques and tools for your organization—and your customers. Table 2.2 aligns suggested techniques and tools with the topical areas of ISO 9004:2000, including paragraph references.

Now that the primary focus of an organization stepping up to ISO 9004 has been clearly identified—i.e., customers—the next concern is providing the resources needed to support that strategic direction. Chapter three explores some of the principal resource issues.

ENDNOTES

1. ACSI—The American Customer Satisfaction Index, initiated in 1994, is a cross-industry measure of the satisfaction of U.S. household customers with the quality of the goods and services available to them, both those goods produced within the United States and those provided as imports from foreign firms that have substantial market share or dollars sales. The ACSI is produced by the National Quality Research Center at the University of Michigan Business School, in partnership with the American Society for Quality and the CFI Group of Ann Arbor, Michigan. About 16,000 customers of companies surveyed are contacted each quarter. Scores may be obtained at *www.theacsi.org.*

2. LCALI is a methodology developed by R.T. Westcott & Associates for its clients.

3. Reichheld, Frederick F. and Claus Fornell. "What's a Loyal Customer Worth?" *Fortune,* December 1995. The authors presented a formula for computing a customer's worth.

4. Hammer, Michael. *The Agenda: What Every Business Must Do To Dominate the Decade.* New York: Crown Business, 2001.

CHAPTER 3

Focusing on Resource Management

Competent personnel and appropriate resources are critical to ensuring quality

You often hear the phrase, "People are our most important asset." But how can an organization ensure that it has competent people performing all the functions that affect product quality?

For your organization to produce a consistently value-added product that meets customer needs and future expectations, it's essential to start by hiring quality-adaptive people with the aptitude and attitude to become competent in producing your product (remember "product," in ISO-speak, is a physical product or a service).

ISO 9004:2000, Quality management systems—Guidelines for performance improvements expands upon the topic of human resources in ISO 9001:2000's clause 6.2, Resource management—Human resources, along with subclause 6.2.1, Involvement of people, and subsubclauses 6.2.1.1, Competence, and 6.2.2.2, Awareness and training.

To help you understand what ISO 9004:2000 offers in terms of improving product quality, this chapter outlines ways an organization can ensure it has competent people assigned to all functions where the work performed affects product quality. The chapter also examines how an organization can involve its human resources effectively and present a model for individual development and other issues to consider in succession planning.

ISO 9000:2000 defines "competence" in clause 3.9.12 as the "demonstrated ability to apply knowledge and skills." For our purposes, the definition has been expanded to include knowledge, experience, skills, aptitude and attitude (KESAA). If employees are your organization's most important assets, then having competent personnel in the broadest terms will ensure product quality and the life of the organization.

HOW TO SELECT THE RIGHT PEOPLE

The people an organization hires should meet at least the basic requirements to do the job, but this is often easier said than done. For nearly every job in an organization, some basic requirements should be stated for each KESAA factor.

To comply with discrimination and all other laws as well as demonstrate common sense, what's required for each job as far as the five factors are concerned should be validated. This means an effort should be made to analyze each position to be filled and to document the minimum requirements.

With the possible exception of skills (*S*), each factor is somewhat difficult to define. However, think of the consequences of hiring someone with inadequate knowledge (*K*), insufficient or inappropriate experience (*E*), and little aptitude (*Ap*) for the work, and/or an attitude (*At*) contrary to the performance required. Now examine a typical "job description," and most likely you'll find it inadequately addresses most if not all the KESAA factors.

Usually what must occur is a "task analysis," a process to uncover the *K, S* and *Ap* required for a job. How much *E* your organization needs in a new hire will depend on how much training time you plan to invest and how long a learning curve your business can tolerate. A person's *E* might need to be evaluated closely if your organization has a corporate culture or business processes that the applicant may be resistant to because of his or her past experience.

Attitude can be the most challenging factor to assess. For example, hiring a top-ranked person from a prestigious college sounds great. However, if the new hire must undergo a long-duration management-training program followed by rotation through a series of mundane assignments, *At* could become a problem.

If the person comes in with an *At* of superiority, high confidence, and expectations of rapid promotion, the disillusioned fast-tracker might prove unproductive and soon leave. The organization then has to fill the position again. On reflection, the fault lies in wanting the best possible new hires but not designing the job assignments to match the *K, S, Ap*, and *At* you should expect to find in such a recruit.

From a human resources perspective, an organization must think of employees as customers buying a product (i.e., positions within the organization). If the position doesn't meet customer specifications—and how the supplier "sold" the position (i.e., product) the organization will fail to achieve customer satisfaction, i.e., employee satisfaction.

If the need is to hire a fully competent person who can step into the job and do it from day one, then a very detailed hiring specification is needed as well as careful hiring practices. This is especially true if no one in the organization is capable of properly assessing the job candidates' KESAA factors. Outside guidance might have to be retained to help evaluate such candidates.

Figure 3.1 diagrams the application of the KESAA factors in achieving a quality hire.

The quality of the people selected for hire depend equally upon how well the hiring specifications are defined and the candidates are recruited and matched to the specifications, *and* the decision to hire candidates adheres to the standard established. This leads to another concern: Are the people responsible for compiling the job requirements and recruiting, screening, selecting, and assimilating new-hires competent to perform these tasks? How effective is the internal system for doing all this?

HOW TO ASSIMILATE THE NEW HIRE

What happens—or doesn't happen—during the first few days a new hire is on the job can significantly affect the organization's product quality. The following might seem unlikely, but assume a person with all the right KESAA is hired. He or she comes to work on day one a little nervous but highly motivated to do a good job and the following scenario plays out:

■ Filling out benefit forms takes hours, and no one is around to answer questions.
■ The orientation program starts late because the executive who will welcome the new employee is busy and delayed or won't be available.

Figure 3.1

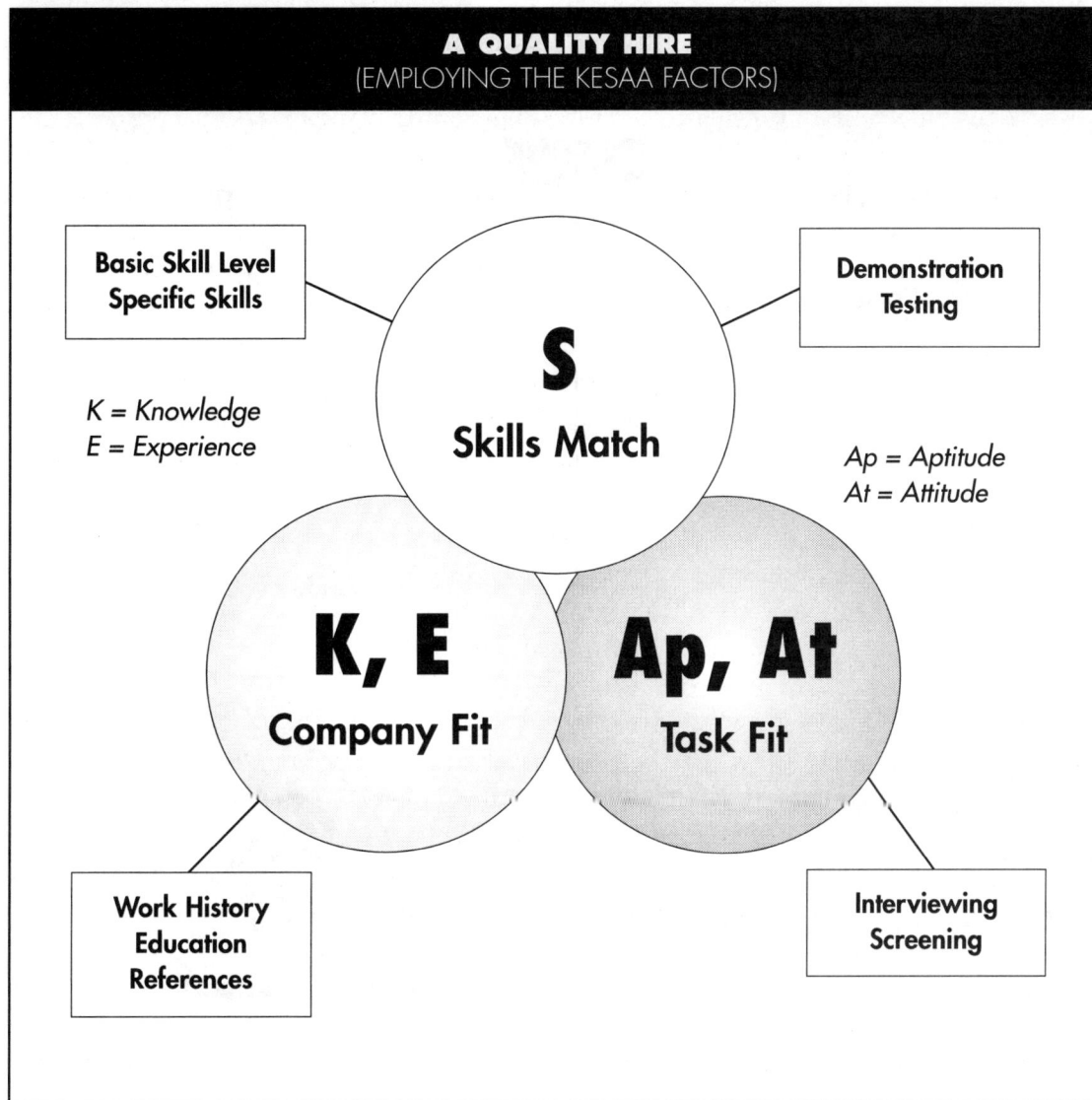

A QUALITY HIRE
(EMPLOYING THE KESAA FACTORS)

S
Skills Match

K, E
Company Fit

Ap, At
Task Fit

Basic Skill Level
Specific Skills

Demonstration
Testing

K = Knowledge
E = Experience

Ap = Aptitude
At = Attitude

Work History
Education
References

Interviewing
Screening

- A planned tour of the facility is postponed because a tour of visiting customers takes precedence.
- The immediate supervisor is unavailable to explain the expectations for the new job, and a reluctant co-worker is forced to show the new hire the ropes.
- The new hire is left alone to figure out what to do next, where the restroom and work supplies are found, and how the telephone and computer systems work.

If days two and three are anywhere near as unmotivating, they can seriously affect the new hire's approach to producing a quality product because no one seems to care. The old adage, "People start a new job motivated—it's what is done to them afterward that makes a difference" appears to be a recent discovery for too many managers. However, most organizations have known all along that if you treat employees with dignity and respect, most likely they'll treat the customers well.

Figure 3.2

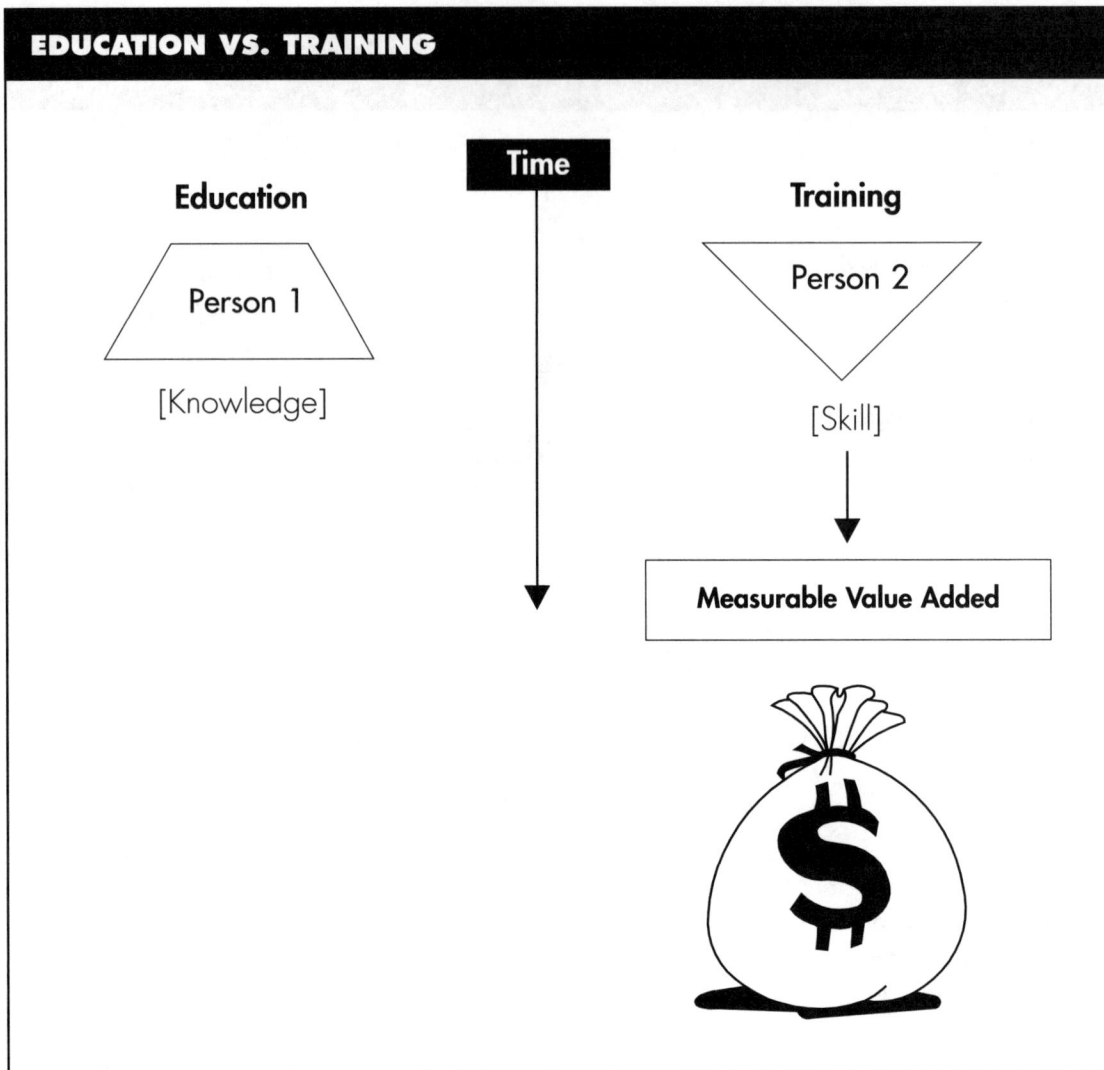

EDUCATION VS. TRAINING

Education — Person 1 [Knowledge]

Time

Training — Person 2 [Skill]

Measurable Value Added

To assimilate a new employee effectively, a supervisor must spend time with him or her discussing the organization's strategic direction, goals and objectives, and key policies as well as each other's expectations. They must agree on some personal objectives to support the new worker's performance for an initial learning period—from a few days for an entry-level worker up to three months or more for a professional. These start-up objectives must reflect both what the supervisor expects from the worker and what the worker expects from his or her supervisor.

This start-up time should include some basic orientation to the organization, its products and how and where they are used, its customers, its suppliers, and the production processes. Some basic education and training might be needed, depending on the level of K, E, and S possessed by the new hire. Certainly the organization's work protocols must be addressed (e.g., how a phone is answered; how a customer is treated; what procedures to follow; what forms to complete; and what personnel, quality and legal rules, regulations, and standards must be met).

Figure 3.3

TRAINING SYSTEMS MODEL

Mandated need
Expressed need
Needs analysis

Support

Management

DESIGN

Instruction

Evaluation

Delivery

Administrative
procedures

Facilities

Media

Instructor-facilitator

Participants KESAA

**TRAINING
DELIVERY**

EVALUATION

OUTPUTS

Enhanced K, S

Improved:
• Performance
• Attitude

OUTCOMES

Quality

Customer service

Productivity

Profit/payoff

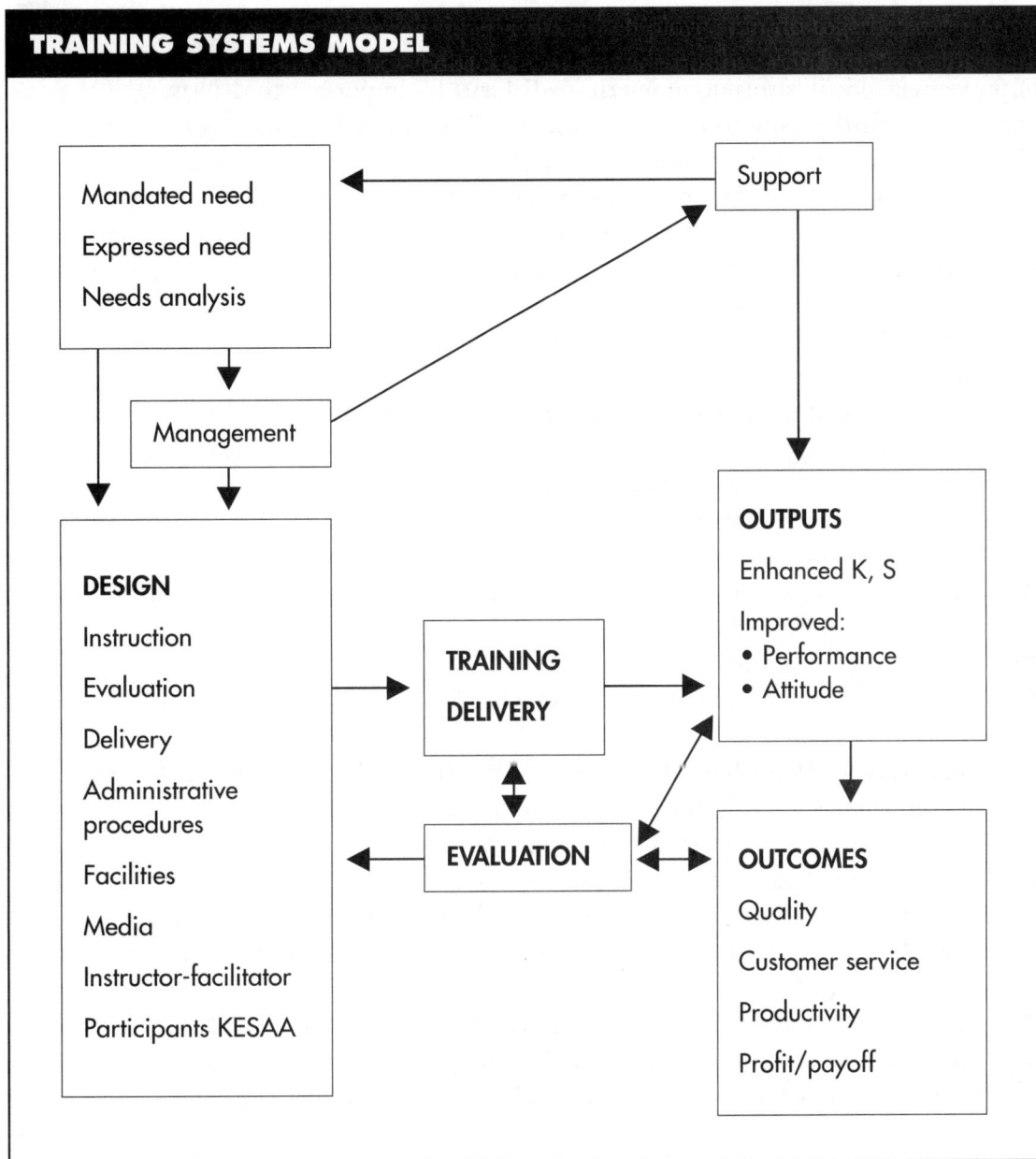

The supervisor, in a coaching role, must provide continual guidance and support during the start-up period, with that role lessening as the employee reaches the desired competency. Frequent performance feedback is of greatest value to the employee during this period and should reinforce what the expectations are, convey what the observed performance is, and produce agreement on what the supervisor and employee can do together to improve the employee's performance. The feedback must provide positive reinforcement for work done well, and this reinforcement must address incremental improvements as they occur.

EDUCATION OR TRAINING?

Once a new hire's assimilation to the job is complete, additional education and training will likely be required over time for both the employee's and the organization's continual improvement. How is this need determined? First, it's important to determine if the employee needs further education (to increase the K factor) and/or training (S). Is the effort intended to broaden a person's knowledge or develop a specific skill set? Education, or K, is evaluated through testing for acquisition and comprehension. On the other hand, training is measured by determining if the trainee has attained the expected skill set (S), can demonstrate the skill-set's application, has incorporated the skill into his or her job performance, and if there is a measurable dollar payoff from the employee's new skills.

Figure 3.2 depicts the relationship between education and training. Given two employees with similar KESAAs, the purpose of education is to broaden person one's K over time, while the purpose of training is to develop person two's specific skill or set of skills that can be measured when applied and that will produce a dollar payoff for the organization.

Figure 3.3 is a training system model that can be applied regardless of the medium used to provide the training. The order of approach is important. The first step is to answer why training is required:

■ Is there a new regulation, a new or changed procedure, or a new strategic direction that requires new or expanded S?

■ Who needs the training?

■ What S and K do the trainees need, and what S and K do they already possess?

Comparing a task analysis of the job requirements with an analysis of the employee's present competency level(s) provides the answer; this is known as the "needs analysis."

The second step is to determine the design of the training:

■ What method(s) of instruction will be used (e.g., lecture, Socratic questioning, experiential, simulation, or demonstration-practice), and what media will be needed (printed material, computers, or projectors)? How will the outputs and outcomes be measured and evaluated?

■ How will the training be delivered (e.g., on-the-job, computer-based, or workshop)?

■ What procedures must be followed and what records are needed?

■ What instructor or trainer will be needed (consider also availability, competence, internal, or external)?

■ How are participants to be selected (e.g., present competence levels, amount of training needed by different employees, or application of skills to each employee's job)?

During and after the training, each factor involved in the training's design as well as its delivery should be evaluated. Table 3.1 lists the levels for training evaluation. Note that the training results are measured. A basic rule of thumb is if you can't show a return-on-training-investment at least three times larger than the investment, training shouldn't be conducted—except where mandatory.

In addition, has your organization trained people who can back up employees in case they're off the job for an extended period? Back-up personnel are important at every organizational level. In long-range terms, make sure succession plans are in place for your organization's key positions.

Table 3.1

TRAINING: LEVELS OF EVALUATION	
Level	**Measurement/Results**
1. Reaction	Smile sheets
2. Learning	Tests
3. Behavior	Application on the job
4. Results	Pre- and post-analysis
5. ROTI*	Payback
*ROTI = Return On Training Investment	

Succession planning is critical to your organization's viability and growth. Everyone occupying a key position in the organization should be included in succession planning, regardless of his or her organizational level. A few of the issues to consider include:

■ If the employee were no longer available, what would be the effect on the organization (consider strategic goals, structure, core competency, knowledge base, stakeholder relationships, image to outsiders, or employee morale)?

■ Are the organization's policies and practices relative to rotational assignments, promotions, and developing successors supportive of succession planning?

■ Should the organization wait until a vacancy occurs before attempting to fill the opening?

■ What might be the confidentiality concerns, e.g., should a person know who is being groomed for his or her position?

■ What effects could nepotism create?

■ How much time and cost is involved to train a successor?

COMPETENCY: AN EMPLOYEE PERSPECTIVE

How aware are employees of your customers' needs and the consequences of not meeting customer requirements? You'll probably initially respond by thinking, "Why, that's common sense, and I can't imagine any company where employees aren't aware of customer needs and the consequences if they don't." However, you also know that the reality is very different, even though you might not think it makes a big difference in meeting customer requirements.

Some years ago I was working with an automotive assembly plant, where I became aware of the limited understanding the average assembly-line worker had of the processes involved in producing the final product. Every worker knew what a car was and what his or her job involved—I was working with windshield installers—but many were unaware of how a car was manufactured and assembled, other than the windshield. They were constantly reminded to do "quality work" and were punished if they didn't, but they had no real understanding of the effect their processes had downstream or their ability to affect the quality of what they received from an upstream process. The modus operandi seemed to be "get it off the line and let the rework teams or the dealership take care of any problems."

By comparison, I was later involved with a small manufacturer of thermal measuring instruments and equipment. It had grown from a home garage to a primary source for high-tech devices. All new hires, regardless of their job, underwent a rigorous one-week program to indoctrinate them on how every product was made, their uses, and typical customer requirements. The product catalog, which was loaded with technical specifications and nomenclature, was the basic text. As a result, any employee could discuss a customer's needs with a moderate level of intelligence and direct the customer to a more qualified person if need be. Employees were extensively cross-trained and compensated well for their combined KESAA factors. This company prospered and grew, while the auto assembly plant (now closed) struggled and suffered from poor employee performance and *At*.

An organization that makes its employees aware of what it does and how it does it has a better chance of conveying the importance of each employee's contributions. An organization should consider inviting customers to the facility to take a tour and speak with the employees. Employees must know how the products they produce are used and how important it is to the customer to receive a quality product. Employee involvement is a two-way street: The organization must share information with the employee, and the employee must take responsibility for his or her actions. (Appendix D outlines considerations for when employees visit customers.)

In former days, management and engineering professionals decided what was to be done and how. Workers performed the tasks as assigned and were watched carefully by supervisors. In progressive organizations today, workers are expected to assume greater responsibility not only for completing their tasks correctly and on time but also for contributing suggestions on process improvements. Higher-level KESAA factors are clearly required for this enlargement of the job scope.

In many industries, workers are empowered to make certain types of decisions, within boundaries. This empowerment heightens a worker's sense of commitment, instills pride in what he or she does, and rewards him or her with the respect that results. Customers are more satisfied when knowledgeable people address their needs. The organization can also prosper in the marketplace with its enhanced core competency. The transition to any empowered workforce requires higher-level KESAA factors and an investment in training—particularly to train supervisors on how to allow an employee to become empowered and how to handle mistakes and/or poor judgments an employee might make. Brand-new companies, founded and managed by progressive thinkers, often have an advantage in not having as much to unlearn. (See appendix E for more detail on how to improve workplace competence.)

COMPETENCY: AN ORGANIZATIONAL PERSPECTIVE

From a broader perspective, competency is often referred to as an organization's "core competency," or what an organization is good at. This competency represents all the KESAA factors of all employees and might also include the facilities and equipment used by them. When you market your organization's capability to produce and deliver a product that meets all your customers' requirements, you're talking about the core competency of your organization—what's behind that product. In today's highly competitive marketplace, an organization's core competency is its foremost asset.

This leads to thinking about the strategic goals, objectives, and plans for your organization, which were discussed in chapter one. In this regard, ISO 9004:2000 suggests that an organization's management consider five needs [6.2.2.1, Competence]. They are:

- Future demands related to strategies and operations
- Anticipated needs for management and the workforce, especially as they relate to employee succession or replacement. (The composition of management and workforce might require change as strategies and organizational goals change.)
- Potential need to change organizational processes, facilities, tools, and/or equipment
- Continual evaluation of employees' competence to perform under existing and projected requirements
- Mandates that might now or in the future affect the organization, its customers, suppliers, and other interested parties.

An organization's core competency is only viable as long as the organization remains competitive in the marketplace. These days, competitive forces that can affect an organization often come from an entirely new technology or product that completely replaces any need for your product (e.g., your company survived the transition from manual to electric typewriters but got knocked out as personal computers replaced virtually all need for electric typewriters). The organization must catch up or leap ahead in its product offerings and prepare for obsolescence.

A new process technology might become available that, when your organization installs it, will make part of your trained, competent workforce unprepared or unneeded. You might retrain some workers but a layoff is more likely, and new workers will have to have the required set of K, E, S, and Ap factors. Your organization's core competency will have changed and possibly its competitive position. The change resulting from technological innovation might also mean that a wider range of organizations may be able to produce the same products as your organization and do so just as well.

To summarize, competency is a concern, both at an individual and organizational level. It's both a current and future issue with a direct bearing on your organization's product quality today as well as the marketplace's perception of your organization's capability to meet ever-changing needs in the future.

LEADERSHIP AND MANAGEMENT

Leadership and management are both important for effectively operating and improving an organization, its people, processes, and, ultimately, products. "Leadership" consists of the people designated or perceived to be the head of an organization or initiative, but it can also refer to the approach or process by which leadership is achieved. Technically, a leader "earns" this designation as others follow his or her lead. A leader can also be a manager but not always. The term "leader" is also used to describe an organization that's the model, or benchmark, for its competitors or all organizations—the innovative organization out in front.

"Management" typically is described as comprising those responsible for operating an organization. "Top management" usually means the few individuals at the very top of the organizational structure. Technically, a manager manages processes and organizational units, in contrast to a leader, who simply leads people. "Manager" is the title given to a person by a higher authority. A manager can also be a leader but isn't necessarily so.

Comprehensive studies of types of leaders and management styles have been done for years, and many report examples of mismanagement and inappropriate leadership. Some studies report that it might be desirable to work for an understanding, pleasant boss who allows you great latitude in what you do and how you do it, factors found to be important in some organizations.

Other studies indicate that such a management style is damaging in some organizations. Indeed, some of the most successful corporate leaders were ruthless toward their employees. This isn't to condone such behavior but to stress the need for a management style that suits the organizational culture and structure, and balances the best interests of all parties. Suitable leadership approaches and managing styles are integral to an organization's core competency and the effect on interested parties.

The next question, then, is: "What kind of investment should your organization make in employee development?" It's important to recognize the paradigm shift that's taken place. The paternalistic view that the organization is responsible for the growth and personal development of its employees no longer applies. The individual is now considered responsible for his or her development, and management's role is to provide the resources, opportunities, and support.

Figure 3.4 is a diagrammatic view of the development process. The premise is that an individual is selected based on his or her growth potential (center of the model). The individual is the product of a multifaceted background: life and work experiences, education, capabilities, personality traits, and personal aspirations. The roughly drawn shape in the

Figure 3.4

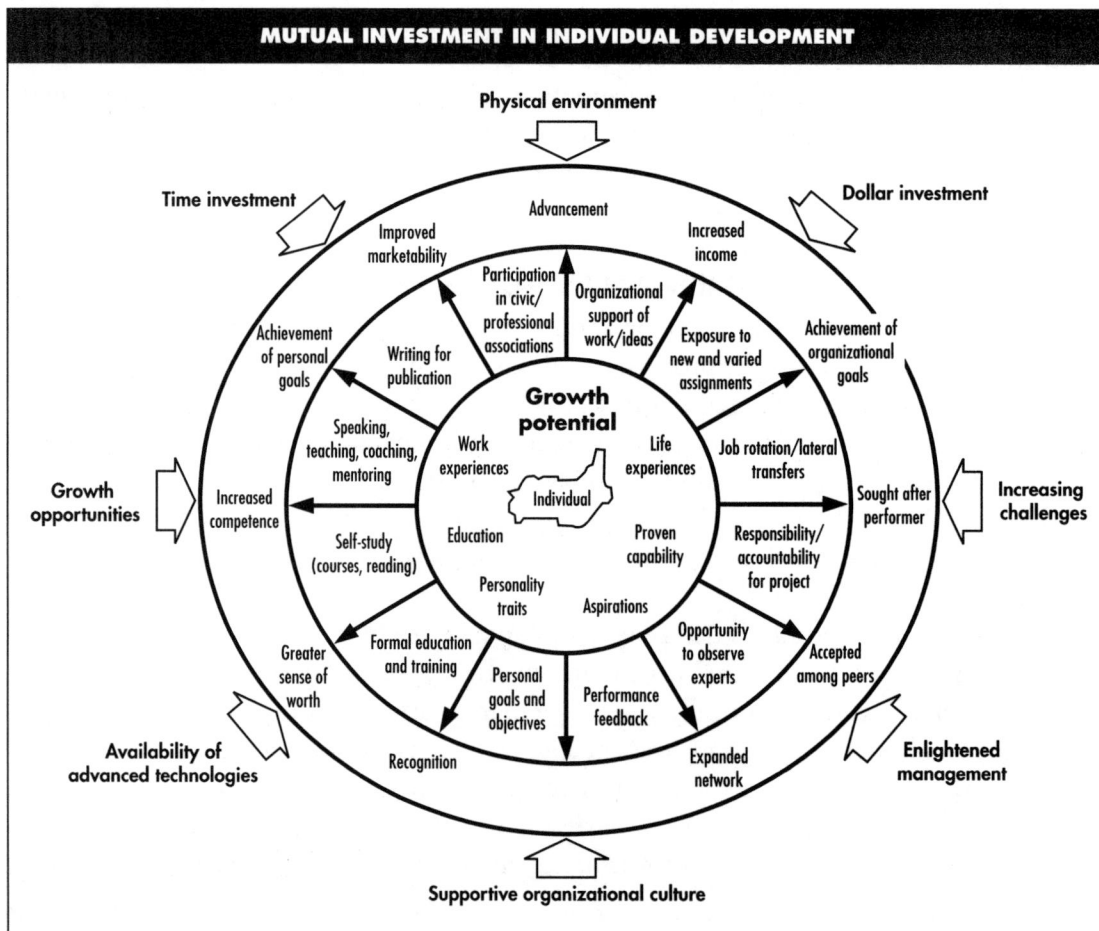

MUTUAL INVESTMENT IN INDIVIDUAL DEVELOPMENT

center suggests individuals have many facets and that the symbolic representation would differ for each individual.

Listed in the first concentric ring, from the center, are some opportunities management can provide to aid the individual's development and growth. Examples of some of the potential outcomes the individual might obtain as he or she develops are shown in the outermost ring. The arrows on the periphery highlight the investment the organization must make for the individual to achieve his or her potential. Intended as a conceptual model, the figure makes no attempt to identify every conceivable development tool.

Using the analogy of a prize-winning garden, plants will blossom to the highest standard when a plan is developed and implemented. The best seed must be selected and sown. The right nutrients must be applied. The conditions for growth must be present and appropriate. Weeding, pruning, and sometimes replanting will be required. However, the plants must grow on their own if both the plant and the gardener are to benefit.

Two types of risk that management might face due to the development an employee does or doesn't receive are:

- The employee might become unproductive and disgruntled or quit if opportunities to develop and grow aren't provided.
- When an employee has the opportunity to develop into a competent employee with marketable K and S, he or she might be recruited or seek advancement elsewhere.

This picture is incomplete, but despite the risks, an organization usually benefits by investing in an employee's development because it will produce a return on investment for as long as the organization retains him or her. Creating and/or harboring an unmotivated, unproductive, uncaring employee who has little opportunity to develop—or has chosen not to use the opportunities offered—can be the root cause of multiple problems and nonconformities over time.

In spite of periodic ups and downs, two renowned companies—IBM and GE—have prospered by using a development model. Admittedly, they have "graduated" many employees to jobs in other organizations, but they clearly view this as being worthwhile because many employees will stay and continue to grow, and it ensures the company will get the most from individuals while they're with it. Development opportunities also attract employees possessing the best KESAA because being with the company helps the individual develop, even if it's only to leave for a better opportunity. Most important, such a corporate culture conveys to employees the value of development and upward mobility.

Development helps provide a pool of competent future managers and leaders at other organizations, some of which will be customers and suppliers. It also helps the economy, upon which all organizations depend for future growth.

OBJECTIVE EVIDENCE

Basic records concerning competency, awareness, and training are part of the ISO 9001 quality management system. If the measurements and evaluations have been documented, you'll have more than satisfied ISO 9001's requirements for "effectiveness of actions taken" [subclause 6.2.2]. But what more can be done to increase the benefit as your organization steps up to ISO 9004:2000?

As your organization develops and deploys its strategic planning process, it's important to measure and document the link between its top-level objectives and the contributions made by developing workforce competencies. The approach is analogous to identifying customer requirements and fulfilling them. Is your organization meeting its top-level objectives, and if so, how effectively? Understand that the object of employee education is to disseminate information and build employees' knowledge, while training's objective is to develop measurable skills. Each has its place and benefits. Your organization needs S to get the job done today. Its employees need enhanced K to improve processes and foresee and meet future needs.

Your organization will have stepped up to ISO 9004's subclause 6.2.1 when it has:

- Recognized the connection between a competent, highly motivated, and empowered workforce and retaining satisfied customers
- Provided employees with ongoing training, continually reviewed their needs, and evaluated their competence relative to their assigned work, before and after training
- Encouraged employees to participate in continual improvement—including giving them the K, S, and positive reinforcement to do so.
- Made every employee aware of the role he or she plays in producing the organization's outcomes, and the effect of his or her contribution on all interested parties (e.g., customers, suppliers, the community, and co-workers)
- Taken the actions needed to build and sustain a marketable core competency, one that will enable it to adapt with the forces of change

Current literature talks about the learning "organization." Simply stated, it's an organization dedicated to continual learning. The combination of concepts explored in this chapter present some of the means for becoming such a learning organization.

RESOURCES OTHER THAN EMPLOYEES

When it comes to an organization's ability to meet customer requirements and achieve customer satisfaction, resource management considers people the company's most important asset. But does that attitude make it any less important to manage all other assets in the organization? After all, when ISO 9001:2000 addresses human resources, it does so with only brief, general requirements for suitable infrastructure and work environment.

Perhaps the baseline quality management system requirements in *ISO 9001:2000, Quality management systems—Requirements* focus on human resource management because that's been the traditional area of concern in any organization, while efforts to manage all other resources is the sign of an organization stepping beyond the baseline. In reality, managing all other resources an organization has or uses will either affect how employees perform their jobs and the organization's ability to meet customer needs, or will be affected by employee performance.

This section examines the guidance ISO 9004 provides in section 6's clauses concerning managing resources other than employees. These clauses, and those discussed earlier, expand considerably beyond the minimum requirements of ISO 9001. Clearly, resource management and continual improvement thereof is a major factor in stepping up to ISO 9004. We'll examine each clause to show how ISO 9004 can be used and how each resource provides the foundation for those that follow, as captured by the hierarchy of resource types shown in figure 3.5.

Figure 3.5

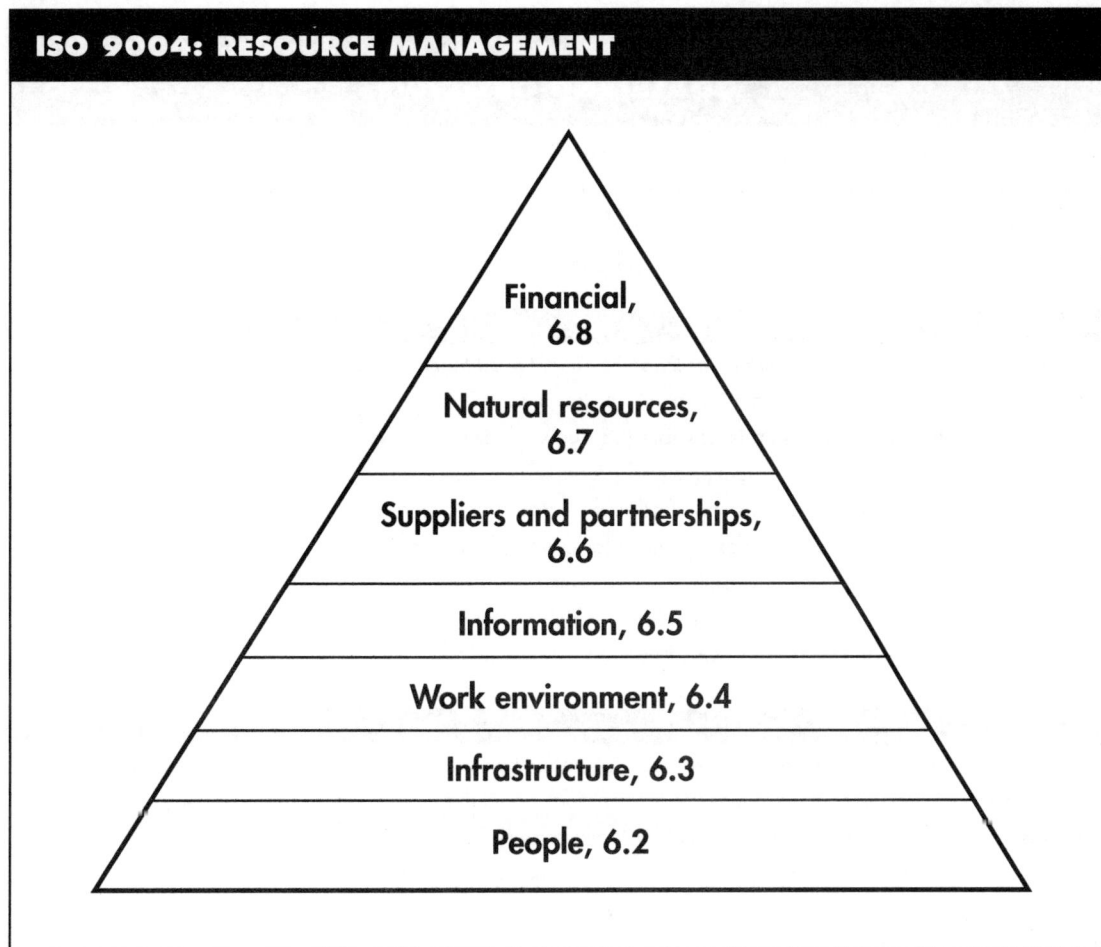

Infrastructure

Clause 6.3 addresses infrastructure, but what does that mean? *ISO 9000:2000, Quality management systems—Fundamentals and vocabulary* defines "infrastructure" as the "[organization] system of facilities, equipment, and services needed for the operation of an organization [3.3.3]." This includes the physical resources required to ensure quality in its product realization processes—that is, the buildings (or occupied space in buildings), workspaces, equipment (production as well as transportation), and tools. Infrastructure also includes technology such as information systems (e.g., an enterprise resource planning system) and communications systems (e.g., telephone, fax, e-mail, Internet, satellite and mail).

ISO 9001:2000 also requires your organization to identify the existing infrastructure and the maintenance needed [Clause 6.3]. To step up to ISO 9004:2000, you'll want to look into future requirements. That is, what are your organization's strategic goals and objectives, and how will they affect your infrastructure? Table 3.2 provides a detailed look at the infrastructure elements that might need to be changed if your organization plans to meet future quality and business targets, objectives, and goals.

To ensure your organization builds and sustains its capability to meet customer's requirements for quality product, a method of ongoing measurement and evaluation is needed.

Table 3.2

INFRASTRUCTURE CHANGES TO MEET STRATEGIC GOALS AND OBJECTIVES

As part of your organization's QMS and business-planning processes, strategic goals and objectives will be developed, but pursuing and fulfilling them might require changes to the infrastructure. The following list of infrastructure elements provides a look at questions and decisions you might face as your organization pursues goals and objectives aimed at maintaining and/or increasing its competitive edge.

Facilities

How do you define your organization's facilities? You might need to make decisions based on these questions:

- Do we locate near our customers, suppliers, or labor pools?
- Do we locate where expansion is possible (i.e., upward or outward)?
- Should we own, rent, or lease facilities and property?
- Do we need facilities that can be modified to accommodate changes in processes?
- Do we choose facilities in the safest locations for our employees, products, customers, suppliers, investors and/or owners, and the facility itself?
- Have we weighed the costs vs. the benefits of facility options, including concern for replacement costs in the event of a disaster or obsolescence?

Workspace

What types of working space will your organization need to meet its objectives and targets so as to balance the best interests of relevant parties? The following questions about the workspace should be answered:

- Does it enable the organization to meet customer requirements?
- Will it provide for the safety, security, and social needs of employees?
- Can it facilitate process flow and minimum cycle time in terms of:
  - ❑ Material and product flow?
  - ❑ Information flow?
  - ❑ Optimal uptime of equipment?
  - ❑ Facilities maintenance?

- Does it convey our organization's concern for quality?
- Will it encourage employees to pursue continual improvement?

Equipment and tools

What types of equipment and tools will your organization need to achieve its objectives and goals? Have you selected the equipment and tools that best suit the:

- New and changed customer requirements?
- Expanded competence of your workforce?
- Changing technologies used in your operations?

(Continued)

Table 3.2—Continued

Supporting services

What types of additional services might be needed to address your organization's outreaching of strategic goals and objectives? Consider the following opportunities for outsource services:

■ Process steps (e.g., welding, painting, computer programming)
■ Equipment maintenance
■ Tool maintenance (e.g., calibration and sharpening)
■ Administrative functions (e.g., accounting, personnel, printing, distribution)
■ Education and training for employees

For education-business alliances should you:

■ Pursue research and development?
■ Conduct market research?
■ Explore product design innovations?
■ Ensure curriculum attuned to your organization's hiring needs?

For engaging in interorganizational personnel interchanges (i.e., temporary loans or swaps):

■ To offset a temporary shift in business workload
■ To allow an expansion of your organization's core competency
■ To allow the professional development of key individuals

Environmental concerns

What issues and concerns must your organization address to ensure its survival, growth, and success in the future? The following questions about its environmental impact should be answered:

■ What responsibility do you have to the communities in which your facilities are located in terms of air, water, noise, and ground usage quality (Do you have filtration systems and/or engage in waste recycling, containment, or removal)?
■ Has your organization researched the compatibility of its products, the types of processes used, and the workforce employed with the needs of the community?
■ Has responsible end-of-useful-life disposition of product been considered in design and development and post-sale services?

Corporate citizenship

What issues and concerns must your organization address to build and sustain good relations with the community? Does it:

■ Promptly pay required taxes?
■ Promptly address any situations it has caused for which the community has concern?
■ Contribute to the community by "loaning" employee time and expertise to community projects, making available new, used, or refurbished facilities, equipment, or tools for community betterment, or providing funds to support community activities?

(Continued)

Table 3.2—Continued

Risk assessment and management

What must be provided to ensure you make the optimum response to potential risks to your organization and its effect on all stakeholders? Is it prepared for the following:

■ Marketplace shifts, including the unplanned obsolescence of product, changes in the customer mix, and loss of a major customer segment?

■ Financial setbacks, such as an economic downturn where decisions must be made about handling employee layoffs and/or a facility closing?

■ Technology changes that might increase/decrease the need for certain employees?

■ Catastrophic loss and its effect on your operations? Recent history has provided two examples:

❑ The destruction of facilities and equipment due to natural disaster, civil unrest, military action or terrorist attack. Is your organization prepared to deal with resulting inadequacies (e.g., inadequate safety, security, and backup facilities and personnel, insurance and/or financial reserves to cover recovery costs)?

❑ A computer database becomes unusable and all key information is lost or destroyed. Does your organization have contingency plans in case backup data wasn't maintained and available, the data security measures in place proved inadequate, or the business interruption insurance was insufficient?

Suggested approaches for developing and implementing maintenance methods to ensure the infrastructure continues to meet the organization's needs include:

■ Establishing organizational objectives and measurement criteria to address each of the areas noted in table 3.2

■ Setting up internal audits to monitor the achievement of the objectives and pinpoint opportunities for continual improvement. This will likely require the organization to do the following:

☐ Train personnel to conduct infrastructure audits (different types of expertise might be required to assess each of the diverse areas)

☐ Develop a review schedule of all areas to ensure that quality is being maintained

☐ Require audit result reviews as part of the periodic management review meetings and continually evaluate the viability of infrastructure audit activities

☐ Designate a person to identify areas of concern and bring those concerns to management for possible action (e.g., when the infrastructure planning and audits may be inadequate).

Work environment

If your organization has been exploring the guidance offered in ISO 9004, you've already considered its personnel concerns as addressed in clause 6.2 and the infrastructure as addressed in clause 6.3. That brings you to clause 6.4, Work environment, which ISO 9000:2000 defines as the "set of conditions under which work is performed [3.3.4]." By fulfilling clauses 6.2 and 6.3, your organization will have developed individual competency and ensured the appropriate facilities, equipment, and tools for all employees to do their jobs. Building a work environment that motivates and satisfies employees and the organization is all that remains to be done.

What exactly is a "suitable work environment?" To define this for your organization, you must answer the following questions:

- Are there opportunities for individuals to become involved in continual improvement?
- Are health and safety rules, guidance on how to comply with the rules, and suitable protective equipment furnished to ensure employee well being?
- Are continual efforts made to improve work methods and practices to prevent chronic physical and mental illnesses? For example, are ergonomically sound equipment and tools used?
- Is the workplace's physical layout and location effective, from both a process efficiency perspective and the worker's ease in performing the work?
- Does the level of social interaction at the workplace balance the best interests of the individuals and the organization?
- Are there adequate and well-maintained rest rooms, eating and recreation areas, secure personal storage areas, and adequate and safe parking and/or mass transit access?
- Are the temperature, humidity, noise and vibration levels, light and air quality, and cleanliness of the premises the best they can be?
- Are the work hours and rest periods planned with employee well being in mind?
- Are alternative work arrangements available to accommodate family care and religious obligations? Are facilities and staff available to assist with child care?
- Are arrangements in place to provide on- or off-site medical, counseling and legal services, particularly in response to emergency situations?
- Is there a plan for emergency evacuation in case of a fire, explosion, natural disaster, civil unrest, or terrorist attack? Do trained personnel exist to manage in such emergencies? Are there periodic drills to test such measures' effectiveness?
- Do employees regard the organization's product as safe for customer use, and does the product meet acceptable ethical and moral norms?
- Do employees perceive members of management as ethical, fair, and competent in their actions, both within and outside the organization?
- Do employees feel good about their work assignments, working conditions, and about working for the organization?
- How do employees portray the organization to outsiders (e.g., customers, suppliers, family, friends, community)?

Information

How do organizations manage their operations consistently and effectively, decide what must be corrected, and how to improve processes? An important ingredient is information, which ISO 9004 treats as a resource to be managed and without which the organization will lose its competitive edge. "Information" is defined in ISO 9004 as "meaningful data" [3.7.1]. Information is actually the second stage in a hierarchy: data when manipulated (i.e., sorted or aggregated) becomes information. Further, when used for a purpose, information becomes knowledge (e.g., the means to make a decision), which over time can become wisdom when it's accumulated, correlated, evaluated, transformed, and/or reconfigured. See figure 3.6, which shows the hierarchy of data to wisdom.

Information, as far as being a resource management consideration, isn't addressed in ISO 9001. The issues and concerns relating to information are left for those organizations

Figure 3.6

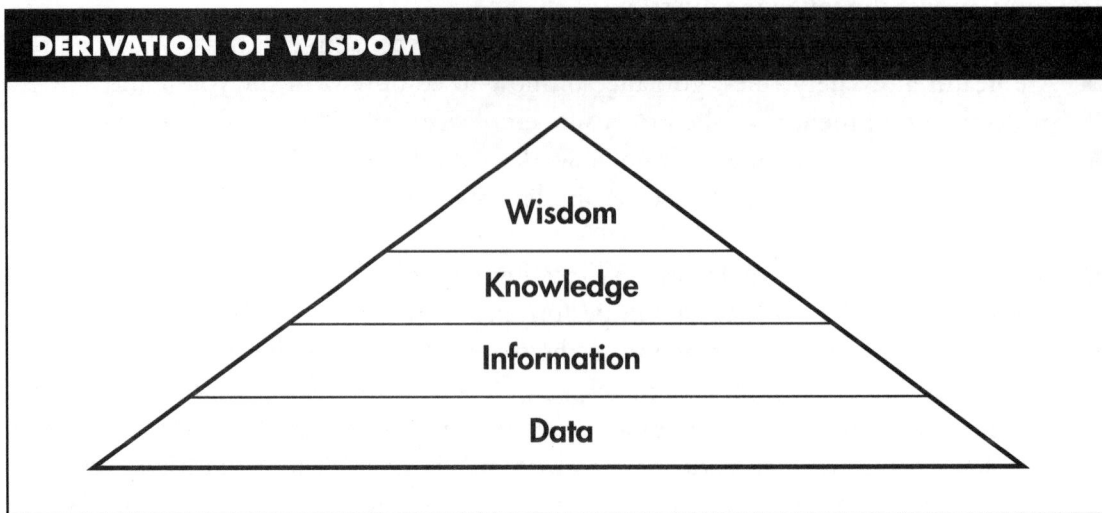

DERIVATION OF WISDOM

Wisdom

Knowledge

Information

Data

stepping up to ISO 9004 to manage. On the one hand, many organizations are swamped with data, much of which is never transformed into information, never mind being further processed into knowledge that can benefit the organization and its interested parties. On the other hand, many organizations fail to collect enough data—or the right kind—to generate knowledge that can enable the organization to operate effectively.

Looking at information resources from the organizational perspective, a first step in managing this resource is to determine why your organization needs and has data. For what purpose is data collected, and do they satisfy the intended purpose(s)? What should be added or deleted from the types of data collected? Consider conducting the value-added test; a revised list will most certainly result from this evaluation. From this list, identify what information is to be generated and for what purpose.

The hierarchy of strategic organizational goals and objectives as deployed throughout the organization should be the guide. Establish objectives for the information, including measures of effectiveness. This effort will identify the types of:

■ Data needed and their sources
■ Information needed and the purposes for each type.

Next, you must establish the means to either collect data or extract them from what's already collected. Then you must determine what type of data collection methodology to use—usually one aided by electronic data capture. This effort will require that you:

■ Accumulate the identified data needed in a form that can be used in the next step
■ Appropriately store and safeguard the data collected.

At this point, the accumulated data must be transformed into usable information. This will likely involve manipulating the data (e.g., coding, sorting, categorizing, measuring, computing, summarizing, extracting). Once appropriate data manipulation is completed, the data are usually prepared in tabular or graphic form.

After analysis and further processing, the information is transformed into knowledge to assist in formulating the organization's strategic direction. As this knowledge is captured, either within the thoughts and ideas of individual employees or as an organizational knowledge base, it becomes the basis for wisdom.

For example, computer programs, called "expert systems," built from an analysis of accumulated information and augmented by human knowledge, can be used to make consistent decisions for granting a loan or extending credit to a purchaser. Wisdom can be applied when overriding the computer's decision becomes necessary.

At the process or workforce level, transforming data into wisdom is more easily understood. For example: A worker is instructed in what he or she needs to know to do a job, which is the data that parallels the skills he or she is taught. As he or she applies the data learned, it's transformed into information he or she uses to perform the job more competently. As the worker accumulates information and his or her skills mature, the information becomes a storehouse of knowledge that allows him or her to perform at a more effective level and contribute to continual improvement. If the job and/or the product change, the worker can draw upon his or her collected wisdom in adapting to new circumstances.

For most organizations, the problem is how to capture, store, access, and use the knowledge accumulated by individual workers. This knowledge proves most valuable if it can be used to train new employees and aid teams in continually improving the organization's processes.

An emerging field known as "knowledge management" focuses on converting tacit knowledge into explicit knowledge. *Explicit* knowledge is that which is captured, recorded, and available for transmission between individuals (e.g., procedures, processes, standards). Tacit knowledge is the difficult-to-capture and -articulate "know how"—the expertise and ways of doing things that are contained within individuals and typically not recorded (and often can't be recorded—yet). When people speak of documenting "lessons learned" from the context of quality improvements, that's explicit knowledge. When the thought processes and expertise that brought about the improvements are successfully captured, that would be tacit knowledge converted to explicit knowledge.

Another field that has emerged, championed by marketers, is called "data mining." Given the vast amount of data accumulated by many organizations, ways are being found to use computers literally to "mine" this data. The objective is to look for correlations that could be useful to better manage an operation or exploit a trend.

When you present a credit or debit card at a retail checkout counter, you might suspect the retailer is collecting a wealth of data about you, such as:

- Who you are (including age, family status, and gender) and where you live
- What store you're buying from and at what time of day
- What products you're buying, including whether you used coupons (and what savings you obtained)
- How you're paying for the purchase

When this plethora of data are transformed, it might inform the retailer about:

- Traffic patterns by store
- Product sales—by item, quantity, time of day, and day of week
- Buying habits—by individual and demographic type
- Methods of payment (ratio of store card, general credit/debit card, check and cash purchases) by store

The information derived from this data can aid in the following:

■ Planning store openings and closings
■ Identifying staffing and inventory needs
■ Evaluating the effectiveness of different types of marketing
■ Determining what customers are buying and how frequently
■ Quantifying the value of stimulating use of store cards

Over time, the data can be mined further to seek correlations that might be meaningful, such as changes in buying habits due to the weather, economic changes, and news events.

Data are an asset only when they've been put to beneficial use by deriving information or knowledge. Data are expensive to collect and transform into information, so it's critical for an organization to establish the means to measure the effectiveness of its data collection and use. A simple return on data investment (RODI) is a place to start, with RODI equaling the value of collecting certain data divided by the costs of collecting them. Computing RODI will, at least for larger organizations, probably require segmenting the types of data to get a meaningful metric. An objective should be to refine continually the data collected and how they're used based on their value to the organization. (Appendix G discusses how to demonstrate a return-on-investment in more detail.)

Suppliers and partnerships

Suppliers' abilities to supply product in accordance with an organization's requirements (which are often derived from customer specifications) is addressed in ISO 9001:2000 subclause 7.4.1, Product realization—Purchasing process. However, the standard doesn't address the need to treat suppliers as a manageable resource. However, if your organization relies on suppliers and other partners in making a product or providing a customer-oriented service, the suppliers and partnerships can be the most critical resource you have. Your organization's experience might indicate that managing suppliers will produce one of the greatest improvements.

When your organization steps up to ISO 9004, managing supplier relationships, alliances, and partnerships should be a critical concern. As an organization matures, the need for consistency and efficiency in entering materials into the system becomes important. Moreover, the availability of reliable suppliers becomes necessary for effectively performing processes, and the following might become desirable:

■ Optimizing the number of suppliers with which business is done
■ Maximizing interorganizational communications to facilitate rapid response to and resolution of problems
■ Cooperating to find ways of continually improving supplier product and/or material and processes (e.g., providing the supplier with training in the use of quality tools)
■ Involving suppliers in new product design
■ Reducing and/or eliminating inventories
■ Reducing and/or eliminating the need for incoming inspections
■ Providing incentives to suppliers to ensure gains are maintained while their input and services are continually improving (e.g., long-term contracts)

To achieve these goals involves establishing a new type of relationship with suppliers and abandoning the traditional adversarial approach. The accepted approach should be one of mutual cooperation and fairness in all dealings, with benefits for all. Reaching this state with your suppliers will require your organization to do the following:

- Establish very clear, two-way communications with suppliers to relay what's expected of each party and how it's to be delivered
- Make suppliers aware of the criteria to be used to evaluate their performance and what the consequences will be for performance ranging from unacceptable to excellent
- Keep suppliers informed as to how their performance is perceived (suppliers can use this information in satisfying ISO 9001:2000 subclause 8.2.1, Customer satisfaction)
- Involve suppliers in product or process design where their input can be beneficial
- Offer assistance to suppliers in improving their processes and practices
- Provide incentives for suppliers as a reward for good or excellent performance as well as a measure of the mutual benefit to be gained from cooperation

As your organization's supplier relationships improve, alliances—i.e., where both parties work together for a common purpose—might be the next stage. Partnering goes further, in that both parties collaborate in enhancing the effort to "pull product" effectively through the supply chain, sharing the gains and absorbing the losses.

Supplier relationships and evaluations derived from periodic assessments should be a topic for management review. Such relationships should be continually improved. (Appendix F offers a checklist of questions that can be used to assess supplier relations.)

Natural resources

ISO 9004 recommends that an organization have adequate contingency plans to avert potential misuse of natural resources [clause 6.7, Natural resources]. There are also many positive actions that should be considered in conserving and using natural resources. An organization has an obligation to the community or communities in which it locates to minimize the depletion or degradation of air, light, and water quality as well as noise and other types of pollution. It should also strive to use land and water rights wisely. For example, consider establishing a proportion between the land used for the organization's facilities and access roads and the amount retained in a natural state or as open space.

To be effective in managing natural resources, the astute organization will have strategic goals and objectives to sustain an acceptable or better quality level in using natural resources. To ascertain how effectively the organization meets these objectives, measurements must be taken and evaluations done. A periodic assessment of effectiveness and management review of the evaluations is indicated. As appropriate to your organization, reference to the standards for environmental management systems, ISO 14001 and ISO 14004, can be useful.

Financial resources

Clause 6.8, Financial resources, alludes to the connection between an effective and efficient QMS and obtaining positive financial results. Clause 6.8 suggests that an organization should pursue "development of innovative financial methods to support and encourage improvement of the organization's performance."

As with any other performance measurement, financial resource objectives should be established and the needs and sources from which they might be obtained should be determined. Plans for using such resources and for comparing financial resources expended should be made. The adequacy of financial resources certainly must be integral to the factors considered in each management review.

How an organization manages its finances must be left entirely up to the organization. Clause 6.8 addresses whether appropriate financial provisions have been made for obtaining, maintaining, controlling, and continually improving its performance.

With ISO 9001/2:1994-registered QMSs, resources and resource management were treated rather lightly. With the advent of ISO 9001:2000, concern for resources has attained greater significance. Concern for the resource management must be even greater when an organization chooses to step up to the recommendations in ISO 9004:2000. Remember, if people are your organization's most important asset, you must manage all the resources people will need to do their jobs, as well as all those that affect or are affected by people. Employees are the central focus, but they're surrounded by critical resources that must meet the organization's needs if the customer is to be satisfied.

Every organization is faced with risks, both those inherent in what they do and those derived from external sources. Chapter four will explore risk management.

CHAPTER 4

Assessing and Managing Risk

Understanding and preparing for risk is critical to ensuring quality.

Anyone who's ever worked for or invested in a business knows that it involves risk, whether it is a high-tech startup or a low-tech manufacturer that's been around since the Industrial Revolution. Given the collapse of the dotcom stock market bubble, the events of September 11th, the Enron and Arthur Andersen debacles, everyday fraud cases, and even natural disasters, you and your organization should understand two things about risk:

■ Negative events whose effects range from minor disruptions to a major catastrophe can affect your business no matter where you're located.

■ Negative events take many forms, and each will affect an organization differently; what's a minor disruption to one organization can be a catastrophe for another.

In light of this, it's important to remember that a risk that becomes a negative event has the potential to disrupt your organization's processes and prevent you from meeting customer requirements. Your quality management system (QMS) should be flexible enough to allow you to pursue customer satisfaction under even potentially adverse conditions. When your organization is prepared to perform in a risk-filled marketplace, that information will benefit the organization.

Clearly, *ISO 9001:2000, Quality management systems—Requirements*, which is a generic baseline QMS standard, shouldn't be expected to require risk assessment and management because risk is neither generic in nature nor a basic element of a QMS. *ISO 9004:2000, Quality management systems—Guidelines on performance improvements* doesn't have a section or clause devoted to risk assessment and management. However, subclause 7.1.3.3 suggests five tools for product/process risk assessment.

This isn't necessarily an oversight because risk assessment and management probably is a topic the ISO 9004 drafters subsumed in many sections of the standard—a practical approach, given that risk can affect any process or QMS element.

Because of risk's potential to affect quality—and even an organization's very existence—this chapter explores some risks that could affect an organization's processes when going beyond baseline requirements of ISO 9001:2000 and stepping up to ISO 9004:2000. It also suggests ways in which your organization can assess and manage such risks.

Table 4.1 provides a list of risks that could affect your organization. This is a less-than-exhaustive list. Perhaps more sobering than this list is many organizations' overall lack of attention and preparation for such unexpected losses. Very likely you work for or know of a company that operates under this "it won't happen to us" outlook regarding potential risks. In reality, some risks can close down an organization for good and leave its owners indebted for life.

The savvy organization, regardless of size, makes some assessment of the potential risks to which it's exposed and establishes feasible means to manage the risks of loss.

THE RISK MANAGEMENT PROCESS

A QMS is a series of interrelated management processes for an organization. Its goal is to help the organization:

■ Evaluate these processes for effectiveness and then ensure they're used consistently and as intended

■ Ensure that each process works with all others to provide a stable, effective, and efficient series of processes for product creation

■ Establish risk management, as a preventive process, to ensure no other processes are interrupted or corrupted

To establish an effective risk management process, you must take the following five steps:

1. *Plan* the means by which your organization will:
   ☐ Identify and define its potential exposures to loss
   ☐ Quantify the potential financial and nonfinancial risks
   ☐ Examine the feasibility of alternate risk management techniques
   ☐ Select the best risk management technique(s)

2. *Do* implement a test on the chosen risk management technique(s)
3. *Check* the technique's effectiveness and make necessary adjustments or select a new alternative
4. *Act* to implement the full process
   ☐ Implement the tested technique(s)
   ☐ Monitor the techniques for adequacy of protection

5. *Improve* the implemented techniques (return to "plan")

These steps constitute a plan-do-check-act (PDCA) approach, which is basic to an ISO 9001-based QMS focused on continual improvement. An organization using this approach seeks to continually improve its effort to lessen exposure to loss.

Determining your organization's exposure to loss, although a sensible idea, is easier said than done. One recommendation for accomplishing this is to consider the following four questions when identifying exposure to loss:

■ What's exposed to a potential loss? Items worth considering include:
   ☐ Property (e.g., real estate, facilities, equipment, product, material, intellectual property)
   ☐ Net income (both short- and long-term)
   ☐ Liability (both short- and long-term)
   ☐ People (e.g., employees, customers, suppliers, community members, investors)

Table 4.1

TYPES OF RISK THAT COULD AFFECT AN ORGANIZATION	
Legal action	Noncompliance with regulatory requirements
Environmental violations (perceived as unacceptable)	Customer errors
Customer payment delinquencies and nonpayment	Supplier errors
Raw material defects	Subcontractor nonconformances
Errors and omissions	Financial investments (e.g., unexpected or unacceptable yield)
Failed projects or inadequate return on investment from projects	Product liability
Employee wrongdoing (e.g., failure to comply with safety and other rules, theft, physical harm to co-workers, giving incorrect answers, falsifying records)	Sabotage
Accidents	Catastrophic loss (e.g., fire, hurricane, tornado, flood, earthquake, blizzard)
Civil unrest or terrorist attack	Damage from military action or political upheaval
Vandalism	Product obsolescence
Inadequate or omitted controls (over processes, finances, employees, suppliers, or subcontractors)	Inattention to danger signals from controls
Illegal or unethical behavior on part of management	Disqualification for certifications, licenses, permits
Unwanted buyout/takeover of organization	Unexpected death, disability or departure of key persons
Other business-interrupting situations	

■ What situation, event, or peril could cause a loss for each exposure?
■ What are the financial and other business consequences of such a loss?
■ What entity might potentially suffer the loss?

Table 4.2 provides a detailed look at exposures relating to these four factors.

You've heard it said that hindsight is twenty-twenty, and this is especially true with risk. Although it's often easy to see what could have been done after a loss occurs, seeing what could happen that would adversely affect your organization—and then taking steps to eliminate or minimize those vulnerabilities—is more difficult. However, techniques and tools exist for identifying and analyzing loss exposures.

EXPOSURE ANALYSIS TECHNIQUES AND TOOLS

Following are ten techniques and tools your organization can use to identify and analyze loss exposures. Analyzing potential exposure is as difficult as identifying the exposure itself. (Note that the list isn't intended to be all-inclusive.)

1. *Analyze reported incidents involving potential or actual losses.* The first place to look is within your own organization. Analyze records to find information about:

■ Payouts for losses for the previous two or three years, including any fines and out-of-court settlements
■ Indications and severity of bad debts and delinquent customer payments
■ Indications of any losses due to fraudulent actions by suppliers or employees
■ Indications of losses due to any revocation of licenses, registrations, or certifying authority
■ Potential loss when a patent period expires

Table 4.2

DETAILED LOOK AT POTENTIAL EXPOSURES TO LOSS			
Loss Exposure	**Causes**	**Financial Consequences**	**Potential Entity Suffering Loss**

Property
■ Tangible
  • Real estate (land, facilities, things that grow on it)
  • Products
  • Material
■ Intangible
  • Licenses
  • Leaseholding interests
  • Intellectual property (e.g., trade secrets, proprietary processes)
	Natural
	■ Fire
	■ Wind
	■ Flood
	■ Earthquake
	■ Storm (rain, hail, snow)
	
	Human
	■ Theft
	■ Vandalism
	■ Misuse
		■ Replacement cost
		■ Functional replacement cost
		■ Actual cash value
		■ Economic or use value
			■ Ownership interests
			■ Secured creditors
			■ Sellers and buyers
			■ Tenant interests
			■ Employees
			■ Community

Net income *(Revenues-Expenses)* ■ Near-term ■ Long-term	**Decrease in revenues** ■ Business interruption ■ Loss of anticipated profits ■ Reduced rental income ■ Decreased collection of accounts receivable **Increase in expenses** ■ Increased operating expenses ■ Increased rental expenses and expediting costs	■ Decreased profits ■ Decreased market share ■ Decreased stock price ■ Less capital ■ Reduction in improvements	■ Business itself ■ Stockholders ■ Customers ■ Employees ■ Contractual interests

Freedom from legal liability
(Arises from an entity being sued for having breached a legal duty or allegedly harming another; becoming obligated under contract to pay for a loss that another entity has suffered)
■ Near-term
■ Long-term
	Classified by entity to whom duty is owed
	■ Criminal
	■ Civil
	  • Contract
	  • Tort
	
	Classified by source of legal duty
	■ Common law
	■ Statutory law
		■ Legal costs, including:
		  • Judgments against the entity
		  • Attorney fees
		  • Punitive damages
		■ Time value cost
		■ Loss of reputation
			■ Business itself
			■ Stockholders
			■ Customers
			■ Employees
			■ Contractual interests

Personnel loss
■ Key persons
■ Employees
■ Customers
■ Suppliers
■ Community members
	■ Death
	■ Disability
	■ Retirement
	■ Resignation
	■ Employee benefits
	  • Contractual liability
	  • Criminal or civil liability
		■ Temporary vs. permanent losses
		■ Normal vs. above-normal losses
		■ Fringe benefits
			■ Stockholders
			■ Customers
			■ Employees
			■ Contractual interests

Adapted from material provided by the U.S. Small Business Administration

Next, request data from insurance carriers regarding the types and amounts of claims paid on your organization's behalf (e.g., liability, health, and accident/disability claims). Also obtain data from any pertinent industry association.

Also analyze community records for the past few years regarding local incidents that caused losses. Not only could such incidents be repeated in your organization because they're common to the community, but they also might inspire copycats to accuse your organization of the same. Sources for community records include:

■ City/town hall records and historical archives
■ Local newspaper archives
■ Local library sources
■ Local police blotters and fire department records

2. *Collect data from internal sources.* Conduct cross-functional brainstorming sessions with your employees and conduct surveys to collect examples of where potential risks may lie hidden.

3. *Audit financial statements and supporting documents.* Financial incidents are a frequent cause of risk exposure for most organizations, and they're among the most cost-effective to fix or prevent. Every organization is required to report financial information to a number of entities, including the Internal Revenue Service, and most companies rely on internal and external accountants to verify this information. Examining these statements to confirm they match what management knows, indicate where discrepancies lie, keep accountants on their toes, and your executives out of jail.

4. *Complete and analyze process maps.* Map your key processes. This will involve convening a representative group of employees who provide input to a given process, perform the process, and receive output from the process. From the process map(s), brainstorm where there might be points of risk in the process. Supplier and customer representatives can also be helpful in the analysis. A supplier-input-process-output-customer format is useful here (See figure 4.1).

Figure 4.1

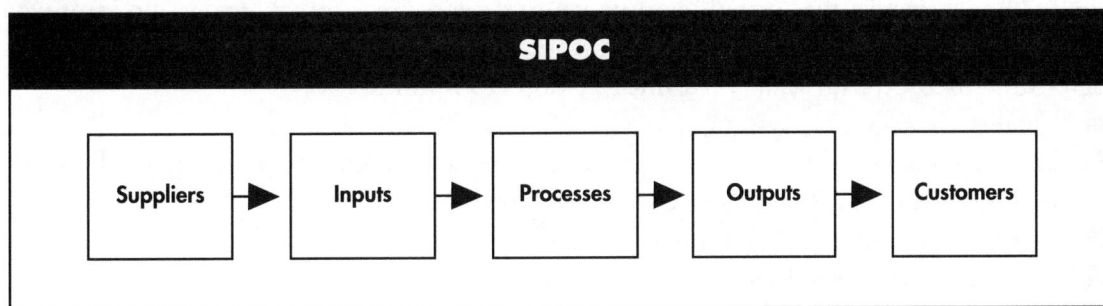

SIPOC

Suppliers → Inputs → Processes → Outputs → Customers

5. *Conduct a "what if" brainstorming session.* Convene a group of key personnel and, using a 7-M cause-and-effect diagram like the one shown in figure 4.2, explore as many possible risk situations as time and feasibility allow.

6. *Conduct periodic inspections and process audits.* Health and safety inspections not only look for lapses in compliance with regulations but also for opportunities to decrease risk. Surprise "drills" keep response teams vigilant and prepared. Questions to identify potential

Figure 4.2

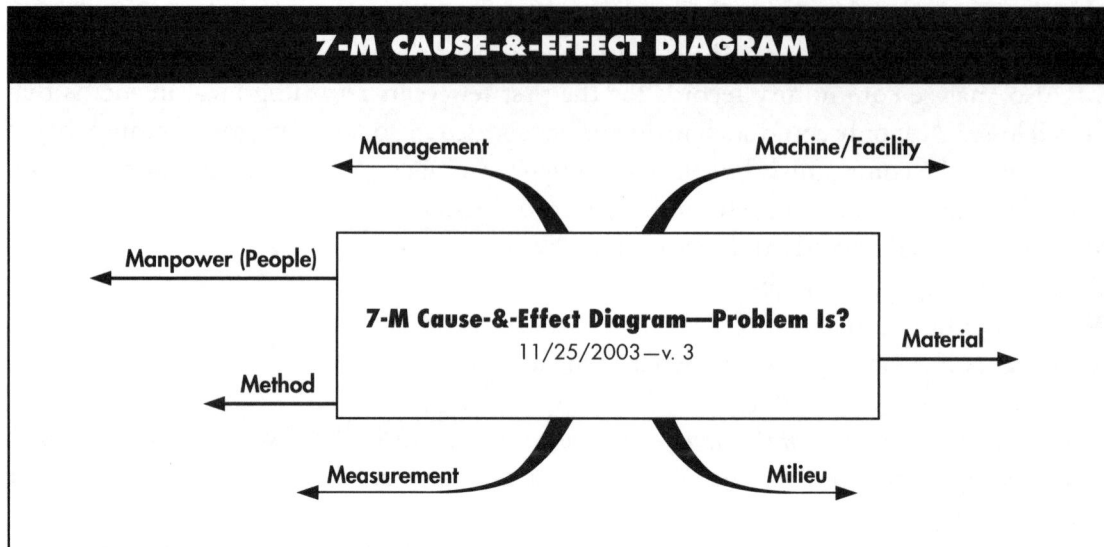

risks can be incorporated into the internal auditing of the QMS as well as product audits. Continually question if your product, in the end-user's hands, will be safe to use during its life cycle, including its disposal.

7. *Employ failure mode and effects analysis (FMEA).* This is an effective technique for determining what could go wrong and what effect it could have on your processes and product. The intent is to prevent such failures and their effects. The elements of a FMEA are listed in table 4.3.

8. *Assess management systems' effectiveness.* This isn't the internal auditing undertaken to verify conformance to one or more standards and seek continual improvement, although it could be achieved as part of those audits. Here, the point is risk assessment to determine if any "holes" exist in your management system(s) and processes that could leave or are leaving your organization exposed to loss. It's never too late to minimize or eliminate exposures; therefore, every future assessment your organization undergoes should include an evaluation of how effective that system is in preventing exposures and what must be improved and/or corrected to decrease exposures. Further, you should assess the following systems to determine their exposure and what must be done to minimize it:

- Quality management system
- Financial management systems, including supplier payments, revenues, payroll, investments, asset management, and contingency reserves
- Intellectual property management systems
- Safety and security systems
- Environmental management and other systems

9. *Contract out surveillance services.* Hiring an outside organization to examine your operations can provide feedback regarding property and personnel security, regulatory compliance, and compliance with nonregulatory requirements (e.g., ISO 9001).

10. *Consult exposure statistics.* Insurance carriers, trade associations, and regulatory agencies can provide your organization with statistical information about common potential expo-

Figure 4.3

FAILURE MODE & EFFECTS ANALYSIS (FMEA)
1. Identify process functions and requirements
2. Brainstorm potential failures and effects
3. Assign a severity code
4. Brainstorm potential causes
5. Assign a likelihood rank to each cause
6. Identify current process controls
7. Assign a likelihood (detection) code that control will fail to identify a problem
8. Compute risk priority number (severity x occurrence rank x detection)
9. Identify corrective actions for high RPN items
10. Determine responsible person and target date
11. Monitor action taken
12. Reassess occurrence ranking and detection code and recompute RPN

sures. These statistics can offer guidance regarding where to look for potential exposures based on your sector's history—because history is known to repeat itself—and what the costs of such exposures could be.

RESPONDING TO RISK EXPOSURES

Identifying your organization's risk exposures is a critical step, but you also must determine how to respond. There's no guarantee you'll be able to respond to all exposures. Once your organization has identified its risk exposure and computed the potential for financial loss, one or more of five actions may be warranted:

- Find a way to avoid the exposure
- Find ways to reduce the potential loss
- Find ways to prevent the occasion for the loss to occur
- Segregate the loss exposures to concentrate efforts on those most likely to occur and/or cause the greatest loss (e.g., perform exposure triage: minimum, medium, maximum)
- Transfer the risk (e.g., through insurance or other contractual arrangement)

Aside from obtaining insurance to cover all or a portion of the potential risk, your organization can establish various contingency plans, including setting up loss reserves, which is a form of self-insurance. However, the single most effective prevention approach is to train employees to recognize hazards and potential areas for loss.

For example, one company conducted a series of employee seminars on potential hazards and risks. At one session, an employee mentioned that his late father, a long-time employee, had told him a story about the damages caused when the adjacent river crested fifteen feet above normal after an unusually snowy winter upstream. The members of the organization's present management, who had joined the company within the last five years, were unaware of this potential for loss. This was an especially relevant "heads-up" notice because the organization recently added facilities—full of expensive new equipment—along the riverbank.

In another company, one employee looked into product liability payouts after a similar training program. She isolated the reported causes and suggested that engineering explore ways to engineer the products to prevent customers from misusing them—the cause for the greatest number of occurrences. A resulting engineering design change substantially reduced the number of occurrences as well as the average payout for the few misuse claims remaining. As a result, the insurance premium was decreased.

Another effective prevention approach is to assess potential risks for a new product at the design and development stage and to take actions in response to the assessment. Clearly, one critical tool to use in this assessment activity is an FMEA. The U.S. automotive sector has standardized an industry-specific approach in the Big Three's *Failure Mode and Effects Analysis* reference manual, but there are many ways to conduct an FMEA.

For example, a small organization, engaged in bidding for military contracts for high-tech devices, successfully used an FMEA to identify and assess risks for a new type of product. The FMEA aided in evaluating design inputs, ensured that potential failure modes were identified and addressed, helped identify the failure modes' root cause(s), determined the actions necessary to eliminate or reduce the potential failure mode, and added a high degree of objectivity to the design review process. The FMEA also directed attention to design features that required additional testing or development, documented risk reduction efforts, provided documentation to aid future FMEAs, and ensured the design was performed with a customer focus.

The FMEA methodology used by this company involved sixteen steps:

1. Define the device design inputs
2. Investigate similar existing designs, if available
3. Identify a failure mode (i.e., what could go wrong)
4. Identify potential failure effects (i.e., how the internal or external customer becomes aware of problem)
5. Rank the severity of the effects using a one-to-ten scale, where one is "minor" and ten is "major and without warning")
6. Establish what the root cause(s) would be
7. Rate the probability of occurrence for the failure using a one-to-ten scale
8. Document the present design controls
9. Rate the likelihood of detecting the failure using a one-to-ten scale
10. Compute the risk priority number (i.e., RPN = severity X occurrence X detection)
11. Recommend preventive and /or corrective action (e.g., what action, who will do it, and when.) Note that preventive action is listed first because you're dealing with the design stage.
12. Return to step three if other potential failures exist
13. Build and test a prototype
14. Redo the FMEA after test results are obtained and any necessary or desired changes are made
15. Retest and, if acceptable, place in production
16. Document the design process, including the FMEA, for the knowledge base

Collaborating with employees who've been involved in design, development, production, and customer service activities is critical because their knowledge, ideas, and questions about a new product design will be based on their experience at different stages of product realization. Furthermore, if your employees are also some of your customers (i.e., end-users), obtaining and documenting their experience is very useful. This experiential input, along with examinations of similar designs (and their FMEAs, nonconforming product and corrective action records, and customer feedback reports), often is the best sources for analysis input.

All expenditures that consume organizational assets incur risk. Thus, a critical step in risk analysis is determining the financial risks related to capital expenditures and projects. Because catastrophes or other type of risk-related problems affect your organization, management and everyone else will judge the effect by how it affects the bottom line.

Bankruptcy is often the result of an organization's failure to analyze the risks of its expenditures and projects and failure to take adequate precautions. Techniques for exposing and examining risks associated with capital expenditures and projects include:

- Brainstorming
- Obtaining stakeholders' input
- Reviewing outcomes of previous expenditures
- FMEA
- Benchmarking with other organizations (covered in chapter eight)
- Collecting and analyzing data from trade associations, government publications, manufacturer's claims, and recalls of similar products by other producers
- Internal analysis of potential yield from investment in terms of:
  - ☐ *Benefit-cost analysis*—the ratio of projected benefits to projected costs
  - ☐ *Payback period*—the time it takes to recoup the investment from net cash flows
  - ☐ *Net present value*—evaluation taking into account the time value of money. Consider inflation and other factors (e.g., a dollar earned now is worth more than a dollar received n years from now, and it can be invested for n years more than the dollar received in the future).
  - ☐ *Internal rate of return*—means of comparison with the minimum cost of capital acceptable to the organization
  - ☐ *Potential ROI*—the payoff potential
  - ☐ *Estimated return on assets or net assets*—the payback of an asset over its useful life

- Portfolio analysis (i.e., comparative analysis of proposed expenditures used to prioritize a new proposal with others pending or already implemented)
- Decision analysis—considering all pertinent factors related to a proposed expenditure, both financial and nonfinancial payback (e.g., fit to the organization's overall business needs, core competency, market strategies, consumer climate)

COMPUTING POTENTIAL LOSS AND DETERMINING ACTIONS

Without delving into sophisticated mathematical modeling techniques, such as actuarial tables and the like, you can produce a credible estimate of your organization's potential for loss. The following steps will assist you.

After identifying the risks and the risk priority (see discussion of FMEA above), prioritize the identified risks (by RPN) using a Pareto chart. Identify the top eight risks and group the remainder under an "all other" category.

■ For each of the top risks, envision a worst-case scenario. List all the consequences that could occur (brainstorming and mind-mapping are effective techniques).

■ Categorize the consequences into clusters of similar happenings (an affinity diagram is a useful tool).

■ Assign dollar estimates of losses to each cluster. Some of the line items you might consider assigning a value for include:

☐ Legal defense costs and claim settlements
☐ Claim settlements for loss of human life
☐ Temporary business loss or business closing
☐ Product recall costs
☐ Erosion of confidence in your organization and/or its products
☐ Increase in insurance premiums
☐ Increase in surveillance costs
☐ Replacement costs: people, facilities, and tools
☐ Product obsolescence
☐ Shortages of raw material, energy sources, transportation, and staffing

■ Determine what it would take (i.e., cost of additional resources) to mitigate or eliminate the accumulated potential dollar loss for each cluster/scenario. Factors to consider include:

☐ Insurance or other ways of spreading the potential loss
☐ Improved environmental scanning and forecasting methodology
☐ Improved response and preparatory procedures (e.g., contingency plans)
☐ Decentralization of risk-associated functions and facilities
☐ Relocation of facilities to less risky geographic areas
☐ Discontinuing production of product with high potential risk

■ Compute the cost of additional resources relative to total value (i.e., the risk ratio) for each cluster.

■ Decide what action(s) would be in the balanced best interest of all the organization's stakeholders.

■ Decide whether to take action.

■ Periodically reassess the decisions made and make necessary adjustments.

SUMMARY

This review discusses some of the factors an organization should consider when creating and sustaining a customer-focused quality organization. It's intended to build awareness of the need for assessing and managing risks that can affect the organization. Remember that not every organization that's won the coveted Malcolm Baldrige National Quality Award or other quality award has survived. This has had less to do with the company's success in meeting the Baldrige criteria than it has with how it managed its business so as to withstand the risks encountered.

Some of the massive business failures of late have had little or nothing to do with product or service quality problems and everything to do with failing to identify, assess, and manage potential risks. It really won't matter if you have the world's best ISO 9001-registered QMS when a mudslide from the hill behind your plant wipes out your business because you failed to identify the risk and had no contingency plan to address it. The same fate awaits an organization if its CEO absconds with the employee pension funds, or its capital equipment replacement project fails to produce the intended payoff and the organization defaults on its loan payments.

Furthermore, in this litigious society, organizations must assess their potential liability from legal actions carefully, including actions arising from alleged product failures, inappropriate actions of employees, or alleged health and safety violations or negligence. Such legal actions often result in horrendous payouts to the litigant if the company is found guilty or is forced to reach a huge out-of-court settlement regardless of alleged responsibility.

Failing to sustain a viable organization that fulfills customer requirements and support its workforce is a quality failure—that is, a quality of management failure.

In chapter five we'll discuss how to produce the right product for the right customer in the right way.

CHAPTER 5

Focusing on Product Realization

Produce the right product for the right customers the right way.

In the eyes of its customers and its managers, an organization's most important activity is producing a product or providing a service. After all, this is the core of the organization's business.

Making changes to improve production and service provision processes should be viewed as critical to your organization's long-term success and survival. However, two significant dangers exist when one considers a change: waiting too long to implement the change, and underestimating the effort required to achieve the best results.

In transitioning from ISO 9001/2/3:1994 to ISO 9001:2000, a common observation is how easy the process will be: "All we have to do is renumber our 1994 based procedures or create a cross-referenced list, and we're done."

Perhaps that approach would work for your organization, assuming you want to meet the minimum requirements or if you are significantly exceeding minimum quality management system (QMS) requirements. But this approach fails to consider that the real goal is to establish consistent, effective, and efficient processes that will improve your production and/or service provision operations—efforts that will satisfy the customer and lead to product and/or service improvements over time.

One seldom-discussed aspect of the ISO 9000:2000 revisions is the importance of, and value in using, *ISO 9001:2000, Quality management systems—Requirements* and *ISO 9004:2000, Quality management systems—Guidelines for performance improvements* with ISO 9004 as a consistent pair. Anyone who has compared at ISO 9001 and ISO 9004 side by side understands that if only the minimum requirements in ISO 9001:2000 are implemented, it's difficult to improve a management system.

In truth, if all you achieve is conformity to ISO 9001, you're squandering your organization's limited resources by ignoring the greater benefits available to you. When you commit to using the consistent pair to move up to an ISO 9004-based organization, numerous opportunities present themselves for upgrading your QMS to benefit your organization and its performance.

ISO 9004:2000 emphasizes a process approach for achieving continual performance improvement to promote organizational excellence. Recommended actions that your organization could benefit from pursuing are spelled out. Communications, training, teams and work groups, measurements, analysis, and review are stressed.

Ways in which personnel can promote innovation by improving customer satisfaction, using resources wisely, and promoting waste reduction and greater efficiency—all of which are essential for continual improvement—are explored.

Where ISO 9004:2000 can provide the greatest support for moving beyond a baseline QMS is in section 7, Product realization, subclause 7.1.3, Managing processes. This assumes you have, at a minimum, identified your mainline processes and support processes. One accepted approach for identifying these processes is a SIPOC analysis such as the one shown in figure 4.1 in chapter four. It requires you to examine all processes relating to product flow, from the materials provided by suppliers to delivery to the customer. Flowcharts, process maps, and process identification tables also are effective approaches to use.

Subclause 7.1.3 suggests that your organization develop an operating plan to manage the processes you identify. An operating plan must provide greater detail, including:

■ How the identified processes align with the organization's strategy, quality policy, and planned objectives
■ How design inputs and outputs will be developed
■ How the processes and products will be verified and validated
■ Specifications and resources relating to the inputs and outputs
■ Identification of subprocesses or activities within the primary processes
■ Identification of support processes (e.g., information management, maintenance activities, marketing support, training, finance-related infrastructure, and work environment and safety-related support)
■ How processes will be monitored, measured, controlled, and improved, including the identification and prevention of nonconformities
■ How personnel competence will be established and maintained
■ How process reliability and repeatability will be established and maintained, including the equipment capability
■ How the environmental impact of processes and resultant product will be addressed
■ How risks will be assessed, including risks over the life cycle and disposal of the product. Clause 7.1.3.3, Product and process validation and changes, suggests five tools for risk assessment. (See chapter four for information about risk assessment and management.)
■ What documents and records will be needed
■ What will be done to ensure a focus on continual improvement

Some organizations fail to consider including "other interested parties" when defining mutually acceptable processes for communicating effectively and efficiently. This is covered in clause 7.2, Processes related to interested parties.

Clause 7.3, Design and development suggests, "The organization should consider life cycle, safety and health, testability, usability, user-friendliness, dependability, durability, ergonomics, the environment, product disposal and identified risks." This might not be pertinent if your organization can justify excluding product design from its QMS.

PRODUCT PLANNING

Is design and development of product—remember that "product" includes services, software, hardware, and processed materials—included within your organization's purpose? If so, you must employ a method for translating, through a logical analysis, the requirements of the customer and other interested parties into inputs to determine how best to fulfill these needs with the resources available. Quality function deployment (QFD) is such a methodology. QFD translates customer requirements into your organization's technical requirements and, through a cascading hierarchy of matrices, deploys these requirements throughout the appropriate parts of the organization. A unique feature of QFD is its ability to identify design changes before the design is formalized on paper or the computer. Because of the shape it takes, the QFD matrix—also known as the "house of quality" (see discussion in chapter two)—depicts the following:

- What the customer wants or needs—also known as the "voice of the customer"
- A weighting of the relative importance of each customer requirement
- An assessment of what customers think the competition is providing
- How the in-house processes meet customer needs—the "voice of the company"
- The organization's objectives (i.e., targets or product characteristics) for meeting customer requirements
- A technical assessment of how much is needed to meet customer requirements
- A correlation matrix showing the strength of the relationship between customer requirements and process or product requirements
- A weighting of the relationship between customer requirements and the organization's technical requirements (usually weighted "nine" when strongly related, "three" when moderately related, and "one" when slightly related)
- A ranking of the relative importance of each factor (sometimes probability factors can be introduced before ranking)

In a sense, the cornerstone of the house of quality is the goal the organization seeks to achieve through its processes, and that goal should be kept in mind when using QFD methodology. The QFD matrix relates to and interacts with a series of matrices that should be deployed to move the organization through a process that begins with a customer contract specifying requirements for a product or service to the output of a product or service that results in customer satisfaction. Table 5.1 shows how this hierarchy of matrices flows from one to another in a typical situation.

Another product realization tool that suits an ISO 9004 approach is failure mode and effects analysis (FMEA), an analytical methodology used to assess the probability of prod-

Table 5.1

A QFD-BASED HIERARCHY OF PRODUCT REALIZATION MATRICES
A typical hierarchy of matrices correlates
⇩ Customer requirements with internal design requirements
⇩ Design requirements with parts requirements
⇩ Parts requirements with process requirements
⇩ Process requirements with production requirements
⇨ Leading to customer satisfaction

uct failures and their effect. Widely used in the automotive industry, an FMEA typically is prepared for two stages of product development: in design (using DFMEAs) and in the production process (using PFMEAs).

The DFMEA is used to ensure that all appropriate product design characteristics have been identified and reviewed. Before beginning production, the PFMEA is used by a manufacturing team to uncover potential process problems. A PFMEA is a dynamic document subject to revision when new potential failures are identified. (Chapter four discusses FMEAs in greater detail.)

When using a DFMEA, the following should be considered for each potential failure:

■ Potential effect of failure
■ Severity code ranging from "minor" (one) to "hazardous without warning" (ten)
■ Potential cause of failure
■ Occurrence code (ranging from one to ten) estimating the likelihood that failure will occur
■ Existing design controls for verification and validation (i.e., types of testing and prototyping)
■ Detection code (ranging from one to ten) estimating the likelihood existing controls will fail to identify the problem
■ Risk priority number (ranging from one to 1,000), obtained by multiplying the severity code by the occurrence code by the detection code
■ Recommended action(s)
■ Responsibility for action(s) and target date(s)

In conducting a PFMEA, the following typically are analyzed for each process:

■ Process history
■ Failure mode
■ Effects of failure
■ Severity of effect
■ Root cause
■ Probability of occurrence
■ Existing process control methodology
■ Rating of likelihood of detection
■ Risk priority number
■ Rank
■ Recommended corrective/preventive action(s)
■ Responsibility for action(s) and target date(s)

In addition to applying FMEA, the *Advanced Product Quality Planning* manual (available from the Automotive Industry Action Group) provides other value-added checklists and forms that can help in addressing clause 7.3, Design and development. These tools also are useful for design-responsible organizations outside the automotive sector.

PURCHASING

ISO 9004 encourages organizations to link electronically with suppliers to optimize communication subclause 7.4.1, Purchasing. This is intended to ensure that both the supplier and organization address the same requirements, such as material and product characteristics, price, and delivery. In some electronic applications, the customer can enter an order directly into the supplier's production schedule. Anything that can be done to close the potential gap between what your organization requires and what a supplier will deliver is an improvement. In many industries, an order confirmation is almost nonexistent, and miscommunication is frequent.

It's recommended that the customer (i.e., your organization) evaluate the cost of purchased product. In essence, this involves breaking the total cost of a product down to its cost elements. This analysis is aimed at providing better information for formulating quotations and bids. Extending this further, compiling cost of quality metrics (e.g., warranty replacement for nonconforming purchased product) will provide the stimulus to drive improvement.

Access to suppliers' facilities in order to gain a better understanding of their processes can lead to improved logistical and technical support and, ultimately, to supplier partnerships. Transforming the customer-supplier relationship from the traditional adversarial relationship to one of mutual respect, cooperation, and benefit is essential in stepping up to ISO 9004.

Making an effort to narrow the number of qualified suppliers is also suggested. A number of approaches—including careful analysis of supplier resources and past quality history, identifying more readily available materials and sources, changing to a pull system of product fulfillment, developing ship-to-stock parts replenishment, and determining applicability of long-term contracts—can all lead to reducing the supplier base and managing supplier relations more cost-effectively. In reality, your efforts will be geared toward eliminating the weakest links in your organization's supply chain and increasing purchases from the most consistently reliable suppliers.

Subclause 7.4.2, Supplier control process, suggests six additional actions to improve supplier selection and/or retention (see appendix F for additional assessment questions). They are:

- Evaluate current suppliers against their competitors relative to performance and achieving customer satisfaction
- Review existing suppliers' responses to requests for quotations, reports of problems, and requests for corrective action
- Evaluate suppliers' potential capability to supply product effectively to meet future demands
- Assess suppliers' comprehension of and adherence to pertinent statutory and regulatory requirements and ability to meet desirable ethical behavioral norms
- Evaluate the financial stability of suppliers and the references provided
- Appraise the suppliers' image in the community, industry, and society at large

The goal should be to make improvements in the supply chain so you can serve your customers more effectively while sustaining your organization and meeting the needs of other interested parties.

If you look in either ISO 9001 or ISO 9004 for guidance pertaining to inventory management, you won't find any. The word "inventory" appears only once, and in an offhand way, within clause 7.4.1. Inventory, treated as a potential waste, is a factor to be considered when applying lean thinking (see chapter seven for more detail about this concept). Nevertheless, inventory management can't be ignored as a critical subprocess within product realization.

An insight into inventory management that is both fascinating and educational can be found in the *Handbook of Best Practices*, chapter twelve, by Chris Christensen.[1] For example, he gives eighteen definitions for the term "inventory" and discusses the balancing act of having enough inventory vs. too much. He also explains how to conduct cycle counts and states that "the savings generated by taking the physical inventory are none." Christensen summarizes the practicalities of an A-B-C inventory system and how to manage within each inventory category.

In *Let's Fix It! Overcoming the Crisis in Manufacturing*, Richard Schonberger discusses the effect of inventory as a competitive factor and how an emphasis on inventory turns can cause companies to "game the system" to appear successful.[2] Clearly, how well your organization manages its inventory system, and how diligent it is in continual improvement, will represent one substantive effort to step up to ISO 9004 and beyond.

INTERNAL OPERATIONS CONTROL

The specific characteristics of a product usually derive from either or both the internal design function and customer-provided specifications. However, other input requirements should be considered, including:

- Statutory and regulatory requirements
- Industry standards
- Internal workmanship norms and instructions
- Competent workers qualified to perform the tasks assigned
- Competent and qualified suppliers
- Suitable work environment, including facilities, equipment, tools, and materials
- Suitable safeguards and communication pertaining to:
    - ☐ Worker health and wellness
    - ☐ Handling of hazardous materials
    - ☐ Product traceability
    - ☐ Segregation of nonconforming product
    - ☐ Handling, packaging, storage, preservation, and delivery of product, including damage, deterioration, or misuse of product throughout its lifecycle
    - ☐ Handling, storage, and preservation of customer-supplied product, material, tools, intellectual property, and proprietary information
    - ☐ Handling of measuring instruments

- Means for validating that the product meets the use intended by the customer
- Means for measuring, monitoring, correcting, and improving processes
- Means for ensuring that measuring and monitoring devices are properly identified, fit for use, and maintained at the appropriate level of accuracy in conformance with applicable standards
- Means for ensuring processes are cost effective
- Ethical and moral organizational and individual behavior
- Environmental and resource conservation issues

For the organization that designs its product, most of the previous requirements will have been considered during the design and development stages. For the organization that produces its product or provides its service based on customer-supplied specifications, takes orders for standard stock items and/or responds to calls for service, many of the above input requirements are likely to be pertinent.

Consider an organization with a basic QMS that conforms with ISO 9001:2000 and has prepared those procedures and work instructions deemed necessary to plan and produce its product. When stepping up to ISO 9004, the organization must pay greater attention to the list above. Indeed, many organizations will choose to augment their production planning and scheduling systems and documents to address certain of these requirements.

For example, a typical production routing document might be modified to include references to applicable regulations, an industry standard, organizational workmanship standards, operator qualifications, and handling of hazardous material and nonconformities. The purpose isn't to complicate the document unduly but to extract and make more readily available pertinent information from the more voluminous requirement documents. The true purpose is to list the essentials of what the operator needs in order to produce a quality product. It's a more complete list to ensure that the operator is doing the work correctly, consistently, and effectively—and to enable the operator to take greater responsibility for his or her own work. While operator training and qualification can prepare an operator for much of what he or she needs to know and do, for some product realization activities omissions or missteps can, and often do, occur.

We all appreciate that airplane pilots are well trained in operating very complicated and sophisticated equipment in a wide range of situations. Do the airlines rely on their pilots to remember all that they must do? No, they don't. Checklists and protocols must be followed. For example, a variety of equipment checks and tests, instructions for abiding by noise abatement laws, and communication protocols are included. Do pilots consider these checks an insult to their personal competence and expertise? Probably not. They understand and accept that the checks are there to help them better safeguard the lives of their passengers, their crews, and themselves.

A personal example: As a young boy, I had an after-school job delivering newspapers for a prestigious publisher in a large city. My employer, unlike other distributors, furnished each delivery person with a book of "his" customers' orders. Although many orders required only "standard" delivery (i.e., drop at customer's door), quite a few required that I adhere to special delivery instructions (e.g., fold the paper, tuck in doorknob, and ring bell). Each of us was trained in proper dress, how to respond to customers, and how to deliver the papers. The book of orders provided us with the specific customer requirements and also directions we needed for successful delivery (e.g., obtain building key from janitor and return upon completing deliveries). In addition to fulfilling its promise of content quality, this publisher also pursued quality of delivery, and we were an important part of that supply chain. Incidentally, a customer complaint resulted in a pink slip in one's box and a discussion with the distribution manager. A second slip could result in suspension or termination, depending on the complaint.

The above anecdote addressed several of the suggested actions listed in subclause 7.5.1, Operation and realization, including:

- Training
- Communicating and recording pertinent information
- Infrastructure improvement
- Problem prevention
- Methods of processing and monitoring

One issue not specifically addressed but implied in clause 7 is the interactions with internal customers. Any organization consisting of more than one person has both providers (internal suppliers) and receivers (internal customers) of product, including services, material, data, and information. These internal interactions have been referred to as "next operation as customer." How well these interactions are planned and controlled directly influences not only internal operations' effectiveness and efficiency but also the external customer's satisfaction. (Appendix A discusses this critical issue in more detail.)

Many organizations consider compliance to ISO 9001:2000's clause 7.5, Production and service provision, as nothing new—and they probably see it as one of the clauses they need to worry least about when transitioning from the 1994 to 2000 edition. In stepping up to ISO 9004:2000, the opportunity exists to make substantial improvements in your QMS, an improvement that can have long-term effect on your organization's longevity, growth, and prosperity. In *The Agenda, What Every Business Must Know To Dominate the Decade*, Michael Hammer includes creating a process enterprise as one of his nine management innovations.[3]

So far the chapters in this book have addressed the development of an effective strategic planning and deployment process; techniques and tools to strengthen and manage our customer focus and customer relationships; upgrading resource management; and assessing an organization's vulnerability to risk and identifying means for lessening them. In this chapter we've reviewed the means to get the right product to the right customer the right way. Now the question is: How are we doing? Chapter six delves into the realm of measurement and analysis.

ENDNOTES

1. Christensen, R.T. "Manufacturing Controls Integration," chapter 12 in *Manufacturing Handbook of Best Practices,* Jack B. ReVelle (editor). Boca Raton: St. Lucie Press, 2002, pp. 261–280.
2. Schonberger, Richard J. *Let's Fix It! Overcoming the Crisis in Manufacturing.* New York: The Free Press, 2001.
3. Hammer, Michael. *The Agenda: What Every Business Must Do to Dominate the Decade.* New York: Crown Business, 2001.

CHAPTER 6

Focusing on Measurement and Analysis

Quality data for decision making is critical to any organization.

If you don't know where you are, how will you know how far you must go to get where you want to be? This may sound like a metaphysical problem for philosophers, but fundamentally it's the question every organization's management should ask while pursuing effective business management and organizational success.

In today's competitive global marketplace, it's difficult to imagine any situation that wouldn't call for some form of data measurement and analysis to decide whether a current process is producing a product or organizational outcome as desired.

Section 8 of *ISO 9001:2000, Quality management systems—Requirements* and *ISO 9004:2000, Quality management systems—Guidelines for performance improvements* are titled "Measurement, Analysis and Improvement," with the expectation being that the first two activities will lead to the third. The fact that measurement and analysis are covered at the end of these standards might imply that the best was saved for last. Or it might mean they're considered a necessary afterthought compared with the other clauses in the standards.

In reality, measurement and analysis interact with all other processes covered in ISO 9001:2000 and ISO 9004:2000. The goal is to use them to bring about improvement. What section 8 recognizes is that everyone measures and analyzes all sorts of data relating to performance.

We measure and analyze during much of our waking hours. For example, measurement can consist of an experienced technician "eye-balling" a product to determine if the finish is acceptable. It can also involve placing the product in a sophisticated instrument to scan and assess the finish against a pre-programmed standard.

Other examples come to mind. Remember when you were a child and your mother made you periodically stand up straight in a doorway so she could place pencil marks on the doorjamb to "measure" your growth? Likewise, isn't the farmer who walks his field and stops to pull back the husk on an ear of corn to check its maturity and the absence of corn borers measuring and analyzing? And, as you commute to work, aren't you constantly "measuring" the distance you maintain from other vehicles and road obstacles and analyzing that data to determine if a corrective action is needed?

How you go about your daily activities and conduct yourself is based on the data you collect, analyze, and correlate with past experience. The same is true with an organization.

Its continued existence, growth, and improvement depends on establishing the right metrics; monitoring, measuring, and collecting data; then analyzing and communicating the results and making data-based quality decisions.

Although ISO 9001:2000 requires an organization to continually improve the QMS based on data collected by several QMS processes, it doesn't specifically require the organization to make fact-based decisions in managing its business activities. However, section 8 of ISO 9004:2000 offers guidance that will improve fact-based decision-making within your organization and lead it beyond the baseline results that the standard provides.

This chapter focuses on a few techniques and methods that can take your organization beyond the ISO 9001 conformance level—techniques that, when fully assimilated and enhanced over time, can move your organization toward world-class status.

A number of major QMS elements and activities can help move an organization toward critical improvement, including:

■ Strategic objectives
■ Customer satisfaction
■ Self-assessment

Inherent in a discussion of each is what data are important and what results are expected that will improve decision-making. How improvement is triggered by the information derived from the data is the subject of chapter seven.

STRATEGIC OBJECTIVES

For the purposes of this discussion, it's assumed your organization has done strategic planning and established strategic objectives (see chapter one). Keep in mind that with any objective, measurements are necessary to determine when the organization has achieved the objective, and how well. Top-level measurements often are referred to as "key indicators" or critical success factors.

For example, one division of a large professional association might establish the following:

■ *Strategic objective*. To increase the division's membership to 65 percent of the association's total membership by the end of its fiscal year
■ *Key indicator*. Division membership as a percentage of the association's total membership

With any strategic objective, tactical plans (i.e., action plans)—complete with responsibilities assigned, measurements defined, and milestones set for reviewing progress—must be established to detail the actions required of the department's subgroups to achieve the objective. Key indicators are recommended, but within reason.

One company, a packaging material printer, attempted to manage its business by establishing seventy-six separate key indicators (KIs). As a result, management quickly became caught up in metrics mania, spending a disproportionate amount of time and resources on collecting and analyzing data to the detriment of sales, production, and delivery management and performance.

An antidote to that scenario is the balanced scorecard.[1] As the term "balanced" implies, this concept involves an organization developing a scorecard that includes metrics from several primary sources. One organization might select primary sources (e.g., customers, employees, shareholders, and processes) that differ significantly from another company's

Figure 6.1

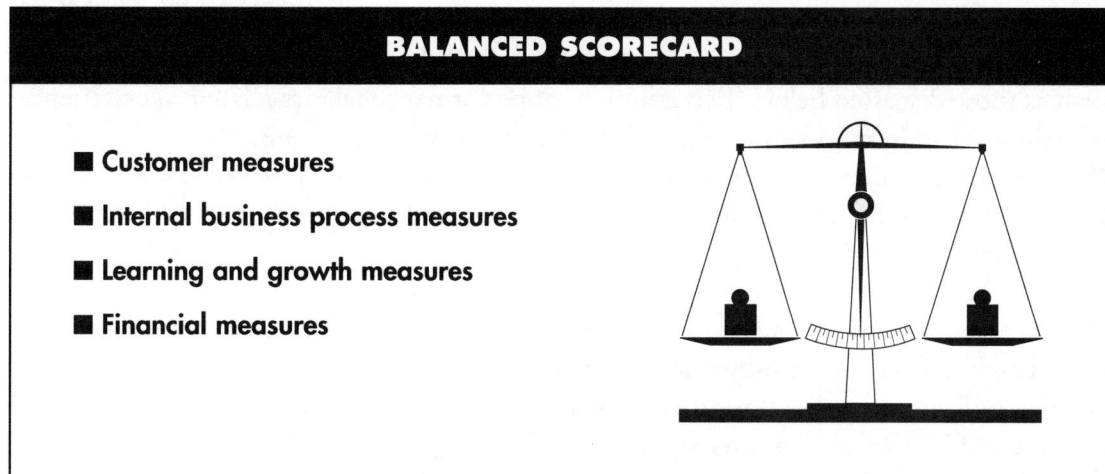

(e.g., customers, internal business processes, learning and growth, and financial). Figure 6.1 depicts typical categories measured with a balanced scorecard.

To succeed with this approach, be careful not to suboptimize when an organization reacts to each metric—keep everything in balance. Further, ISO 9004:2000's subclause 8.1.1, Measurement, analysis and improvement—Introduction, cautions that there should be a "review of the validity and purpose of measurements and the intended use of data to ensure added value to the organization."

In Let's Fix It! Overcoming the Crisis in Manufacturing, Richard Schonberger separates those metrics that can be measured and watched but shouldn't be managed from those of more pressing concern.[2] Indicators that have the least lag between cause and effect are the most useful for frequent attention and management.

At a strategic level, an organization will determine if objectives have been achieved by reviewing the measured results derived from management's responsibility for, and commitment to, the QMS and its customer focus (section 5); effective management of the organization's resources (section 6); efficient and effective product realization (section 7); and the effectiveness and efficiency of the QMS (section 4).

When top management makes decisions based on macro-level metrics such as those incorporated in a balanced scorecard, it's stepping up to total-system thinking. This will move the organization away from the fragmented, element-by-element quality system approach fostered by ISO 9001/2/3:1994 and direct it toward improvements driven by objectives that are supported by facts. But how do you know if the change is working and whether it's good or bad?

For a given measure, a baseline is the basis against which future measurements are compared to determine change. It's the starting line. There can be no meaningful measurement of progress—or lack of progress or even regression—without knowing what the baseline was before change was initiated. To be comparable, baseline measures must be of the same type as future measures (i.e., dollars vs. dollars, percentages vs. percentages, volume vs. volume).

Choosing measurements that are relevant and important to your organization and its quality objectives not only will focus your company, management, and personnel on useful improvement efforts but also on achieving goals that are meaningful to them and thus more likely to gain needed support.

Baselines are established for key indicators that are most critical for the organization, such as those discussed below. Two examples of performance factors related to occurrences or actions taken by an organization with regard to a key indicator are:

■ Number of customer complaints received per customer segment in Greater Los Angeles
■ Percentage of the Central Illinois mortgage loan market currently serviced by the organization

The "snapshot" of the status of such measures at the start of an improvement initiative is the baseline from which subsequent change is measured.

Key indicators are those measures of select critical factors that an organization uses to determine if it's on track with its organizational strategy, goals, and objectives. KIs may be either *leading* (i.e., driving) or *lagging* (after the fact) indicators.

Leading indicators might include customer retention or process improvements underway. Lagging indicators could be inventory turnover or return on assets. A key indicator's metrics can be objective (i.e., based on hard numbers) or subjective (i.e., based on perceptions or opinions).

Lagging indicators tend to be based on objective measures, while leading indicators are based on either objective or subjective measures. Seven factors often serve as key TQM key indicators and are worth noting.

1. *Customer satisfaction.* ISO 9004:2000's subclause 8.2.1, Measurement, analysis and improvement—Measurement and monitoring of system performance, recommends using "effective and efficient methods" to monitor and measure information pertaining to customer perception of whether the organization has met customer requirements. ISO 9004 suggests approaches for accomplishing this, including internal audits [8.2.1.3], financial measures [8.2.1.4], self-assessment [8.2.1.5], measurement and monitoring of processes [8.2.2], and measurement and monitoring of product [8.2.3].

Each approach requires establishing a baseline or starting point for measuring improvement—or lack thereof. Examples of questions an organization should seek to answer pertaining to overall customer satisfaction include:

■ Do the organization's internal audits examine the handling of returns of nonconforming product or the reworking and/or replacement of services the customer complained about?
  □ Were improvement objectives set?
  □ How has the organization improved its processes to decrease the number and severity of these nonconformances?

■ Does the organization have a viable cost-of-quality system in place?
■ Does this system adequately differentiate among prevention, appraisal, and failure costs?
  □ What improvement targets have been set?
  □ Is there a favorable balance of cost types and is it reflected in both lower total quality cost and improved customer satisfaction?
  □ Are there targets for improving customer-related internal systems and processes contained within the QMS itself?

☐ Is the system effectively capturing and using customer feedback data?

☐ Are efforts based on the feedback data demonstrating improvements?

■ Is there an appropriate correlation between measurements of internal processes and customer perceptions? For example, an organization measures computer availability time at 98.7 percent, but feedback indicates service representatives can't resolve customer billing problems because "the computer is down."

■ By what means does the organization determine how customers perceive the product and services delivered? Are the approaches used to gather customer feedback data sufficient to create an unbiased picture of customer perceptions? A single approach is almost never sufficient. And if the focus is primarily on approaches that yield data only when there's dissatisfaction, this bias could lead to inappropriate change efforts.

2. *Market penetration.* Although not addressed directly in ISO 9004:2000, market penetration (i.e., market share and the extent of product and/or service distribution) is an organizational outcome that can be measured to determine if the company's strategy and goals are producing favorable results, depending on the market.

Examples of questions an organization should seek to answer in terms of market penetration include:

■ Is there a method in use to monitor and measure the organization's relative market position compared with its competitors? How effective is the methodology in alerting management when the organization's market penetration changes?

■ Have meaningful improvement objectives been set?

3. *Core competencies.* These include the specific attributes that distinguish an organization (e.g., exceptional workforce skills, innovative applications of state-of-the-art equipment, using methods and materials that leverage the organization's culture, research-and-development reputation, and speed and accuracy in fulfilling orders) and enable it to provide products and/or services that attract certain customers and "secure" their business.

ISO 9004:2000's clause 8.2.1.3, Internal audit, is one tool that can be used to answer questions relating to an organization's core competencies, such as:

■ Have the organization's core competencies been identified?

■ Were objectives set for sustaining and/or improving core competencies?

■ Are the means in place for measuring and monitoring how these core competencies are maintained?

4. *Financials.* All organizations track, measure, and work to improve their financial performance data. ISO 9004 recommends that management consider converting data from QMS processes into financial information "to provide comparable measures across processes and to facilitate improvement of the effectiveness and efficiency of the organization [8.2.1.4]."

Examples of questions an organization should answer in making this conversion include:

■ Are the financials reported downward to a sufficient level so that those who affect the numbers can use the data to make improvements?

■ Has a return on investment been computed to evaluate the value received from continual improvement?

5. *Employee development.* Subclause 6.1.1, Resource management—General guidance, introduction, lists people as a resource that top management should ensure is available. Subclause 6.2.1, People—Involvement of people, recommends that management "encourage the involvement and development of its people."

Thus, in ISO 9004:2000 employee development is critical to organizational capabilities. Indeed, subclause 8.2.2, Measurement and monitoring of processes, recommends that an organization cover the needs and expectations of interested parties—including "the effectiveness and efficiency of the organization's people"—as part of its process performance measurements.

Examples of questions an organization must answer as part of its employee development effort include:

■ Have employee qualifications (e.g., knowledge, skills, experience, attitude, and aptitude) been established for every type of task or job (i.e., group of tasks)?

■ Are the qualified individuals for each task or job periodically checked to determine if they've maintained the required competency levels and refreshed as needed?

■ Are improvement objectives set for enriching the jobs?
  ☐ For cross training?
  ☐ For upgrading to a higher-level job?

■ Are there sufficient means in place to collect, analyze, and act upon concerns employees might have with the organization?

■ Are there sufficient means in place to collect, analyze, and provide performance feedback to individual employees to enable their improvement?

■ Does the organization have policies and procedures to facilitate the personal development of its employees? Are there measures of effectiveness?

6. *Operations effectiveness.* Improving an organization's operational effectiveness is the goal of QMS performance improvement. That's because process performance can measure how well the organization meets customer and other stakeholder needs and whether its processes are optimally effective. Subclause 8.2.2, Measurement and monitoring of processes, recommends that organizations "identify measurement methods and should perform measurements to evaluate process performance."

Examples of questions an organization must answer in selecting measurements and evaluating operations effectiveness include:

■ What's the purpose and/or objective for measuring operations effectiveness?

■ Are there objectives for continual as well as breakthrough improvements?

■ Are there planned results for improving operations effectiveness?

■ What's the process to be measured?

■ Is the capability of each key process known and measured?

■ Are there measurements of key day-to-day operations (8.2.2)?

■ When is it best to take the measurement?

■ Where is it best to take the measurement?

■ Who is the best person to take the measurement?

■ What's to be done with the measurements taken?

■ What measuring tools are available?

■ What data collection and analysis technique or tool is best to use?

■ How and to whom will the information be presented?

■ Are areas for improvement identified and acted upon?

■ What decisions are expected from the results?

■ How is progress toward improvement to be evaluated and effectiveness determined?

7. *Community effect.* Finally, it's noted in subclause 8.2.4, Measurement and monitoring the satisfaction of interested parties, that society's needs—with "society" most often seen as the communities near an organization's facilities—should be met as part of an organization's processes. Although in the past a company was almost always welcomed into a community because it meant jobs and economic stimulus, many communities today evaluate an organization's effect with an eye to what it costs the community to have that organization located there (e.g., infrastructure, traffic, environmental effects).

Because it's critical for many organizations that communities view their presences favorably, organizations must address such community-focused questions as:

■ Are there objectives and measures for continually improving relations with the communities in which the organization's presence has an effect?

■ Are there sufficient means in place to collect, analyze, and act upon concerns the community might have with the organization?

Subclauses 8.2.2, 8.2.3, and 8.2.4 list dozens of areas for consideration in measuring, monitoring, and improving an organization. However, ISO 9004:2000 only implies that organizations must have baseline data as well as know how to set objectives and establish measurements. The standard doesn't say how to do this—it's up to you to know how.

MEASURING AND ANALYZING CUSTOMER SATISFACTION

ISO 9004:2000 lists examples of customer-related information from internal and external sources that are available in written and oral form (8.2.1.2, Measurement and monitoring of customer satisfaction). Such feedback can include verifiable facts as well as perceptions and opinions. As discussed in chapter two, an accumulation of data relating to customers must be converted into usable customer information.

It's the correlation of customer information from multiple sources that provides the basis for management to make informed decisions. Although an organization presumably will achieve conformance to customer requirements with its ISO 9001-based QMS, by stepping up to ISO 9004 it should focus on delighting and retaining a larger percentage of its good customers as well as expanding its customer base.

This makes it critical to listen more effectively, efficiently, and proactively to customer perceptions. By the time a customer complains, returns your product, or buys a similar one from a competitor, it might be too late to salvage that customer, even though your organization has useful customer-related data. Therefore methods are needed to help you learn what customers are thinking *before* a new need or complaint drives them to a competitor. The following scenario should help you understand what proactive listening means:

A small town has one supermarket. A customer checking out casually mentions to a cashier that she wished the store would carry her favorite brand of cereal. Another customer, on a rainy day, comments to the shopping-cart attendant that she wished the store would do something about the big puddles in the parking lot. Another employee, still wearing her supermarket ID, is shopping in the card shop several stores down when a stranger tells her how frequently he gets home and finds that some of his purchases aren't in his bags, necessitating a ten-mile roundtrip drive to the store's customer service counter—a waste of his time and gasoline.

Are these random data of value to the supermarket's management? If the data were isolated and infrequent, they probably would attract little attention even when known. However, with a methodology for capturing, categorizing, and correlating the data into meaningful information over time, the information could provide early warnings of impending customer dissatisfaction or uncover opportunities to provide improved or even new services or products.

Indeed, this information will prove more important over time if the supermarket is to prosper when the town does. After all, what will happen when the population in and around the town grows and another supermarket opens nearby? How important will customers' perceptions be then?

A method for learning what an organization's customers think, called "LCALI" (listen, capture, analyze, learn, and improve) has been addressed in chapter two and appendix B. LCALI involves setting up designated "listening posts," through which employees report noncritical customer data (procedures for handling critical complaints are or should already be in place). This random employee input data is then sent to a central person for analysis and trending and then disseminated to the management of the functions to which the information is pertinent. In response, management must determine if action will be initiated or if the subject of the information is to be put on a "watch list."

Usually, overall trends are discussed at management review meetings, but not the type of unsolicited customer data that originate from the infinite variety of interactions with customers. Such input typically isn't heard or, if heard, typically isn't captured, quantified, and presented as trends because there's no process for doing so, and the data's potential importance hasn't been recognized or communicated. It's only when the data are accumulated and analyzed that developing trends (i.e., information) can be noticed and action taken.

Every employee, from the CEO to the warehouse stock handler, might come in contact with an organization's customers (or might be a customer), and they might express opinions of its services and products. Salespeople talk with buyers, engineers talk with customers' engineers, and delivery-truck drivers talk with shipment receivers. The points of contact are nearly infinite, and negative perceptions aren't the only ones expressed. In your organization as in any other, the people responsible for generating these perceptions, both negative and positive, need feedback on their performance.

In some cases, data collected through listening posts can have little value, but there might also be "hidden gems" (e.g., data about a change in a competitor's strategy or news that a customer is contemplating moving or closing its operations). Consider the following case of the disappearing customer:

A public utility employed account representatives who periodically visited its large customers. The utility intended the visits to serve as a way to offer services, learn of any new needs or dissatisfaction, hear about future plans, and maintain good relationships. When the utility cut its budget, the number of account reps, and thus the frequency of account visits, was curtailed. At the time when a visit would have occurred previously, a large customer decided to close its plant in the utility's district and moved operations to another state before the next scheduled visit. In effect, the utility lost its chance to offer incentives that might have influenced the customer to remain in the district.

SELF-ASSESSMENT

Internal auditing has been a mainstay of the ISO 9001/2/3-based QMS since the inception of the ISO 9000 series. ISO 9004:2000 suggests a broader and more in-depth scope for internal auditing [8.2.1.3, Internal audit]. It provides the following examples of subjects that should be assessed:

■ Effectiveness and efficiency of process implementation
■ Capability of processes
■ Effectiveness and efficiency of the organization's use of statistical techniques, information technology, and quality cost data for decision-making
■ Using all resources effectively and efficiently
■ Measuring and improving process and product performance

Another suggested use for internal audits is to collect evidence of, and report on, excellent performance to promote employee recognition. Clearly, expanding into any of these suggested areas probably would involve more sophisticated assessment tools and a higher degree of internal auditor competence. Self-assessment must be recognized as a primary tool for identifying areas for improvement, so steps should be taken to build the needed competency and the internal auditor's repertoire of tools.

ISO 9004's appendix A, Guidelines for self-assessment, provides a comprehensive set of assessment questions that an organization can use to augment the traditional internal auditing of its QMS. Besides evaluating the system's maturity, appendix A also can be used to link the assessments to benefits the organization expected from its objectives.

An organization must also consider the cost of quality (both the costs of the QMS's process and product nonconformities). But organizations producing many different products or product families often don't know the segmented costs. When they do learn the applicable costs, they sometimes find that a given product segment is costing far more than they realized. This information can have an obvious effect on pricing, profitability, and, perhaps, a decision to phase out a product.

In stepping up to ISO 9004, organizations should be more concerned about the financial implications of their product, processes, and practices, as addressed in 8.2.1.4, Financial measures. A progressive organization will identify, track, measure, and act upon quality cost data. Many organizations don't understand or ignore the relationships between prevention and appraisal costs, and internal and external failure costs. The ultimate goal is to reduce the total costs of quality so that predominant quality costs in the future consist of investments in prevention.

In the following example, an organization learns how the costs of quality made a significant effect on its business:

> *A company that manufactured computer components from a precious metal initially had little concern for nonconformities. The inspector simply tossed defective parts into a recycle box for return to the melting pot. Although there was 100-percent salvage of material, the cost of detecting, segregating, and reprocessing defective units was ignored. The inspection, material handling, and repeat processing costs were minor compared with the cost of the material involved, but an assessment revealed that there was still a significant cost of waste involved. Once analyzed, the process was selected for improvement and cost prevention.*

It's imperative today for many producers to expand their focus to include analysis of lifecycle costs. Unexpected costs can occur when a product fails sometime after an end-user has placed it in service, and such costs can be catastrophic to the producer. Recent examples from the automotive industry have been highly publicized. And in a growing number of instances, when a product is no longer usable, the cost of environmentally regulated disposal becomes an issue and must be considered by the producer.

Whether or not there's a product liability, potential environmental issue, or other concern, costs are involved in investigation, defensive measures, and possibly claim settlements. Beyond considering defective product, unintended product use, and ultimate disposal, there may be other costs incurred during the product lifecycle that merit consideration. For example, answering customer questions about product use that might involve help desks and call centers, and complying with regulatory requirements (e.g., tracking of medical device complaints).

ISO 9004 addresses the concept that self-assessment can be used to benchmark an organization's performance against others'. Subclause 8.1.2.5, Self-assessment, also cautions against considering self-assessment a substitute for traditional internal quality audits. Perhaps this indicates that two classes of audits and auditors are needed to go beyond baseline performance levels.

ISO 9004's subclause 8.2.2, Measurement and monitoring of processes, expands upon the minimal requirements in ISO 9001's subclause 8.2.3, Monitoring and measurement of processes, by suggesting that the process performance measurements cover the "needs and expectations of interested parties" in areas such as:

- Process capability and dependability, cycle time, and yields
- Effective and efficient application of technology
- Effectively and efficiently reducing waste and other cost allocations
- Employee effectiveness and efficiency

ISO 9004's subclause 8.2.3, Measurement and monitoring of product, expands the phraseology in ISO 9001's subclause 8.2.4, Monitoring and measuring of product, by identifying factors to consider in selecting applicable measurements pertaining to meeting customers' needs and expectations.

ISO 9004's subclause 8.2.4, Measurement and monitoring the satisfaction of interested parties, offers examples of measurements that could be taken for four constituencies having needs relating to an organization's processes. The following examples represent measurements and monitoring approaches the organization could use to assess how well it meets the needs of these parties:

■ For the organization's employees
  ☐ Employee opinion surveys
  ☐ Assessment of individual and collective employee performance and its effect on organizational results

■ For its owners and investors
  ☐ Assessment of organizational capacity to meet its objectives
  ☐ Assessment of the organization's financial performance and return to investors
  ☐ Evaluation of the effect of external factors on organizational results
  ☐ Assessment of the value contributed by the organization's actions

■ For its suppliers and partners
  ☐ Opinion surveys to determine satisfaction with the organization's purchasing processes and relationships
  ☐ Feedback to suppliers and partners about their performance relative to pertinent policies and agreements
  ☐ Assessment of purchased product quality, supplier and/or partner contributions received, and mutual benefits derived from the relationships

■ For society in general
  ☐ Monitoring of data relating to its objectives of interacting satisfactorily with society
  ☐ Assessment of society's perceptions of the effectiveness and efficiency of the organization's performance

Clause 8.3, Control of nonconformity, expands beyond ISO 9001's clause 8.3, Control of nonconforming product, to address:

■ Effectiveness and efficiency of controls
■ Maintaining records relating to nonconformities to assist in learning and improvements
■ A process for reviewing trends or patterns of occurrence
■ The need for competent individuals to disposition nonconformities and record nonconformities corrected in the normal course of work as potentially valuable information for improvement

The fact is that many organizations don't document instances where product or process nonconformities occur, nor do they calculate the time and expense involved to correct the nonconformities or segregate and dispose of nonconforming product. What manager wants his or her workers taking even more time, after dealing with a nonconformity, to record something that's already been corrected or otherwise addressed? Yet, what might seem like a rare instance could be more frequent that anyone thinks, especially if similar nonconformities are dispersed throughout the organization but no one mentions them, at least not to those with the authority to address a pattern or trend.

In one firm that considers its operations efficient, undocumented nonconformities affect only 0.25 percent of production runs and go unnoticed, but if you factor in the time employees spend correcting nonconformities with the cost of the lost product, it equals 2 percent of what otherwise could have been produced. In an organization with $50 million in annual sales, that would equal $1 million in profit. In some companies, that would be this year's profits or a nice addition to the profit-sharing plan *and* the bonuses given to employees for meeting targets.

ISO 9004's clause 8.4, Analysis of data, emphasizes that decisions should be based on facts, and such facts can be derived from:

- Suitable, valid methods of analysis
- Appropriate choice and use of statistical techniques[3]
- Balanced facts derived from logical analysis along with experience and intuition
- Appropriate presentation of decision information, tailored to the needs of the organizational unit to which the information is targeted

One technique often overlooked for self-assessment is the management review. ISO 9004:2000 elevates the review process to evaluating system efficiency throughout the organization (clause 5.6.1). The clause suggests that to add value, top management "should control the performance of realization and support processes by systematic review based on the quality management principles."

Clause 5.6.2 lists review input considerations. These thirteen considerations, which might not all be adopted by a given organization, offer the means whereby top management can step beyond the minimal requirements of ISO 9001.

A useful approach is to treat the management review as a process. Document and follow a procedure that leads the organization through continual improvement to achieving, ultimately, world-class status. At a minimum, it's assumed the process has formalized such elements as review frequency, who shall attend, items to be discussed (i.e., the pre-meeting agenda), and how the problems and situations discussed will be resolved. In addition, it's advisable to evaluate the management review meeting process itself.

At the conclusion of the management review meeting, take three to five minutes to evaluate the meeting's effectiveness and efficiency and identify how the process can be improved. Figure 6.2 represents a sample evaluation form.

Examples of improvements in the management review process made by some organizations include:

- A requirement that all persons who bring information to the meeting do so in a form that can be incorporated into the meeting's minutes for subsequent distribution to attendees, other interested parties, and the permanent file of management review meetings (which are subject to external audit). The format can vary according to the needs of the organization, e.g., hard copy, electronic file on disk, or sent via intranet or e-mail. This action saves the meeting recorder's time and ensures the information is transmitted accurately.
- A resolution that, where feasible, information to be discussed be presented in a graphical form, e.g., trend charts, tables, and pie charts.
- A rule that issues and problems brought to the meeting will have been investigated prior to the meeting, alternative solutions assessed, and a recommended action provided (the concept of "completed staff work")
- A resolution that further problem solving be assigned as an outside-the-meeting activity

Figure 6.2

EVALUATION OF MANAGEMENT REVIEW		
Meeting Leader's Name: _____		Date: ___/___/___
Item	**Question**	**Observation/ Suggested Action**
Agenda	Was a meeting agenda prepared and sent to each participant prior to the meeting?	
Attendees	Did attendees/positions represented conform to QSP5.6?	
Old business	Were all "open" actions from previous meetings closed or extended appropriately?	
Quality policy	Is the quality policy suitable as published? Has the quality policy's content been deployed to all employees? How?	
Quality objectives	Was the quality objectives' status/results reported and discussed? Any modifications suggested?	
Customer satisfaction	Was the analysis of customer returns, complaints, and listening post input reported and discussed?	
Vendors	Was the analysis of supplier performance and status reported and discussed? Any improvements suggested?	
Training	Was the status of training program plans and programs discussed? Any significant changes?	
Auditing	Was the summary status of internal audits reported and discussed? Were any significant findings and actions resulting from internal audits reported and discussed? Was the adequacy of the number of trained auditors discussed? Was the schedule for registrar's audits reviewed?	
Corrective actions	Was the summary status of open and closed CAs reported, including highlights of any significant problems and actions?	
QMS documentation	Was the effectiveness and efficiency of the quality system manual and quality system procedures discussed?	
Document control	Was the effectiveness and efficiency of the document control process discussed?	
Resources	Was the adequacy of resource allocations to maintain and improve the quality system discussed? Any changes?	
Other factors	What other factors that might affect the organization were discussed? Did any decisions result?	
Quality system	Was the overall effectiveness and efficiency of the quality system discussed? Were any significant quality systems improvement plans initiated? Were any improvements reported? Were these improvements quantified (by $, #, %)?	
Preventive actions Reporting	Are new preventive actions required, based on this meeting? Number? Were all reports made in writing as well as orally?	
Critique	Will there be a critique of the meeting discussed by all attendees before leaving the meeting?	
Minutes	Were minutes taken (for distribution to all positions represented by QSP5.6)?	
Next meeting	Was a date announced for the next management review?	
Continual improvement	What actions should be taken to improve the next management review meeting? (Use back of form if needed.)	
Evaluation: My rating of meeting ("5"—highest, "1"— lowest) =		
Attendee Name: _____ *Title:* _____		

- An agreement that any problem requiring corrective action is taken care of outside the meeting and, if necessary, only the resolution is reported

- An agreement that any suspected problem or lingering system deficiency noted at the meeting will be assigned as a preventive action. Notation in the meeting minutes will indicate the action has been transferred to the preventive action system for resolution and follow-up, thereby leaving no preventive actions open in the management review records

- An agreement that all decisions other than preventive actions made at the meeting shall be documented in the minutes, indicating the action to be taken, by whom, by when, and when the progress is to be reported (usually at the next management review)

- A resolution that the entire QMS will be reviewed for effectiveness and efficiency at least once a year. The internal auditing process will perform the assessment. Management review attendees will review the assessment and determine what must be done to the QMS for continual improvement

- An agreement that the organizational objectives relating to the QMS will be reviewed and updated at least once a year, more frequently in critical areas

- A determination that the QMS will periodically be evaluated (i.e., at least yearly) relative to its adherence to the eight quality management principles

It's been found that many external (i.e., registrar's) auditors during their certification audits typically visit with top management first. In this meeting they assess top management's commitment to quality and the organization's QMS. Usually this meeting includes a discussion of the organization's management review process and the objective evidence supporting the reviews. Auditors have been particularly impressed to find an organization that also reviews the effectiveness and efficiency of the management review process itself, and strives for continual improvement of its process.

MAKE SELECTIONS TO AID DECISION-MAKING

ISO 9004's section 8 outlines considerations for any organization interested in moving beyond the basic requirements of ISO 9001. Section 8 doesn't prescribe how an organization should employ these recommendations but leaves it up to each organization to select those measurement and analysis suggestions and techniques that will aid in its decision-making effectiveness and efficiency. Although the emphasis is on making fact-based decisions, experience and even intuition aren't excluded. "What gets measured gets done" is a long-standing adage that should be the motto of managers in every organization.

It's important to emphasize that data shouldn't be collected simply because they could prove useful someday. Likewise, techniques that unnecessarily complicate the effective and efficient management of processes shouldn't be used. Further, don't do the following:

- Jump onto every bandwagon of new ways, techniques, and tools without having a defined outcome and a link to the organization's strategic objectives

- Buy every new technology unless it has real potential for your organization

- Train the entire organization in the latest ideology and tool without a valid reason

- Initiate fragmented approaches that haven't been substantiated by your organization's strategy

Experimentation is costly; plan wisely and execute well.

This chapter has explored some types of data that might be pertinent for your organization to measure and analyze. The remainder of section 8, dealing with improvement, will be covered in chapter seven and will address some of the ways in which the information gathered from measurement and analysis can be more effectively and efficiently used for decision-making.

ENDNOTES

1. Kaplan, R. S. and D. Norton. *Balanced Scorecard: Translating Strategy Into Action*. Cambridge: Harvard Business School Press, 1996.
2. Schonberger, Richard J. *Let's Fix It! Overcoming the Crisis in Manufacturing*. New York: The Free Press, 2001.
3. American Society for Quality. *Draft National Standard: Guidelines for Implementation of Statistical Process Control BSR/ISO/ASQ S11462-1-2001*. Final, published by ASQ (This standard hasn't yet gone to its last stage. ASQ Item # T11462).

CHAPTER 7

Focusing on Continual Improvement

Continual improvement is vital for your organization's well-being.

The concept of continual improvement sometimes seems lost on the management of many organizations. Ever in pursuit of the next dollar and personal agendas, many executives ignore the values and efforts that made their organizations viable in the first place. Although top management might appreciate that their company can't remain static and unchanging if it's to survive, many members of the management team still ignore the benefits available through continual improvement processes.

Chapter six examined ISO 9004's section 8, Measurement, analysis and improvement, and concluded with clause 8.4, which deals with the data an organization should consider collecting and analyzing to ensure its quality management system (QMS) is suitable, effective, and directed toward continual improvement. This chapter focuses on clause 8.5, Improvement, which deals with what your organization must do with the analysis: improve its processes. Although it's the last clause in ISO 9004, it's probably the most important in that it provides the reason why all the other clauses exist.

When it comes to continually improving a QMS's effectiveness, most organizations accept that two primary approaches are possible for producing a process improvement:

■ Step-by-step improvement activities, usually performed by people within a given process and referred to as "incremental improvement" or by the Japanese term *kaizen*

■ A breakthrough project, known as "process reengineering," typically a start-from-scratch approach involving the complete rethinking of how a process should be carried out

ISO 9004:2000, Annex B, Process for continual improvement, provides steps for implementing both incremental and breakthrough improvements.

OBJECTIVES-OUTPUTS-OUTCOMES

Your organization's strategic planning process should focus on its future direction and the strategic objectives by which it can reach that future. Such longer-term objectives can only be achieved when short-term tactical plans are deployed throughout the organization. These take the form of action plans (discussed in chapter one), which resemble mini-project plans in structure and intent. Let this serve as a reminder that QMS objectives must be measurable and achievable. To be effective, any outputs from action plans must contribute to the organization's outcomes. Many organizations focus on outputs without considering what effect these action plans have, or should have, on their outcomes.

For example, based on an action plan to track three aspects of customer satisfaction, a report is generated from data analysis. This report is an output. What the recipient does with it can or should be focused on an outcome. Recall the "data to wisdom" hierarchy from chapter three: Data ⇒ Information ⇒ Knowledge ⇒ Wisdom. Data are analyzed to produce the report (i.e., information). The report's recipient derives the information's meaning (i.e., knowledge) and applies his or her wisdom to the knowledge to make an informed decision about what to do. The result of the decision is an outcome.

To measure the effect on the bottom-line, outcomes typically are stated in dollar terms. When measured thus, the dollar outcomes of several action plans addressing one strategic objective can be accumulated to assess the measurable effect on the organization. Based on the stream of complaints from organizations claiming that their ISO 9001/2/3:1994 efforts were just an added cost and did nothing for them, the astute observer can presume that the complainants approached the registration process as an imposed burden rather than as an opportunity to improve their organizations' processes—and their bottom-line. Likewise, few of those complainants can claim to have made any attempt to measure the effect of any improvements made.

Figure 7.1 depicts the interactions from strategic goals and objectives to outputs, and, ultimately, to measurable outcomes.

ISO 9001:2000, combined with guidance from ISO 9004:2000, attempts to facilitate an organization's journey toward continual improvement. The tools and techniques are available, but they must be picked up and used effectively.

COORDINATE CONTINUAL IMPROVEMENT EFFORTS

Is your organization's total quality management initiative "fragged?" A fragmented approach to TQM can result in unresolved customer dissatisfaction, lost profit, and possible cancellation of your organization's TQM initiative. Following is an example of a "fragged" TQM effort. The elements of a fragmented approach to TQM will be familiar to many organizations:

> *Facing competitive pressure in January 2001, the chief executive officer of QTM Inc. declared, "Put together something that will do more for us than just ISO 9001:2000 registration. Put the QC guy in charge."*
>
> *Thrilled with an apparent blank check, Joe—the quality control guy— hired a consultant to provide statistical process control training for all plant personnel, obtained software and terminals for shop-floor data capture, and bought new calibration equipment. In charge of the organization's TQM initiative, Joe oversaw SPC training, collected lots of data from the shop floor, and calibrated everything in sight.*
>
> *However, he initiated some immediate process changes based on his interpretations of the fluctuating data from the shop floor without making any effort to distinguish between inherent variation in processes and special-cause variation. Furthermore, many of the process changes made were based on little more than unsubstantiated hearsay as to conditions before he instituted change. There*

Figure 7.1

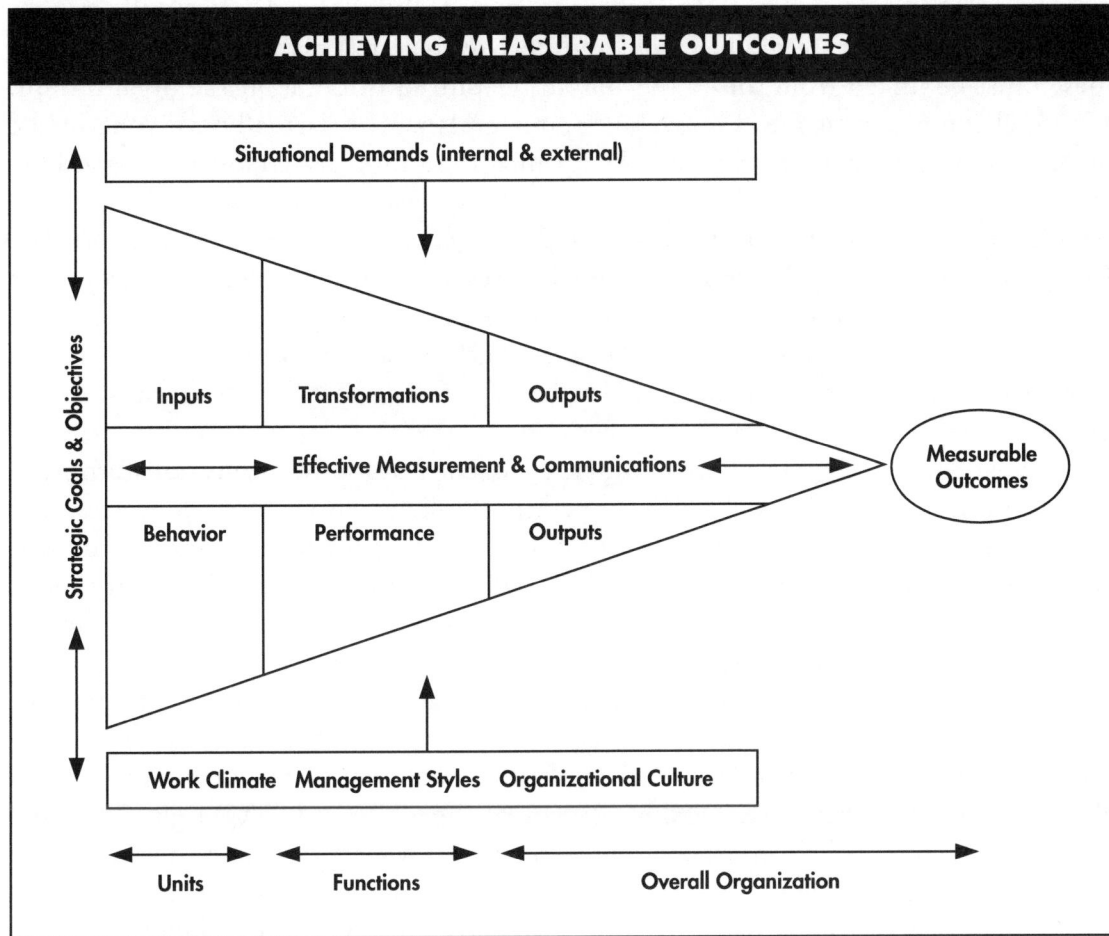

ACHIEVING MEASURABLE OUTCOMES

Situational Demands (internal & external)

Strategic Goals & Objectives

Inputs | Transformations | Outputs

Effective Measurement & Communications

Behavior | Performance | Outputs

Measurable Outcomes

Work Climate | Management Styles | Organizational Culture

Units | Functions | Overall Organization

was also no apparent link between Joe's "TQM" initiative and QTM's corporate strategy.

Top management paid little attention to Joe's frenetic, fragmented approach, although they'd been impressed by his initial burst of activity. But nine months after authorizing the effort, the CEO asked to see the initiative's results. The business situation had become worse, profits were down, no improvements were apparent, and Joe had spent significant money and personnel time on his less-than-effective attempts. The CEO declared the TQM effort a horrendous mistake and prohibited any additional expenditure. Joe is unemployed and wonders what could have gone wrong. All that remains today are shop-floor data collection terminals that continue generating data that no one looks at and a calibration system that has been abandoned.

This story and its outcome are typical of an "all-American quick-fix." Obviously, Joe was totally at fault, right? Wrong! He should never have had sole responsibility for the TQM effort. The CEO should have been personally committed and involved, and the initiative should have been carefully planned and cost-justified.

To avoid a fragmented, disjointed approach, an organization needs a vision of where it wants to be at some point in the future (e.g., five to seven years), an overall strategy, long-term goals, short-term objectives, and near-term action plans and projects. All of these must be linked from top to bottom and deployed throughout the organization. When all the pieces fit into the overall strategic plan, with virtually everyone in the organization participating, you have the formula for an integrated journey toward excellence.

Initiating a TQM effort using *ISO 9004:2000, Quality management systems—Guidelines for performance improvement* as a model represents a culture change. It involves all stakeholders and requires that the organization be permanently dedicated to continual improvement in every aspect of its business. TQM is a philosophy of work-life—a business-oriented, completely dedicated striving to be the best the organization possibly can.

Implementing a TQM initiative, when approached properly, means transforming a company's culture, business strategies, operating policies, procedures, processes, and products to balance its quest for profit or cost containment against a quest to delight customers and satisfy its other stakeholders. TQM is much more than quality tools, training programs, data collection and analysis, cross-functional team meetings, advertising slogans, a coveted quality award, or desperate actions to "buy quality."

TQM isn't sold in a box off the shelf, nor is it packaged in a software program or captured in a set of fixed steps. In any organization, TQM must be homegrown to produce worthwhile results. The seed must be planted, take root, and be nurtured continually during the life of the organization. Beware of the advertised "TQM guru" because TQM can't be installed by an outside source, no matter what his or her credentials. Each organization's culture shapes the TQM initiative into a unique endeavor. The structure and content of a TQM approach reflect an organization's way of doing things and point to ways in which that organization can improve its processes to the highest degree.

ISO 9004:2000 represents a comprehensive checklist for any organization striving to step up to the TQM challenge. Although *ISO 9001:2000, Quality management systems—Requirements* places an emphasis on "process," so does ISO 9004:2000—although with higher expectations. ISO 9004:2000 isn't a set of quality management system or TQM requirements but a full-bodied guide and checklist for building toward a world-class organization through performance improvement.

Considerations and actions your organization should address in establishing continual improvement as its modus operandi include:

- Maturity level of the organization
- Predominant management style in the organization
- Preventive and corrective action
- Cost reduction and loss prevention
- Lean thinking
- Team approach
- Organizational structure
- Improvement cycle
- Return on investment

MATURITY LEVEL

An old Chinese proverb states, "It is very dangerous to try to leap a chasm in two bounds." Similarly, it's usually unwise to attempt an ISO 9004:2000-level approach to TQM or even a certifiable QMS within a very immature organization. "Immature" means the organization's processes haven't been defined, standardized across operations, linked into a cross-functional system, evaluated for effectiveness, and continually improved.

Table 7.1 displays examples of qualifiers for five different levels of maturity pertaining to manufacturing organizations. The table isn't intended to be all-inclusive but should be a useful tool in developing a rudimentary understanding of your organization's maturity level. It will also give you a sense of how feasible achieving level five maturity is, how much you should attempt, and when to launch a long-term approach to achieving that level of maturity.

Even if your organization involves a great deal of service-related activities or is predominantly service-oriented, table 7.1 offers a perspective on what differentiates a dysfunctional system from a world-class one.

Along with maturity, organizational structure will have an effect not only on how "TQM via ISO 9004:2000" is pursued, but the relative success of such an initiative. Organizational structure is concerned with how employees work within the organization. A company that's primarily team-structured might have faster and perhaps greater success in its TQM initiative than one structured in the traditional hierarchical mode.

Likewise, organizations with free-flowing communication and employees involved in using and improving cross-functional processes will have an advantage over those that must break down or work around barriers involving these factors. Many traditional organizations can be in for a culture shock.

PREDOMINANT MANAGEMENT STYLE

In accordance with *Theory X and Theory Y*, Douglas McGregor's book concerning assumptions about people, an organization's predominant management style will influence the success of the TQM via ISO 9004:2000 initiative.[1]

For example, McGregor noted that if management perceives its workforce to be basically lazy and to consist mostly of unwilling workers who have no desire to excel at what they do (Theory X), management's actions would help fulfill this prophecy. As a result, the organization will likely have much difficulty recruiting and retaining qualified personnel and maintaining an acceptable level of product or service quality to meet customers' requirements. It also might be reacting to stakeholders as "the enemy" (e.g., greedy shareholders, untrustworthy employees, stupid customers, unscrupulous suppliers, and other meddlers).

On the other hand, if management's assumption about its people is that they basically want to do a good job and can be trusted (Theory Y), employees will tend to be treated with dignity, their jobs will be made personally enriching, and each will have a genuine desire to serve the organization's customers better. Customers, suppliers, and other interested parties will become entities with whom the company collaborates and focuses its efforts to improve outcomes.

The workforce takes its cue from top management, whether a single boss or a panel of executives. What's the baseline for your organization? Are attitude and behavior adjustments needed before beginning the TQM via ISO 9004:2000 effort, or is the organization about ready to start?

Table 7.1

LEVELS OF ORGANIZATIONAL MATURITY

	LEVEL 1 Dysfunctional System	LEVEL 2 Awakening System	LEVEL 3 Developing System	LEVEL 4 Maturing System	LEVEL 5 World-Class System
	Economy-of-scale focus with long runs preferred. Time-consuming changeovers are the norm. The customer's "voice" is rarely heard, and then only at the top.	Quality steering committee has been formed; quality systems are assessed; quality initiatives are planned. A customer focus is a goal.	Tested practices are deployed to all major areas of the factory. Customer involvement is sought.	Seeks out and learns about best practices. Adapts improved practices for all areas. Customers, suppliers, and employees are integrated into the systems.	Retaining satisfied customers is key. Plant uses single-piece flow with cellular techniques. Improved throughput achieved by reducing bottlenecks.
	Rigid plant layout; nonintegrated systems, erratic workflow prevalent. Buffer stock everywhere. All jobs "rush." "Firefighting" is normal.	Applicable lean management practices have been identified. Training is being conducted.	Flexible production layouts and cells are introduced. Cleanliness and neatness of individual work areas is stressed.	Production system allows short runs, greater product mix, speedy introduction of new products, shorter cycle times.	Plant layout is agile and clean. Workers self-inspect their work. Lean manufacturing tools and techniques liberally applied.
	Machinery run at maximum speed without regard for its life or performance quality. Workplace is unorganized and unclean.	A small project is underway to implement and test improved quality management practices.	Pull-type production system under test in one area. Employee qualification system is in place.	Operating information is provided immediately with computerized displays. Errors are prevented with mistake-proofing devices.	Preventive maintenance ensures availability, optimizes quality, efficiency, and lifecycle cost.
	No teamwork. "Fiefdoms" fiercely guarded from encroachment by other functions. No link between any overall strategy and production scheduling.	Bottlenecks and nonvalue-added functions in process flow are being examined. An equipment maintenance program is under development.	Cross-functional teams promote adherence to standards and ensure continuous improvement.	Teams, some self-managed, aid adherence to high standards, customer focus, and continual improvement.	Management is personally and visibly involved in continual improvement. Quality of information and decision-making at all levels is exemplary.
	Management by command. Poor workforce commitment and involvement.	A cross-functional team is being initiated to work on cycle-time reduction.	Systems are implemented to provide data for performance measurement, improvement.	An effective strategic planning process is instituted.	All employees are highly motivated, involved, and empowered.
	Communication is one-way (downward) with little or no feedback loops.	Weekly production review meetings are held, chaired by the VP of manufacturing.		Overall strategy is linked to production planning and process improvement.	Supplier relations based on collaborative communication.
	Adversarial supplier relationships; focus on price.	A supplier qualification approach is under study.	Supplier certification program in place.	Plant benchmarked by others in industry.	Plant benchmarked by others outside industry.
	Customers frequently get poor quality and delivery.	Overall performance remains below industry norm.	Overall performance is about equal to industry norms.	Performance is above industry norm	Performance is world-class.

What is your organization's level? ☐

PREVENTIVE AND CORRECTIVE ACTION

ISO 9004:2000 doesn't directly supplement ISO 9001:2000's subclause 8.5.3, Preventive action, although subclause 8.5.3, Loss prevention, does address some methods and tools used in preventive action procedures (e.g., failure mode and effects analysis). Perhaps the drafters decided not to provide guidance relative to preventive action because they had as much trouble differentiating between corrective and preventive action as most people do.

To help to better differentiate between these two actions, the following definitions expand upon what's in the standards:

■ A quick fix or "patch" is an action taken to enable a process to continue, presuming more extensive action won't be required. A "patch" might be appropriate for a single occurrence of a problem or error. An example is having an operator strengthen a soldered part. If very infrequent, this action is typically not documented.

■ A "corrective action" is an action taken if patches are required at any frequency, and the process is producing nonconformities. This action is taken when a problem is serious (e.g., happens more than once, affects delivery, involves costly materials and/or labor). Decisions are required: rework or scrap the defective output, downgrade output if it can be sold for another purpose with less stringent requirements, or seek concession from the customer for acceptance of output not meeting original requirements. A corrective action requires documentation of the root cause(s) of the nonconformity, the correction made, and evaluation of its effectiveness. Multiple occurrences of the same or similar occurrences might call for a more extensive overhaul of one or more processes—which is also a corrective action because it addresses the root cause(s) of an existing problem.

■ A "preventive action" is an action taken when a process is suspected of operating less effectively than it might; a process situation might potentially affect the quality of a product or service; a process that's been subject to corrective action and could signal the need for a preventive look at another, similar process; or a process that hasn't been examined for a long period of time. Organizations should develop a "preventive maintenance" program for processes, subjecting processes to in-depth analysis and overhaul on a periodic basis. Preventive actions must be documented and the results of changed processes tracked for a reasonable period of time to ensure the action is preventing problems. Error-proofing techniques can be useful for preventing potential processing errors. Used appropriately, internal process auditing can lead to preventive actions. The "action plan" approach or full project-planning methods should be considered for planning and managing the improvements.

■ A "development action" extends the concept of preventive action toward developing new processes to replace or eliminate existing processes—a process reengineering (or breakthrough) perspective. Such actions would be documented within the preventive action context but usually involve much more extensive research and development activities (e.g., design of new equipment and/or facilities, developing new chemical compounds, employing new service delivery methods). Development actions often result from changes in the marketplace, a need to regain a competitive advantage, and new technological opportunities. Many organizations engage in such actions but fail to recognize they can and should be documented and "counted" as preventive actions.

Although ISO 9001:2000 recognizes only the terms "preventive" and "corrective" actions, the above distinctions appear to help differentiate situations and the types of action to be taken.

COST REDUCTION AND LOSS PREVENTION

The concept of cost reduction is linked with loss prevention, which is covered in ISO 9004's subclause 8.5.3, for two reasons:

■ Cost reduction is readily embraced by the business community but not loss prevention.
■ If pursued correctly, loss prevention can produce outcomes that would cause most of top management to stop viewing cost reduction as an "effective" business tool.

Unfortunately, most organizations engage in various approaches to reducing costs. Some even sabotage critical elements in the name of cost reduction. This cost-cutting disease infects organizations of all types and sizes. When an organization begins to fail, the first reaction is often to close facilities or curtail services (i.e., cut facility costs or lay off personnel). You might ask, "Couldn't the organization see a downturn coming?" Usually the signs are there. If so, could smarter actions have been taken before taking such destructive steps? After all, some organizations won't survive the downward spiral created by such drastic actions. Keep in mind that cost reductions, taken without regard to the consequences, can backfire.

Might it not be a better organizational approach to improve the environmental scanning process so as to detect developing trends that could affect the organization? Would it not be better to apply preventive actions strenuously to improve processes, thereby reducing costs by eliminating waste? And would it not be better to find the means to make more money, or grow revenue, rather than cut one's capability to produce by simply cutting out costs?

Take the example of a professional, not-for-profit association that's feeling the effect of dwindling membership. Management chose to cut costs by eliminating member programs and services, but this further reduced its membership and revenues, necessitating still further cost cutting. The organization is now defunct. Why? The reason was because all efforts had been concentrated on cutting costs rather than finding ways to entice new members—and to make membership retention a priority.

Nothing had been done to find ways in which the association could adapt to the rapidly changing environment and economic swings affecting the membership. Association officials should have recognized during the past few years that the companies for which the membership worked had begun curtailing the financial support that enabled their employees to participate in the association. Instead, these officials buried their heads in the sand and lamented the situation rather than taking preventive action.

Periodically improving processes produces a far greater payoff than focusing solely on reducing costs, which didn't help the association above. This isn't to negate the value of knowing what your quality costs are and using the information to trigger meaningful preventive actions. But it's important to understand that losses, including losses of market share and organizational capabilities due to cost cutting, can be a substantial part of costs. Even more important, preventing losses will not only improve your organization's bottomline but also improve customers' satisfaction.

For example, a small lumberyard stored lumber and other building materials in open areas. Attempts were made to keep the materials covered with huge tarps, but they often blew off in bad weather. The result was that much of the yard's product was prone to damage, requiring personnel to monitor product protection and deal with weather damage. After years of incurring inventory losses and customer complaints, management decided to study the feasibility of erecting permanent sheds to protect the materials.

A careful analysis revealed that the cost of the sheds would be paid back within four years, eliminating the former resistance to spending money on sheds. And customers became much more satisfied with their purchases—dry lumber didn't warp, and dry building materials bought by weight yielded more material per pound. Not only did the lumberyard reduce the cost of nonconforming product and increase customer satisfaction, it also freed up personnel from dealing with product damage and became more competitive with larger yards in terms of both customer service and cost.

We're all aware that accident prevention has a positive effect on the bottom line by preventing lost production time, liability claims, legal actions and increased insurance costs. What if similar attention were paid to inventory loss prevention, scrap prevention, cycle-time loss prevention, lost customers, and employee losses?

It might help to see an example of an organization that engaged in loss prevention. In this case, "Etronics" is an assembler of telecommunications equipment sold exclusively to a network of distributors. A practice implemented years before allowed these distributors to review their inventories once a year and return for credit any product that wasn't selling. This was initially viewed as a brilliant business strategy because it encouraged distributors to try to sell Etronics' innovative products—distributors had nothing to lose and much to gain. As time passed, however, Etronics found it was swamped during each return period with cartons of unsorted, damaged, and often unmarked product, some obviously years old.

To process (i.e., test and re-enter into inventory) this collection of junk required more time and cost than it was worth. Etronics usually scrapped much of the product and gave distributors credit based on each distributor's documentation. While this practice had been the norm for years, Etronics' management finally took a stand and carefully documented the conditions under which material could be returned for credit. All distributors were notified of the revised policy and why it was needed. The response was a mix of protests and comments such as, "Why didn't you do this years ago?" However, no distributor left and all abided by the new rules. The annual distributor-dump was brought under control, at a substantial savings to Etronics.

APPLYING LEAN THINKING

There's a growing trend toward applying lean thinking and lean techniques within the context of ISO 9001-based QMSs, Six Sigma, TQM, and overall preventive action. Attempting to cover lean techniques adequately here is impractical; therefore, the following will provide a brief look at a few of the key tools and techniques.

Emerging from the manufacturing sector, lean thinking and the techniques and tools associated with it are now being applied to nearly all types of organizations. Yet, although few present-day practitioners will admit it, much of this thinking and some of the tools have distant roots in work simplification and zero-defect efforts of half a century ago. As with Six Sigma and TQM, "lean" embraces techniques and tools that have been available for many years. However, as is the case with Six Sigma, lean thinking has materialized as a philosophy as well as collection of techniques and tools.

Lean thinking is a "weight reduction" approach to ridding an organization of redundant, non-value-added activities that consume resources and add costs. Process mapping—an old flowcharting tool with new features—is used to uncover wasteful steps in processes and show where cycle times might be reduced. As speedy and frequent changeovers from one product to another become increasingly necessary, techniques such as SMED (single-minute exchange of die) are used to improve machine setups and reduce downtime. Like an athlete trying to achieve perfect form, the goal of lean thinking is to minimize waste and increase efficiency, thereby making an organization competitive in "the race."

The Theory of Constraints (TOC), derived from Eliyahu M. Goldratt's work and his novel, *The Goal*[2] is another useful methodology. H. William Dettmer[3] categorizes TOC as "a collection of system principles and tools, or methods for solving the problem of improving overall system performance." Within the context of lean thinking, TOC would mean systematically identifying and removing obstacles to a smooth production flow, be they widgets or insurance claim processing. As the primary constraint is removed, the next in line is addressed, smoothing its flow of product.

However, reality in some organizations can conflict with practicality when it comes to TOC. For example, huge machines often are already in place to perform multiple operations in one pass. Although deemed efficient, they might be bottlenecks requiring material to be batch-processed. These "monuments," as the machines are sometimes called, can represent serious constraints for an organization striving to achieve the benefits of "one-piece flow." This is of growing importance as customers look for greater product customization.

A key concept of lean thinking is setting the pulse or pace (known as *takt* time) of the production operation to customer demand. "Pull systems" for producing product (*kanban* in Japanese) eliminate or substantially reduce a need for buffer stock and aid in smoothing the flow of material. "Just in time" approaches provide for delivery of material where it's needed just in time for its use.

Other lean techniques and methodologies exist that your organization might want to consider applying to its operations and are worth a brief mention, including:

- Organizing the workspace into "cells" enables operations to occur in sequence, allowing single-piece flow and more flexible use of operators
- Total productive maintenance involves understanding and minimizing the factors contributing to machinery and tool wear and scheduling maintenance to prevent breakdowns at times least upsetting to the production schedule. This "service it before it breaks" philosophy also conveys a preventive outlook to all employees.
- Mistake-proofing processes (*poka-yoke* is the Japanese term) prevent defects from occurring. Various types of electronic, electrical, or mechanical devices can be used to prevent a process error.
- Continuously updated control charts might be a feature of the more sophisticated electronic data-capture systems in preventing a process from going out of control.
- The "Five S's," another Japanese concept, makes all aspects of a workplace orderly and clean and works to keep it so. Responsibility for the Five S's is delegated to the operator, as is another function, self-inspection. With both techniques, an operator tends to gain

an increased understanding of his or her role in processes and to take greater responsibility for a quality product.

■ Concurrent engineering means engineering works in parallel with production—and often with the supplier and/or customer representatives—to shorten the time from product launch to delivery. Done well, concurrent engineering can substantially decrease the number and costs of engineering changes.

■ Process reengineering, or the redesigning of a process from scratch, is an approach to improving a process that might be suffering from inefficiencies or excess costs, is a cause of quality problems, and/or can't meet new competitive pressures. The redesign of an order processing and delivery system is an example. Sometimes called the "start with a clean sheet of paper" approach, process reengineering focuses on creating a whole new and better process. Some of the old system might be incorporated in the new but only after efforts to find a better method are exhausted.

Lean thinking, as stated earlier, embraces many techniques and tools from many disciplines and uses them to continually improve processes by shortening cycle time, reducing costs, and increasing customer satisfaction. This overview is far from inclusive. Look to the rapidly growing body of knowledge on lean thinking for more in-depth information.

IS TEAMING THE BEST ANSWER?

A multitude of books and articles have been devoted to teams. This vast literary array discusses types of teams (e.g., cross-functional, improvement, natural, project, self-directed, and virtual) and explores how they're structured (i.e., roles and responsibilities), formed, and function (team stages are: forming, storming, "norming," and performing). Many authors also focus on the perils and pitfalls of using teams and the pros and cons of a team's internal dynamics. What's given less attention is when to employ a team approach and for what purpose and benefit? And what approach is best with a QMS geared to continually improving an organization, as covered in ISO 9004:2000's subclause 8.5.4?

Some entire organizations are structured on a team basis, including many of the newer, high-tech companies, and there are redundancies inherent in an all-team approach. Yet, in industries experiencing rapid growth and developing new technologies, the redundancies are offset by the focused direction gained by having teams work on new product design and launches. By comparison, an organization in a more mature and/or stabilized industry might create and support an ad-hoc team (or "task force") to accomplish a specific process improvement. This type of team is typically formed to achieve a near-term objective and then disbanded when the objective is reached. Such an approach has the focused direction without much redundancy, and it answers the questions when to use a team, for what purpose, and to obtain what benefits.

Popular these days are "cycle time" reduction teams that seek to continually devise ways for reducing the cycle time of the process in which they're involved. Frequently, the people responsible for implementing (i.e., designing and documenting) an ISO 9001-conforming QMS work as a team, usually a cross-functional one.

The total reengineering of a process might be accomplished with a dedicated, cross-functional team. Typically used for long-term efforts, such a team often is structured and managed as a parallel organization to the mainstream one. Some types of organizations are totally project-oriented, e.g., a consulting firm. In these cases there's usually a very small core management and administrative group and many project teams headed by project managers.

A newer concept is the virtual team, which relies on teamwork being conducted through conference calls and the Internet. Within the past three years, the author has participated on virtual teams to produce two textbooks. For the first, team members were located in Connecticut and Tennessee. For the second, members participated from Connecticut, Ohio, and South Carolina. Although the team members knew each other, they never met face-to-face during the book projects. E-mail facilitated communication and transmitting drafts, and both projects were completed on time and within budget. Indeed, the budgets were lower because travel and related meeting expenses that would have occurred using traditional team methods were avoided.

Team members rarely are excused from all their day-to-day responsibilities while serving on a team, and that can be both problematic and beneficial. It's problematic in that the team must fight for resources (i.e., time and budget). Which "master" does a member serve, his or her work unit or the team's project? How will management support the member's decision? And it's beneficial because the organization has committed team members who are still grounded in their day-to-day processes. This means team members probably are aware of what's happening in the organization. But it also means they can't focus full attention on the project. Moreover, team members might view their continued role in the "real world" as a guarantee that they'll be able to return to their daily work when the team completes its work. Full-time "transfer" to a team project could make it difficult for a team member to reclaim his or her daily job or missed promotional opportunities when the project is over.

Not every process improvement or problem situation merits a team. Management must consider the costs incurred to create, maintain, and support a team (e.g., staffing shortages, unattended responsibilities, effect on and perceptions of unsupervised workers, meetings, and other team costs). Urgent, life- and property loss-threatening situations rarely are suited to a team process—decisions can't wait. Highly autocratic organizations would likely find it difficult to subordinate much of their decision-making power to a team. Fully participatory-style organizations, on the other hand, could find it difficult to curb the potential for teams to proliferate.

Finally, teams often are ineffective if they lack a trained team facilitator to help them through the stages (see team stages note above) and keep them focused on their objective(s). A mob lacking direction and purpose isn't a team.

IS YOUR ORGANIZATIONAL STRUCTURE LESS THAN EFFECTIVE?

There's no single best way to organize an enterprise, and countless organizational structures have been tried. What works best depends upon a host of factors, including the:
■ Type of personality, vision, values, and goals exhibited by the top executive
■ Type of business and how it responds to its marketplace and other demands from interested parties (i.e., customers, employees, suppliers, investors, community)
■ Organization's core competencies
■ Competitors' strategies and approaches
■ Availability of resources (e.g., employees, supplier products, funding sources)

- Legal and regulatory constraints
- Geographical location(s)
- Cultural differences of various locations and job markets

A company selling state-of-the-art equipment primarily to military customers might require a whole suborganization dedicated to one specific customer or family of products. In a different situation, an organization serving multiple customers with custom-designed products might need a matrix-type organization to best utilize its technical professionals and move discipline-specific people from project to project as need dictates. The point isn't whether a given type of organizational structure is better than another but rather which is best for your organization.

Reflect on the often-disastrous reorganizations that occur following a merger or acquisition. The conquering company tends to force its approach on the conquered, which often forces out the very people who made the acquisition attractive in the first place. Wasting human competence could be considered an unacknowledged crime, yet the "criminal" almost always blames the "victim" for the crime, directly or otherwise.

It usually pays to get an objective view of the effectiveness of your present organization and management style by having an external organizational development expert conduct a periodic diagnosis. But be prepared to make some changes, especially if you haven't done this kind of diagnosis recently. Once your organization has made its changes, build in a review of the organizational structure as a prelude to annual strategic planning.

Perhaps you should consider Michael Hammer's innovative concept of managing without structure?[4]

Figure 7.2

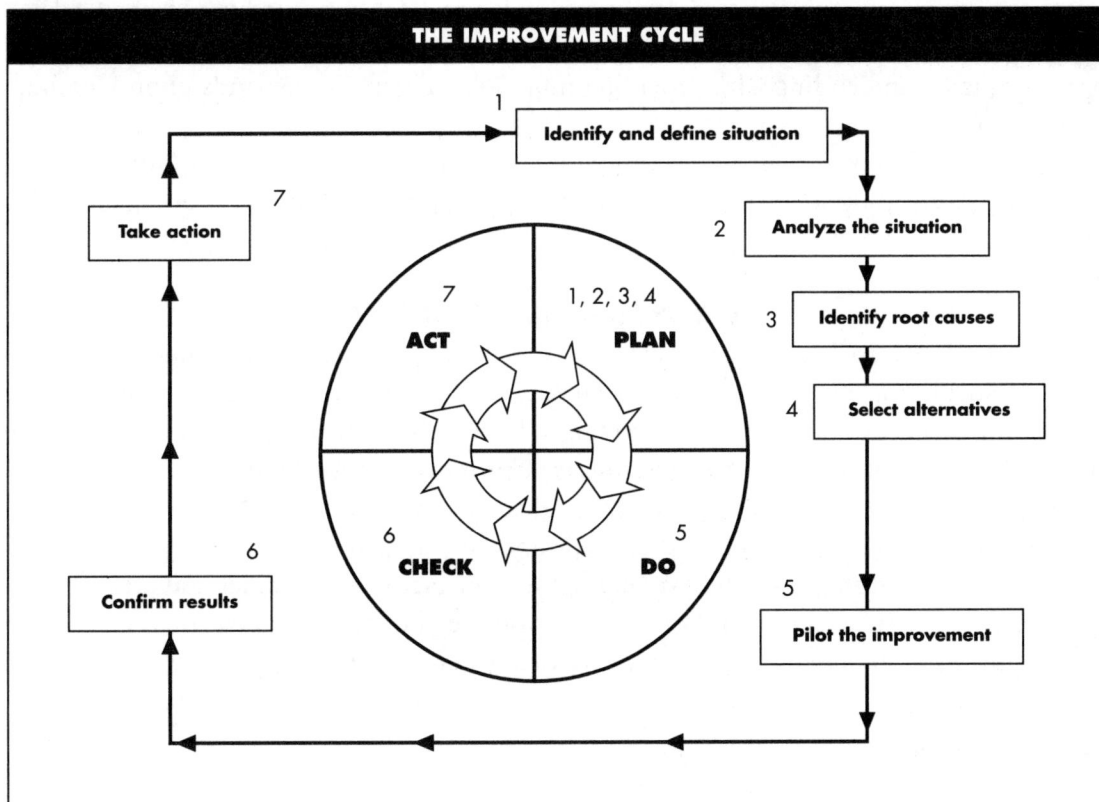

THE IMPROVEMENT CYCLE

1. Identify and define situation
2. Analyze the situation
3. Identify root causes
4. Select alternatives
5. Pilot the improvement
6. Confirm results
7. Take action

ACT — 7
PLAN — 1, 2, 3, 4
CHECK — 6
DO — 5

Figure 7.3

SAMPLE LOQSI LOG				
Date	References to Procedures, Standards, Customers, Suppliers	Initiated By	Description of Improvement (Situation and Action Taken)	Results ($, Qty, %)

IMPROVEMENT CYCLE

One of the most famous and useful models for improvement is the Shewhart/Deming plan-do-check-act (PDCA) cycle. Figure 7.2 superimposes seven substeps. The PDCA model fits virtually any improvement initiative at any organizational level. Use the model extensively in planning and executing improvements.

RETURN ON INVESTMENT

Use ISO 9004:2000's section 8 as a guideline in your efforts. Track return on investment from your first improvement project, and for every one thereafter. Periodically accumulate the value of the improvements made and use these numbers to justify additional improvements. (See appendix G for how to demonstrate the return on investment for quality improvements.) A log of quality system improvements, as depicted in figure 7.3, can be used to capture the data.

W. Edwards Deming introduced the concept of a chain reaction[5] beginning with improving quality and ending with providing more jobs. Figure 7.4 expands upon Deming's original concept.

Following Deming's logic, the conclusion is that effective continual improvement will more than justify using an ISO 9004-based QMS as a major contributor to your organization's outcomes.

BEGIN OR CONTINUE THE JOURNEY

Hundreds of possible approaches exist to achieving continual improvement; this chapter has touched on but a few. Unless you've access to unlimited resources, assess your organization's needs and start by addressing relatively high-priority situations and those that will likely produce early positive results. Get more employees involved to build on these successes, and keep your focus on strategic goals and objectives. Not every effort will be a big success, so learn from mistakes made and keep improving.

Chapters one through seven have highlighted key factors to consider and areas for improvement when stepping up to ISO 9004. Chapters eight and nine draw your attention to two highly useful processes to assist in the effort: benchmarking and project management.

Figure 7.4

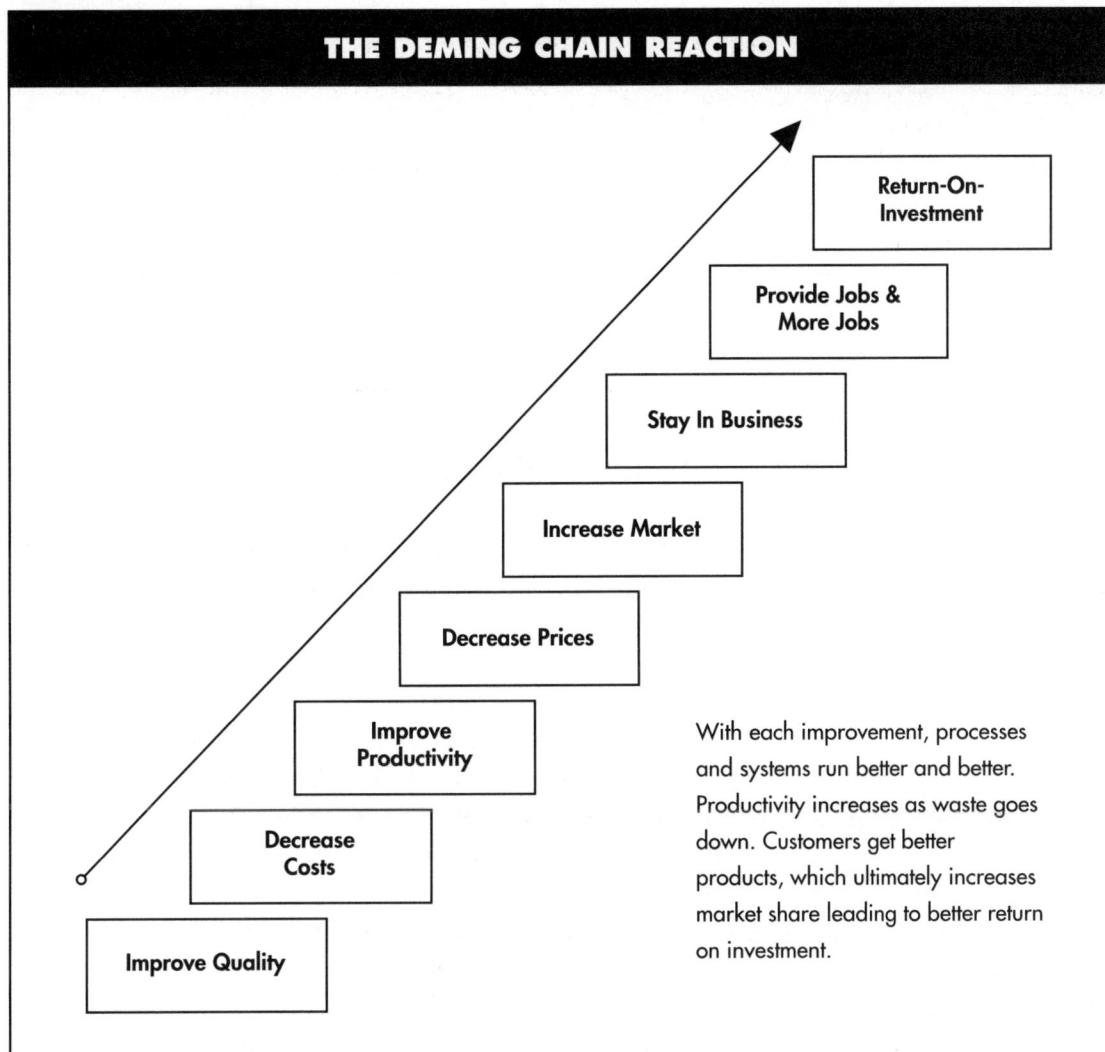

THE DEMING CHAIN REACTION

Return-On-Investment

Provide Jobs & More Jobs

Stay In Business

Increase Market

Decrease Prices

Improve Productivity

Decrease Costs

Improve Quality

With each improvement, processes and systems run better and better. Productivity increases as waste goes down. Customers get better products, which ultimately increases market share leading to better return on investment.

ENDNOTES

1. McGregor, Douglas. *The Human Side of Enterprise.* New York: McGraw-Hill Book Co. 1960.

2. Goldratt, Eliyahu M. *The Goal,* Second Revised Edition. Croton-on-Hudson: North River Press. 1992.

3. Dettmer, H. William. *Goldratt's Theory of Constraints: A Systems Approach to Continuous Improvement.* Milwaukee: ASQ Quality Press.1997.

4. Hammer, Michael. *The Agenda: What Every Business Must Do to Dominate the Decade.* New York: Crown Business, 2001.

5. Deming, W. Edwards. *Out of the Crisis.* Cambridge: Massachusetts Institute of Technology Center for Advanced Engineering Study. 1986.

CHAPTER 8

Benchmarking

Benchmarking is a quality process for continual improvement

If you looked through *ISO 9001:2000, Quality management systems—Requirements* for any coverage of "benchmarking," you'd see it's not required or even mentioned by the standard. In fact, the term "benchmarking" isn't even defined in *ISO 9000:2000, Fundamentals and vocabulary*. Most likely benchmarking is omitted from ISO 9000:2000 and ISO 9001:2000 because it isn't necessary for a baseline generic system. So why bring up benchmarking? Because it's a valuable quality process that can be used to achieve continual improvement of your QMS and overall performance improvements for your organization.

This chapter defines the term and examines how to use the process when stepping up to ISO 9004:2000. It's important to note that references to benchmarking are found throughout ISO 9004:2000, with specific mentions in many clauses and subclauses, including:

- Clause 4.2, Documentation, suggests organizations benchmark their documentation systems
- Subclause 5.4.1, Quality objectives, recommends management use benchmarking when setting objectives
- Clause 7.2, Processes related to interested parties, suggests organizations use relevant process information derived from benchmarking
- Subclause 7.5.2, Identification and traceability, suggests benchmarking performance data can uncover identification and traceability problems, and thus lead to improvement
- Subclause 8.1.2, Issues to be considered, recommends that benchmarking individual processes should be used as a tool for improving processes' effectiveness and efficiency
- Clause 8.2.1.5, Self-assessment, suggests organizations use self-assessment to benchmark performance against external organizations and those with world-class performance records
- Clause 8.4, Analysis of data, suggests using analysis to benchmark performance
- Subclause 8.5.4, Continual improvement of the organization, recommends benchmarking competitor performance and best practices to identify opportunities for improvement

Other entries in ISO 9004 mention benchmarking, but those listed above should give you a sense of benchmarking's potential range of application. But what exactly is benchmarking?

Benchmarking is a continual, organized process for comparing your organization's practices and services with its industry and/or other organizations (e.g., those recognized for their best practices within or outside an industry) for the purposes of learning and identifying ways to improve processes and services to meet or exceed best practices.

It's important to note that benchmarking isn't:

- Industrial spying
- Competitive analysis (i.e., comparing strategic decisions, products, pricing, profits)
- Industrial tourism (e.g., field trips or plant tours)
- Focused as much on numbers as on processes that produce the numbers
- Initiated unless significant potential gains are expected
- A quick or inexpensive process, if properly executed
- For those organizations that don't intend to make the effort to learn, measure, and improve their present processes
- Appropriate without proper protocol and legal considerations
- Worth initiating unless your organization is prepared to make changes resulting from what it learns
- Easily accomplished if your organization has nothing to "trade" with its benchmarking partner
- Usually a one-shot process

A well-planned and conducted benchmarking process will help you uncover ways to do things more quickly and effectively. When your organization's quality initiatives have produced improvements and you believe it's time to look elsewhere for added insights about best business practices, it's time to consider benchmarking.

Benchmarking can help your organization:

- Identify the difference between its performance and the recognized best practices of other organizations and overcome complacency
- Develop support for internal change by making employees aware of the need for continual process improvements
- Trigger an early warning that its process performance might be slipping
- Discover how best-in-class organizations use their resources and what they achieve by doing so
- Stimulate innovative ideas for correcting or eliminating performance problems with a key process or processes
- Learn about emerging new technologies and techniques
- Evaluate the relative benefits of its business approaches vs. those of a benchmarking partner
- Enable the setting of internal targets against which to measure process performance improvement

Considering the potential benefits, you might wonder if benchmarking is applicable (i.e., will produce similar benefits) for all types of organizations. As a rule, benchmarking provides the greatest benefits to organizations that have effective quality management systems (QMSs) and are among the highly successful producers for their size and business type. A mid-level producer (i.e., one that still has much to gain from its own quality initiatives) can gain valuable insights from benchmarking, but it would earn a better return on its investment by first improving its own processes. A lower-level producer—i.e., one with an incomplete or rudimentary QMS in place—will become discouraged by the chasm between its practices and those of a best-in-class producer—and likely will have difficulty finding a benchmark partner because of having little to share.

SELECTING PROCESSES FOR BENCHMARKING

Once your organization has evaluated the results of its QMS and quality initiatives and concluded that internal efforts have done as much as possible to bring about improvements, benchmarking can be used to further organizational improvement. The question then becomes: What process should we benchmark?

Selecting processes to benchmark is critical to success. Organizations that have used benchmarking to improve their performance have applied it to only one or a few processes because it's impractical to benchmark all of an organization's processes against those of another. Good candidates for benchmarking include any process that:

- Consumes a high percentage of your organization's resources
- Significantly affects quality
- Is strategically vital to your business's success
- Is key in distinguishing your organization from its competitors
- Has great potential for—and is capable of—improvement, given your organization's resources, core competencies, and management's support
- Is legal and ethical to discuss with a benchmarking partner

Table 8.1 provides some examples of processes that are good candidates for benchmarking. Once you choose a process to benchmark, you must then choose the level of benchmarking in which your organization will engage. Following are four typical benchmarking levels, each of which has its benefits and drawbacks:

- *Internal benchmarking* compares one function with another, or compares the same process across locations. Data are fairly easy to collect. The focus is limited and possibly could be biased.
- *Competitive benchmarking* compares your organization with its direct competitors locally, nationally, or even worldwide. In this case, the data can be more relevant but difficult to collect. Resistance from a local direct competitor is likely. However, when comparing with organizations outside one's local market area, you might not be viewed as a competitor. Ethical and legal issues, however, can be a concern.
- *Functional benchmarking* compares your organization's processes with those of organizations with similar processes but outside your industry. This level avoids the problems of competitive benchmarking but could produce data that do not relate, in critical factors, with your processes due to industry differences.
- *Generic benchmarking* involves finding organizations that have best-in-class processes and approaches from which you might learn and then translate that learning into improvements applicable to your organization. When you "think outside your box," there's a high potential for discovering innovative practices and usually little resistance to partnering with a noncompetitor. However, translating practices to your work environment could prove problematic and expensive.

Table 8.1

EXAMPLES OF PROCESSES THAT CAN BENEFIT FROM BENCHMARKING
Business Practices

■ Accounting system
■ Staff-compensation system—the system, not the pay structure
■ Purchasing practices, supplier selection
■ Manufacturing, distribution processes
■ Customer database design
■ Cost ratios (direct, indirect)—not the dollars
■ Decision-making criteria for capital investments/improvements
■ Technology, tools and techniques, including:
   • Innovative use of computers and other electronic devices
   • Lean manufacturing
   • Quality tools
■ Facility size, layout, décor
■ Staffing approach, size of staff, training practices
■ Employee empowerment, involvement, recognition approaches
■ Advertising/promotion practices
■ Rent, lease, buy practices

Other Processes
■ Services and products offered ■ Customer acquisition and retention practices ■ Service quality, customer satisfaction, assessment techniques ■ Firm's image, business hours ■ Special practices and incentives

Many organizations conduct benchmarking studies at all four levels. They often join or develop networks of benchmarking partners to conduct studies on one or more levels to benchmark different processes with suitable partners. Table 8.2 provides examples of potential partners for processes that could benefit from benchmarking.

BENCHMARKING PROCESS STEPS

The benchmarking process typically involves ten steps:

1. *Review, refine, and define your existing processes.* You must know what your organization does and that those processes have already implemented internal improvement before you begin to consider benchmarking.

2. *Determine what processes to benchmark.* As mentioned earlier, it's important to select one or a few processes where benchmarking can be applied effectively and where potential results will justify the investment. The following questions should be answered in determining what to benchmark and why:

■ Where's the critical need?

■ What organizational, quality objective, or critical success factor will be aided by the benchmarking information obtained?

Table 8.2

EXAMPLES OF GENERIC BENCHMARKING PARTNERS		
Industry	**Target for Improvement**	**Possible Benchmark Partners**
Airline	Changeover planes quickly	Auto racing pit crew
Bandage manufacturer	Convert material to product	Auto manufacturer
Education	Teach/train students	Industry trainer
Hospital	Bill and collect payments	Credit card company
Pizza delivery	Deploy personnel rapidly	Emergency room; military
Shell casing manufacturer	Make smooth cylinders	Lipstick manufacturer
Municipal government	Pothole repairs (reduce time and material)	Electric or gas utility
Hotel	Maintenance of public spaces	Casino
Professional association	Book and product sales	Internet-based book company
On-call TV repair service On-call plumber Cable TV service Public utility	Truck—stock replenishment or selecting onboard tools and equipment	Fire department, ambulance service, police department
Urban transit company	Bus/trolley car maintenance	Interstate truck stop service center
Sports arena	Processing mailed-in ticket sales	Commercial mail-order company
Metal stamping manufacturer (i.e., job shop)	Time to change over dies for new order	Aircraft carrier—mounting weapons/ammunition on planes
Bank	Handling cash transactions	Sports arena
Assembly plant	Restocking parts just-in-time	Supermarket
Aerospace manufacturer	Large-project management	Major commercial building construction firm
Printer of continuous Web, paper products	Improving operating performance	Manufacturer of rolled metal products
Large high-tech electronics manufacturing and assembly	Establishing customer/public tours and information center	NASA; large public utility

■ What specific information do you seek?
■ When does your organization need the information?
■ What measurements are appropriate?
■ Who will use the information you obtain?
■ What outcomes or expectations does your organization have?
■ What's the baseline for the process to be benchmarked?

3. *Form a benchmarking team.* Obtain and use the answers to the following questions to ensure the team selected will benchmark the chosen processes effectively:
■ Who are the best persons to serve on the team?
■ What are the team members' roles and responsibilities?
■ What training will team members need? How will this be accomplished?
■ What support and resources will the team need?
■ Who will take primary responsibility for the team's work?
■ How much team time will be spent benchmarking?

4. *Identify benchmark partners.* The following questions must be answered when identifying and soliciting potential partners:
■ Does your organization want to benchmark with direct competitors or noncompetitors?
■ Is the objective to benchmark best practices, best-in-class, or world-class performance?

- Does your organization want to join or start its own network?
- What resources are available?

5. *Collect and analyze benchmarking information.* The following questions must be answered before taking this step:
- Have you collected and analyzed your organization's internal information? (Remember that benchmarking is best undertaken after internal improvement efforts have been exploited.)
- How will you gather the data you need?
- How will you organize and analyze the data?

6. *Evaluate your organization's process performance vs. the benchmarking partner's performance.* The following questions should be answered before beginning the evaluation process:
- Does the benchmarked organization match your benchmarking objectives?
- Should your organization's performance target meet or exceed your organization's strongest competitor?
- Is there a potential payoff from meeting or exceeding the benchmarks obtained from your partner?

7. *Determine how upgrading practices will affect your organization.* Consider its:
- Culture, vision, mission, strategic goals and objectives, and policies
- Quality plans (objectives) and critical success factors
- Client focus
- Personnel
- Suppliers
- Profit

8. *Establish your organization's new strategic quality level targets.*
9. *Implement improvements and a system to monitor progress.*
10. *Evaluate the effectiveness and efficiency of the benchmarking process itself.* Make improvements and repeat the benchmarking steps again.

An important preparatory step is to obtain information about benchmarking. For example, you might want to learn more about possible partners and networks your organization could use. Depending upon the benchmarking data to be collected, multiple sources of information might be available. Figure 8.1 presents a hierarchy of information sources that shows both how easy and difficult it is to obtain information from different sources as well as the information's quality (i.e., usefulness).

POTENTIAL PERILS, PITFALLS, AND LIMITATIONS

No activity undertaken to change an organization, its QMS, and its performance is without risk. Risk can mean either failing to achieve the objective or actually harming the organization, its QMS, or its performance. ISO 9004:2000's purpose is to provide an extensive range of considerations an organization and its top management should address when pursuing QMS performance improvement, including benchmarking.

Figure 8.1

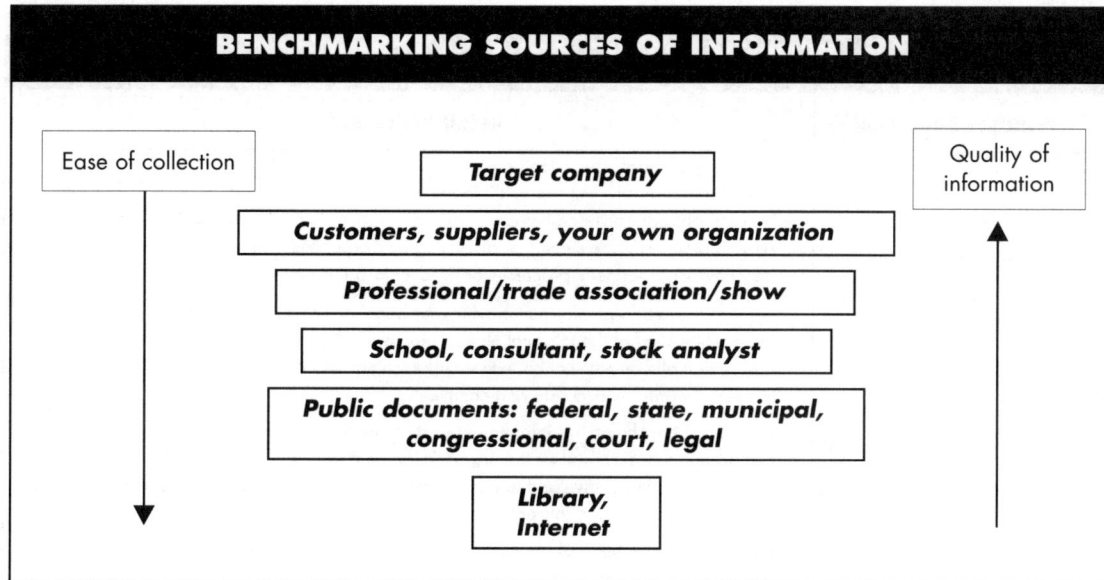

Improvement doesn't take place in a vacuum, nor does it occur without preparation and support. The following is a list of fifteen pitfalls your organization must avoid when conducting benchmarking activities:

- Management commitment is lacking.
- The benchmarking process isn't linked to the organization's strategic goals.
- Significant targets for the benchmarking study weren't identified.
- Insufficient knowledge and expertise exists to carry out benchmarking studies.
- A lack of resources (e.g., people, time, and money) inhibits the study.
- Good project management practices haven't been applied.
- Inappropriate people are assigned to the benchmarking team.
- Ignorance of legal and ethical issues and benchmarking protocol exists.
- Inappropriate benchmarking partners are chosen.
- Undue focus is put on quantitative measures rather than how the process works.
- The benchmarking focus is on noncritical processes.
- The most knowledgeable people for the process being studied aren't involved.
- An assumption is made that every benchmarking project requires a site visit.
- Focus is on benchmarking only the competition.
- Excessive amounts of data are collected.

Table 8.3 outlines some of the provisions that may be included in a benchmarking code of conduct. A formal code of conduct is a recommended approach to engaging in benchmarking for a number of reasons, including the potential legal perils an organization can face by failing to conduct benchmarking in a responsible and ethical manner, even if it intended to do so.

The following are examples of benchmarking-related activities that could occur that might place an organization in a legal liability situation:

Table 8.3

BENCHMARKING CODE OF CONDUCT	
Principle Addressed	**Detail Addressed**
Legality	If a potential legal issue, don't continue. Don't engage in any actions or dialogue that could be perceived as a conflict of interest, restraint of trade, or price fixing. Avoid obtaining trade secrets or disclosing any proprietary information about your benchmarking partner's processes or product to a third party.
Exchanging information	Prepare to exchange information with your benchmarking partner that's of the same importance level of the information you request. Ensure that all communication with your benchmarking partner is clearly understood by the recipient and is accurate and complete.
Confidentiality	Assume all benchmarking information exchanges are confidential, both in regard to individuals contacted as well as the organization as a whole. If any information is divulged to persons or organizations beyond the benchmarking partners, be sure that prior consent is obtained from the information's owner.
Information use	Ensure that information obtained through the benchmarking process is used only as a basis for process improvement within the context of the participating organizations. Never use the name of an individual or an organization from which information is obtained without permission. Never use the benchmarking process as a commodity to sell. Never discuss the benchmarking process or information obtained in any way in which the partner's organization or its employees can be identified, unless explicit permission has been obtained.
Contact with partner	Channel all communication between benchmarking partners through the contact persons designated by each partner. Abide by the culture, practices, and rules of the benchmarking partner's organization.
Preparation	Respect your benchmarking partner's time by being fully prepared before engaging the partner in the information exchange. Prepare all necessary interview questionnaires and an agenda prior to the visit.
Wrap-up	Respond to any commitments made with your partner in a timely manner. Ensure that any agreements made with benchmarking partners are fulfilled.
Sensitivity	Make an effort to understand how your partners want to be treated—and act accordingly. Determine how each benchmarking partner wants the information provided, treated, and used—and act accordingly.

- Soliciting phony bids to gather competitive information.
- Using pressure tactics to force a supplier, as a condition of doing business, to provide volume or dollar figures about a competitor.
- Obtaining a competitor's product illegally and reverse engineering it.
- Photographing or taping processes or discussions without permission.
- Discussing pricing policies, actual prices, or obtaining price lists, which might be perceived as collusion and price fixing.
- Soliciting a benchmarking partner's employee to work in your firm, without permission of the employee's firm.

It's also important to understand the limitations regarding how an organization benchmarks, what benchmarking can provide, and what an organization can or can't do when benchmarking. For instance, don't do the following:

■ Attempt benchmarking unless your organization has an enlightened and supportive management and a culture receptive to change and improvement.

■ Overstep your organization's expertise and resources. If necessary, start with a simple, less complex process to test your capabilities.

■ Approach benchmarking as a student seeking a free education. Instead, improve your organization's own process to make it the best you can, then approach the benchmarking study as an exchange of information.

■ Go on a benchmarking spree unless you've prepared your organization to accept potential changes. If it won't accept the results, you'll be wasting your and your partner's resources.

■ Short-change the benchmarking process. Instead, go into as much detail as your organization's and its partner's resources will allow. Gaining only a superficial view of a process can be misleading and useless. Remember, you're committing money and time, so get what you came for.

■ Take up a benchmarking partner's time if you haven't briefed the partner in advance on what you seek or if your team is unprepared.

■ Steal. Be sure that whatever your organization takes away from a benchmarking visit is with the partner's understanding and permission.

■ Give up easily. A benchmarking study could be unsuccessful, so debrief, find out what went wrong, and learn from the mistakes to ensure that next time will be successful.

■ Forget that benchmarking can produce a significant return on investment when it's properly planned and executed.

WHAT OTHERS HAVE LEARNED

Though important for improvement, benchmarking can produce a range of measurements about an organization, its QMS, its performance, and other results that might be difficult for top management to accept. Some organizations have learned the following from benchmarking:

■ They weren't as great as they thought they were.

■ A full-blown benchmarking study is too expensive for a small organization.

■ Trying to find an organization that's best in everything is impossible.

To avoid the above experiences, consider doing the following:

■ Enlist the aid of governmental and quasi-governmental agencies, such as the Field Engineers Newsgroup, your state's Manufacturing Extension Program, and the National Institute for Standards and Technology's Best Manufacturing Practices Program.

■ Solicit customers' recommendations as to suppliers that can be contacted about their processes and practices.

■ Solicit your suppliers' suggestions about their other customers you might want to contact.

■ Check into benchmarking services such as the International Benchmarking Clearinghouse of the American Productivity and Quality Center, the Benchmarking Exchange, and the "world class by principles" system of assessment and improvement.[1]

It's important to keep in mind that, because it leads the way to breakthrough improvement, benchmarking is a quality process. When a QMS becomes stable (i.e., special causes are eliminated), it's time to look beyond incremental continual improvement, take one or more of those stable processes, and compare what your organization does with others performing similar processes, albeit better than you do. Then learn, adapt, innovate, and make significant improvements to your own processes.

These days we're counseled to "think outside the box." Reworking old ground rarely results in a breakthrough. Benchmarking provides an opportunity to seek out new ideas and approaches. For example, to improve its ability to deplane passengers and baggage rapidly and make a plane ready for another flight, Southwest Airlines benchmarked the pit crews of Indianapolis 500 racecars. From this you can appreciate the value of looking at others' best practices, regardless of the industry. Similarly, in seeking ways to reduce the risk of employee theft, IBM studied Las Vegas casinos.

Joseph M. Juran has told an interesting story worth paraphrasing[2]: Early in the last century, some German generals arranged to follow an American circus. In those days, the circus performed in huge tents that were difficult to set up and take down. They moved quickly from town to town, took the circus down, put everything on a train, and traveled to the next location to set it all up again—a very complicated process. They had a variety of animals and some very unique people to transport, feed, and house—with all their gear. They even used specially designed railway cars. And they were very good at it.

The generals had a similar problem. They had all types of people. They had to move horses, supplies, equipment, tents, ammunition, and food quickly from place to place—set up camps and tear them down. From observing the circus, which had no relation to an army, the generals learned about logistics, deployment, and efficiency.

Though your organization might not exactly resemble a circus or an army, it will benefit from benchmarking if done properly and if appropriate to your organization's stage of quality deployment.

ENDNOTES

1. Schonberger, Richard J. *Let's Fix It! Overcoming the Crisis in Manufacturing*. New York: The Free Press, 2001.
2. Juran, J.M., editor-in-chief. *A History of Managing for Quality*. Milwaukee: ASQ Quality Press. 1995.

CHAPTER 9

Applying Project Management Tools
To Achieve Continual Improvement

Work life is a series of projects—plan and manage them well for success.

It's a safe assumption that many managers and quality professionals have insufficient knowledge, skills, or experience with the proven methodology of project management. Faced with a new project, professionals—technical as well as managerial—often take costly and ineffective actions that result in poorly implemented projects and failure to achieve the purpose intended. The many projects initiated in the name of TQM, reengineering, cost reduction, and ISO 9000 that produced less than desirable outcomes fan the fires of discontent about quality initiatives.

As with most management-oriented methodologies, project management is a mix of time-tested techniques and the art of managing people. Project management, in some form, has been around for quite a while—building the pyramids is often cited as an early example. Emphasis on project management has ebbed and flowed over the years, depending upon the pressures of the economy and business climate. After a long spell of apparent dormancy, project management has once again erupted onto the business environment. With advances in technology, a more discerning and demanding customer base, a more skilled workforce, and economic pressure to "run lean," the project-oriented organization is becoming more prevalent. A wide-range of public courses—college-based, association-based, and consultant-sponsored—are now offered on the subject. The Project Management Institute offers a Certified Project Manager[1] designation to those who pass a rigorous examination and demonstrate their proficiency with planning and managing a successful project. Project management is definitely "in."

Recognize that while an extensive portfolio of project management techniques and tools are available, there's a vast difference in applying these methods to a large, multiyear construction project, a twelve-month ISO 9001 quality management system implementation, or a three-month process improvement and machinery upgrade project. The basic concepts apply in all situations, but the approach must be scaled to fit the cost-to-payoff ratio. A common error is to fail to use the tools and techniques appropriate to the project's complexity and the resources available, thus causing either overkill or underutilizing techniques that could have been effective. Table 9.1 lists common project management techniques and tools.

Table 9.1

PROJECT MANAGEMENT TECHNIQUES AND TOOLS FOR IMPROVEMENT INITIATIVES	
Project purpose and intended outcome • Charter (i.e., contract) • Mission statement • Scope • Goal and objectives • Stakeholder requirements: deliverables ***Analysis of risks and feasibility*** • Cost-benefit analysis • Payback period • Net present value • Internal rate of return • Potential return on investment • Estimated return on net assets ***The team*** • Team formation • Team building training • Conflict management training • Team facilitation ***Breakdown of work to do*** • Work breakdown structure • Resource requirements matrix	***Timelines*** • Gantt/milestone chart • Activity network diagram • Critical path method (CPM chart) ***Person(s) responsible*** • Linear responsibility matrix ***Project budget*** ***Quantifiable measurements*** • Time expenditure • Resource usage • Project costs vs. budget ***Post-project evaluation and lessons learned*** • Outcomes and ROI achieved • Time schedule met • Budget met • Post-mortem of project planning and execution • Documentation to knowledge base

This chapter can't address every known project management technique and tool available. Stated as a caveat, however, organizations will succeed best by selecting, from a limited array of proven practices, the techniques and tools that offer the highest probability in aiding a project's successful completion. "Successful" is defined as achieving the stated outcome for the project within allowable time and costs. For this discussion, it's assumed that top management has determined that the organization will initiate a project to achieve a stated outcome. (Making this assumption means skipping the early feasibility analysis as to whether initiating the project makes sense or not for the organization. We'll assume that's been done and you've been assigned to head the project.)

PROJECT PLANNING PROCESS
A project's lifecycle typically is defined in five stages:
- Concept
- Planning
- Design
- Implementation
- Evaluation and project closeout

Once the project's concept and feasibility have been determined, the plan-do-check-act cycle becomes directly applicable to project management.

Figure 9.1

USING THE PDCA CYCLE FOR PLANNING AND MANAGING PROJECTS

PLAN
- Document project scope, charter, objectives, and stakeholder requirements
- Form project team
- Identify outputs
- Identify and sequence tasks
- Compile timelines and dependencies
- Identify resource requirements
- Prepare budget
- Identify measurements

ACT
- Take corrective actions to keep project on schedule and within budget, or terminate project
- Reinforce progress
- Report on project status
- Complete project and close-out
- Celebrate and disband team

CHECK
- Monitor project, check status at designated milestones
- Measure interim results attained
- Make any needed modifications

DO
- Implement the project plan

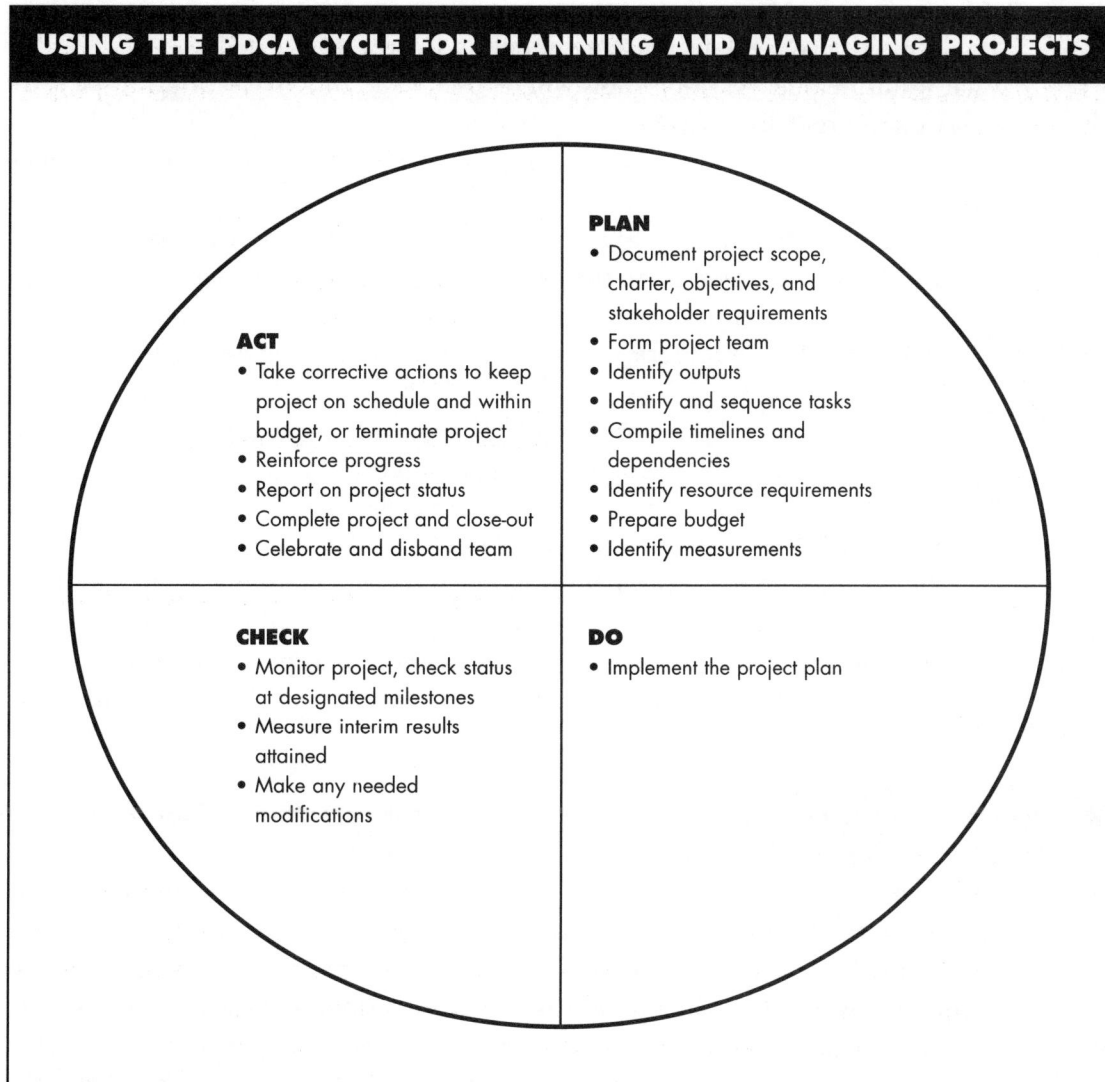

Planning: technique and tools

Define the scope of the project. For example:

■ State when the project is to start and finish. A background document could also describe the benefits for completing the project successfully as well as any consequences for failing to meet the targeted dates.

■ Document a project charter. What are the project outcomes, who will head the project, to whom will that person report, what statutory or regulatory rules are applicable; what organizational policies, protocols, and practices are to be observed; and what constraints might apply.

■ Compile a list of the stakeholders who might be affected by the project and its outputs and outcomes. For larger projects, categorize these stakeholders as "primary" (i.e., directly affected) or "other interested parties" (indirectly affected).

■ Select and form the project team. Considerations for this step include:

☐ How many and what type of people are needed for the team?

☐ Will members be selected only from the work unit affected by the project outcome? Is a cross-functional team needed?

☐ Should multiple disciplines be represented on the team?

☐ What team-member selection tools will be used (e.g., the Myers-Briggs Type Indicator or other tools)?

☐ Will members be required to perform project tasks in addition to regularly assigned duties?

☐ If so, what arrangements are needed to ensure release time for team participation?

☐ If members are assigned solely to the project team, what arrangements are necessary to ensure they can return to their regular work when the team disbands? How will their developmental, promotional, and compensation progression be protected during their absence?

☐ Will a trained team facilitator be required to assist the team during the team stages (e.g., forming, storming, "norming," and performing)?

☐ What training will team members require to be effective members? How, when, and by whom will such training be provided?

☐ Identify the outputs the project team is to produce. These might include documents for project planning and managing, protocols for reporting project status, computer programs, databases, project plans for pre-implementation approval, project implementation plans and schedule, and documentation of post-implementation outcomes.

■ Identify and sequence the tasks required to achieve the project objectives. This generally takes the form of a work breakdown structure (WBS):

☐ The format for shorter, less complex projects can be simply a hierarchical listing, in outline format, of the tasks and subtasks required.

☐ The format for a medium-duration (i.e., several months) or more complex project might be a pyramidal structure of categorized functions and tasks, with each box indicating person responsible, start and complete times, budget allocation, and an identification number for ease in accumulating time and cost data. *Note:* The WBS indicates the hierarchy of tasks but doesn't readily indicate the time dependencies among all the tasks. Figure 9.2 is a partially completed WBS. Responsibilities, estimated time, budget, and a numbering scheme have yet to be added.

■ Develop timelines and time dependencies for the primary tasks or task categories. The format is usually a Gantt chart that lists the tasks vertically on the left, the weeks or months as horizontally headed columns, and the time when each task or category must begin and end indicated in solid horizontal bars. *Note:* For small projects with fewer tasks, the Gantt chart suffices to depict time dependencies among the tasks. Figure 9.3 shows a Gantt chart for an eighteen-month project.

For more complex and longer projects, a more sophisticated chart of time dependencies is needed to enable project scheduling and monitoring. Three tools are available:

Figure 9.2

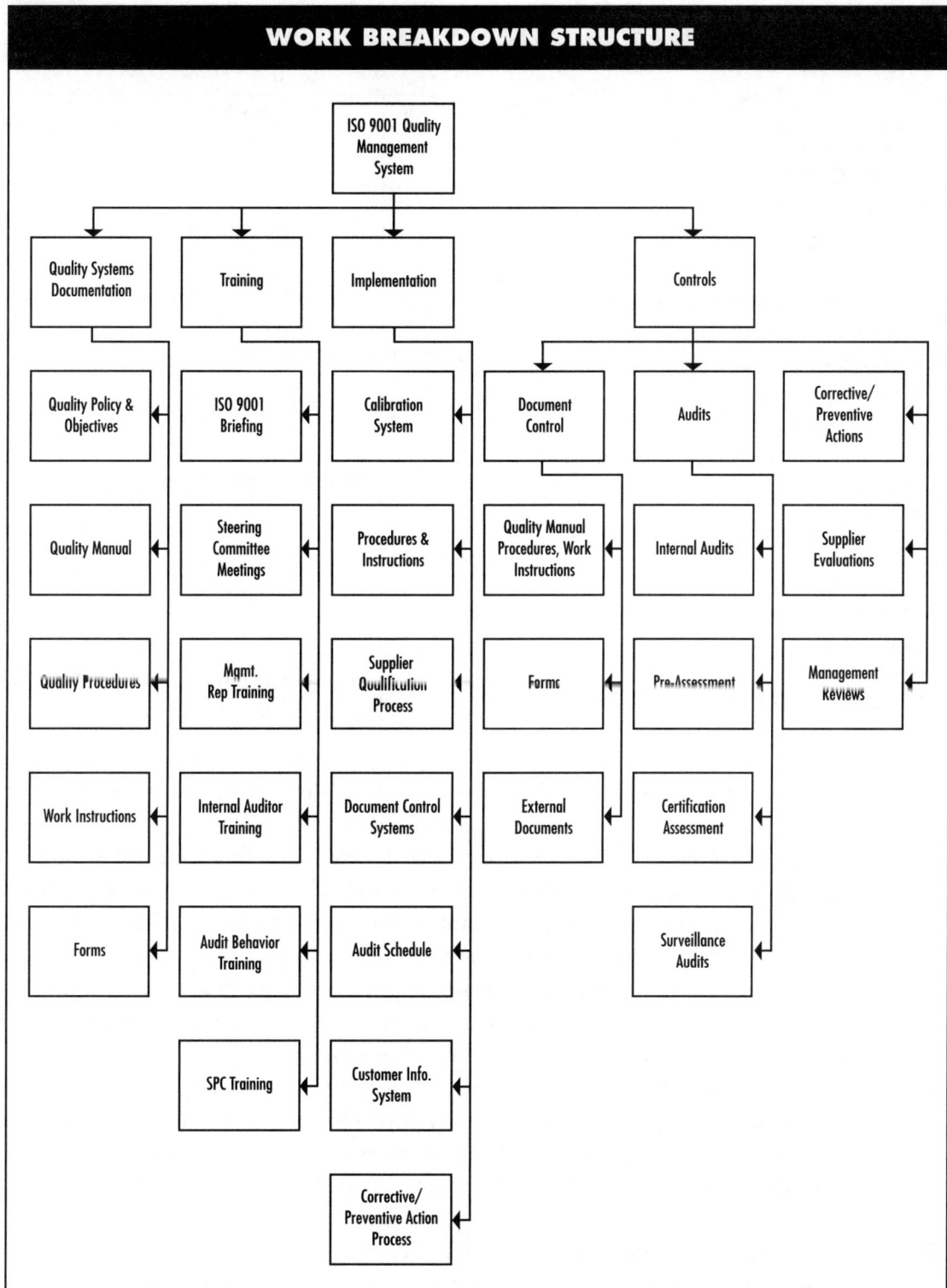

WORK BREAKDOWN STRUCTURE

ISO 9001 Quality Management System

- Quality Systems Documentation
  - Quality Policy & Objectives
  - Quality Manual
  - Quality Procedures
  - Work Instructions
  - Forms
- Training
  - ISO 9001 Briefing
  - Steering Committee Meetings
  - Mgmt. Rep Training
  - Internal Auditor Training
  - Audit Behavior Training
  - SPC Training
- Implementation
  - Calibration System
  - Procedures & Instructions
  - Supplier Qualification Process
  - Document Control Systems
  - Audit Schedule
  - Customer Info. System
  - Corrective/Preventive Action Process
- Controls
  - Document Control
    - Quality Manual Procedures, Work Instructions
    - Forms
    - External Documents
  - Audits
    - Internal Audits
    - Pre-Assessment
    - Certification Assessment
    - Surveillance Audits
  - Corrective/Preventive Actions
    - Supplier Evaluations
    - Management Reviews

Figure 9.3

Task	1-13	14-26	27-39	40-52	53-65	66-78
18-MONTH QUALITY PROJECT (Weeks)						
Select consultant	▼					
Conduct ISO 9000 briefing	▼					
Conduct gap analysis	▼					
Form steering committee	▼					
Prepare quality system procedures	▬▬▬▬▬▬	▬▬▬	▬▬▬	▬		
Prepare quality policy and objectives	▼					
Prepare work instructions						
Employee kickoff meeting		▼▬▬	▬▬▬	▬		
Evaluate registrars			▼			
Train internal auditors			▼	▼		
Implement quality system procedures						
Select, schedule registrar			▬▬▼	▬▬▬	▬▬	
Conduct internal audits				▬▬▬	▬▬	
Prepare quality system manual						
Conduct audit behavioral meeting				▬▬▬	▼	
Conduct preassessment					▼	
Take corrective/preventive action						
Conduct final assessment						▬▬▼
Registration—celebrate!						▼

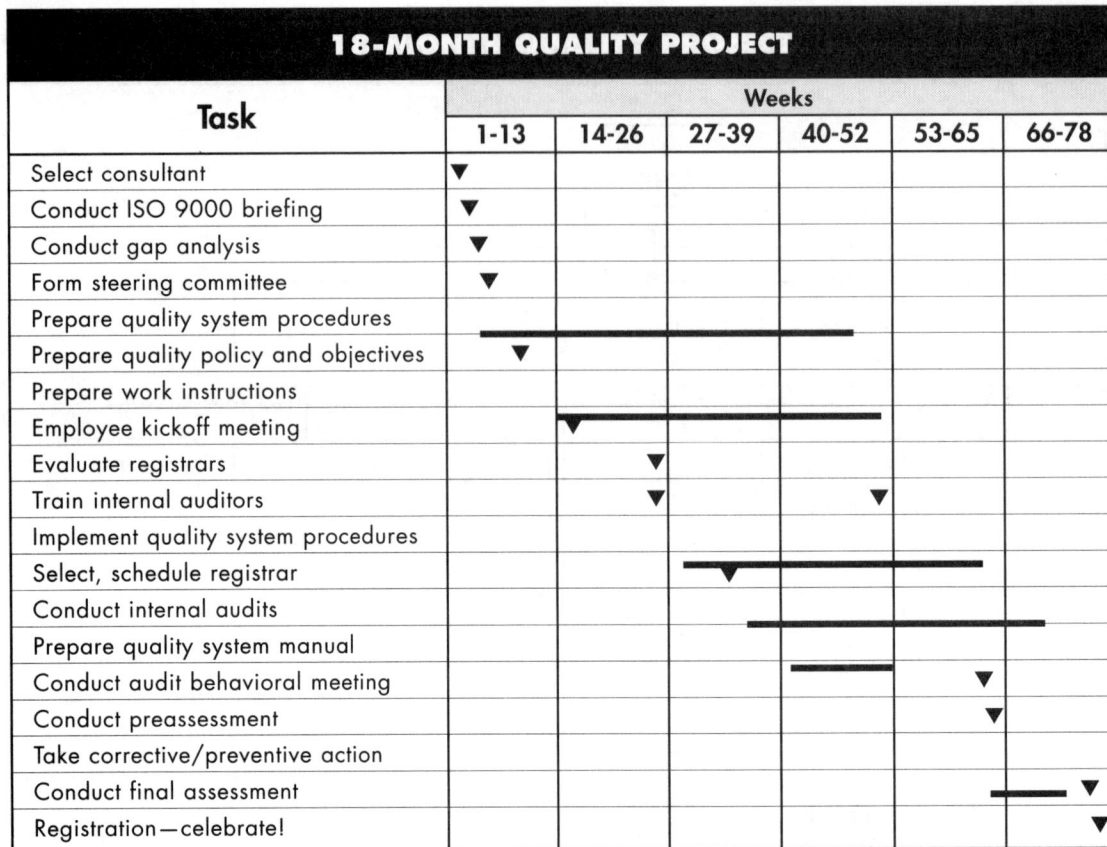

- *Arrow Network Diagram (AND).* This shows dependencies among tasks. However, by itself it doesn't consider task duration and cost.
- *Critical Path Method (CPM).* A charting tool usually used where previous experience allows a reasonably accurate estimate of time durations for each task. Determining the critical path—with the estimated time to accomplish all the designated tasks indicated on the longest path—is based on the single time estimate. The complexity of the projects for which this tool is used generally requires a computer to make the computations and run what-if scenarios. Costs can also be included. Figure 9.4 shows a CPM chart for a medium-size project.
- *Program (or project) Evaluation and Reporting Technique (PERT).* This is used for projects for which previous experience might be lacking. The tool allows for three time estimates—optimistic, most likely, and pessimistic—and requires a computer program to process. Estimated costs can also be included in the computations.

■ Identify and develop resource requirements. These include:
- For smaller, less complex projects, simple listings of the personnel required, along with competency levels and time frame required, might be sufficient.
- For larger and more complex projects, several resource requirements matrices might be needed—e.g., for personnel, facilities, or equipment. Figure 9.5 shows one way to lay out personnel requirements.

Figure 9.4

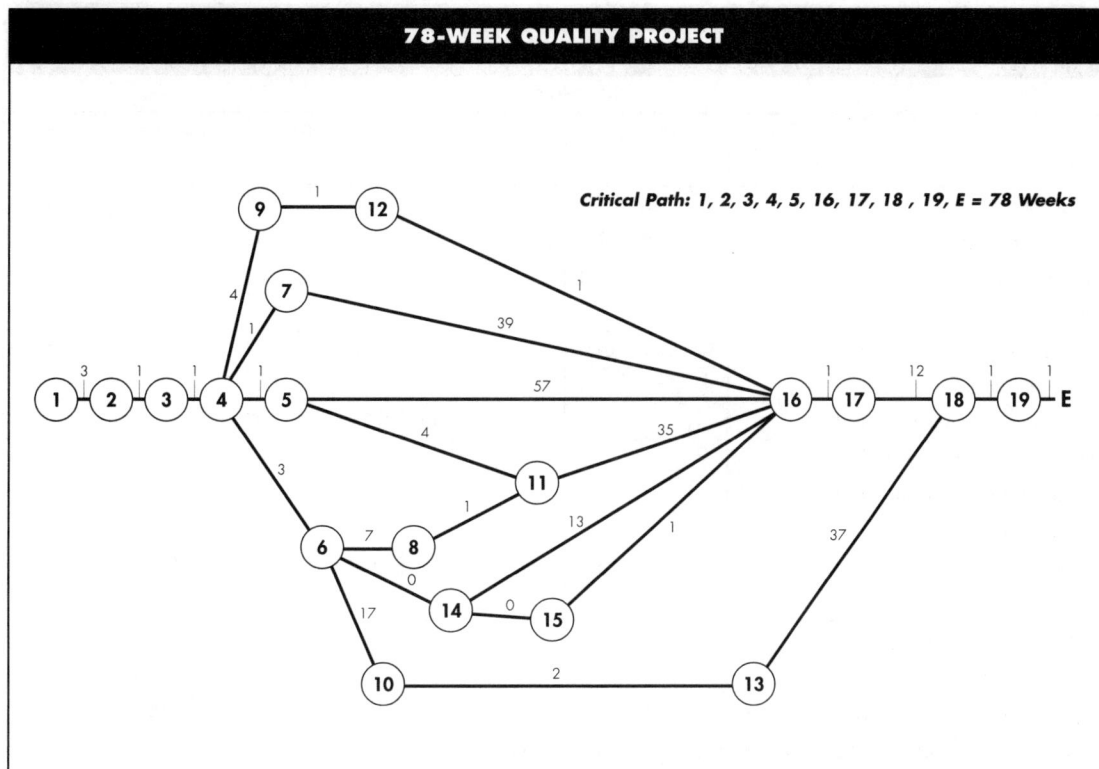

78-WEEK QUALITY PROJECT

Critical Path: 1, 2, 3, 4, 5, 16, 17, 18 , 19, E = 78 Weeks

■ Prepare the project budget. Identify the measurements that will be used to monitor project progress and determine if project objectives and outcomes have been met. Then prepare the final recommended project plan for approval (This might require several iterations until approval or final rejection is received). If the project is terminated, then:
  ☐ The team completes its documentation by debriefing itself and documenting the lessons learned.
  ☐ The team is disbanded.

If the project is approved, then the project team either transitions the project to those responsible for implementing it or (more likely) the team is augmented by additional personnel who will help in implementation.

■ Implementation schedules are prepared using:
  ☐ A task assignment list or implementation WBS
  ☐ An implementation Gantt chart, including interim milestones, or both a Gantt chart and a CPM chart tracking program
  ☐ A format indicating that responsibility for project status reporting is established. For example, a time utilization status (for smaller projects the Gantt chart can be expanded vertically to accommodate status bars and start/finish pointers for each task); a costs-to-budget variance tracking and reporting chart; or a resource utilization tracking and reporting chart.

■ Design of the project content is completed.

Figure 9.5

PROJECT DELTA: PERSONNEL REQUIREMENTS (OCTOBER–MAY)						
DAYS						
Task	**Data Entry Operator**	**Design Engineer**	**Systems Analyst**	**Computer Operator**	**Production Planner**	**Total**
Build test data file	Nov. 15.0	Oct.–Nov. 5.5	Oct. 3.5	Oct. 6.25		30.25
Run desk check of data		Nov. 3.0	Nov. 2.0	Nov. 1.25		6.25
Modify test data	Dec. 1.5	Dec. 1.0	Dec. 1.0	Dec. 2.0		5.50
Run computer test				Dec. 8.0		8.00
Analyze test results		Dec.–Jan. 15.0	Dec.–Jan. 15.0	Dec.–Jan. 5.0		35.00
Make modifications		Jan.–Feb. 25.0	Jan.–Feb. 12.0	Jan.–Feb. 3.0		40.00
Prepare first month data	Mar. 6.0		Mar. 1.0	Mar. 3.0		10.00
Prepare second month data	Apr. 5.0		Apr. 0.5	Apr. 1.0		6.50
Prepare third month data	May 5.0		May 0.5	May 0.5		6.00
Run full-scale production				May 1.5	May 0.75	2.25
Analyze results		May 3.0				3.00
	32.5	52.5	35.5	31.5	0.75	152.75

Note: Action plans, discussed in chapter one are scaled-down project plans suitable for short-term, less complex projects, especially those contained within a single work unit.

Do: implement

Designated personnel implement project plans. Implementation for larger or more complex projects might be on a trial basis and for a limited area of application.

Check: monitor and evaluate

Using the planned reporting methods, the implementation team monitors the project implementation and reports on status to appropriate parties at designated project milestones.[2] Measurements of interim results also may be communicated to relevant parties. The team will make necessary "course corrections" and trade-offs as indicated and approved.

Act: full-scale rollout and project closeout

The implementation team rolls out the project to all affected areas in accordance with the implementation time schedule and budget. When the planned objectives have been met, the team officially closes the project by preparing a final summary of results achieved and subsequent evaluations. These include:

- Objectives met vs. projected schedule
- Resources used vs. those estimated
- Costs vs. budget
- Organizational outcomes achieved vs. planned and unplanned outcomes
- Effectiveness of project planning team (optional)
- Effectiveness of implementation team (optional)
- Team compilation of lessons learned. The documented project can be entered into an organizational knowledge database for use in planning future projects and training project managers.

■ Team participants are recognized for their contributions.
■ Documents citing the recognition can be entered into employee records.
■ A celebratory event can be arranged.
■ Internal and/or external publicity can be arranged.
■ The team is disbanded.

Note: For some projects, many organizations find that conducting a post-implementation assessment several months after the outcomes have been achieved is more valuable.

WHY USE PROJECT PLANNING AND MANAGEMENT TECHNIQUES AND TOOLS?

Project management lends structure and discipline to quality initiatives. It enables an organization to plan for greater customer satisfaction and profitability. When properly applied, project management, with its plans, tools, and controls, provides the organization with a clear path to success. Transitioning to an ISO 9004-oriented organization is greatly helped by project management. Such a transition, much as with a Baldrige initiative, is a long-term, relatively complex reengineering of business thinking and processes. To make the transition effectively and avoid negative results that previous quality initiatives sometimes generate, sound project management techniques must be employed.

As in the earlier disclaimer, many additional project management techniques and tools are available, including some very comprehensive computer software. However, the above tool set should be adequate for most of the projects undertaken for quality improvement.

The concept of continual improvement espoused in the ISO 9000:2000 series implies a continual stream of improvement projects. Implementing lean thinking implies a project approach. Certainly Six Sigma demands a project approach, as does preparing an organization to apply for any of the quality excellence awards. To survive and grow in the future, modern-day quality professionals must add project management competence to their repertoire of skills.

ENDNOTES

1. The Project Management Institute's standards committee has published a document available on the Web (*www.pmi.org*) that can help your organization decide which tools will be most applicable to its situation and identify areas in which organizational competence should be developed. Information about the certificate program is also available.

2. If a larger project is subdivided into stages, there's often a go/no-go decision made at the end of each stage. This point in time is referred to as a "stage-gate."

CHAPTER 10

Stepping Up to World-Class Status

Is there life beyond ISO 9004 and the Baldrige criteria?

Assume you've been using ISO 9004 as your guide for stepping beyond the minimal requirements of ISO 9001. Assume, too, that you've already enjoyed some of the benefits achieved through improvements. You're now exploring whether applying the Malcolm Baldrige National Quality Program criteria makes good business sense for your organization. As for applying for the award itself—well, you can think about that a little later.

Let's begin by understanding these distinctions:

- In an organization's quest for excellence, the Baldrige criteria embrace strategic plans and both internal and external activities. The emphasis isn't on quality alone but on overall performance excellence.

- The Baldrige National Quality Program (BNQP) is designed to enable organizations to apply for the Baldrige Award when they believe their performance excellence merits recognition. However, most organizations that explore and apply the criteria do so with the intent to improve themselves, not to apply for the award.

- ISO 9004 is designed to assist those organizations seeking registration to ISO 9001 in building a more effective and efficient quality management system or enhancing an already registered quality management system (QMS). The emphasis is on moving from an ISO 9001-compliant QMS to one that also operates efficiently and that considers both customers and employees.

- ISO 9004 enhances, but doesn't expand, the coverage of the quality management system to be registered. Its application is limited to those organizational objectives, activities, and practices specified in the certification scope definition. An organization can opt to include marketing, financial, and human resource activities within its scope. However, most organizations limit the processes covered to engineering, production, and product and/or service delivery, along with, perhaps, some customer service and customer billing functions. As typically applied, ISO 9001 or ISO 9004 don't embrace the entire organization. In fact, clause 0.4, excludes "guidance specific to other management systems, such as those particular to environmental management, occupational health and safety management, financial management, or risk management."

The Baldrige criteria don't mention ISO 9001 or ISO 9004 or any other certifications, although ISO 9000 or ISO 9004 could certainly be considered covered within some of the Baldrige categories.

■ Assume an organization were to aspire both to qualifying under the Baldrige criteria and becoming registered to ISO 9001 with ISO 9004-type enhancements. The organization would be best advised to strive for the ISO 9001 registration first, then build on it to reach the Baldrige criteria level. Reasons for first implementing an ISO 9001/ISO 9004 QMS include:

☐ Planning and implementing an ISO 9001/ISO 9004 QMS build structure and discipline through the standard's documentation, ongoing effectiveness assessments, and process improvement techniques. But negative consequences can occur—such as losing certification, and therefore the investment involved—if the system is allowed to deteriorate or lapse. Pressure is introduced to continually improve through the requisite internal and external audits.

☐ The process of preparing for, achieving, and maintaining registration signals to employees, suppliers, and other stakeholders that management is committed to quality and customer satisfaction.

☐ The process, when well implemented and managed, also demonstrates to management and owners the value of continual improvement.

Organizations that have become ISO 9001-registered aren't by this effort alone qualified for the Baldrige Award. Likewise, organizations that have applied for a Baldrige-type award frequently are unprepared for ISO 9001 registration. However, a number of organizations have achieved ISO 9001 registration and moved on to apply for and achieve the Baldrige Award. By doing, so they've mastered two powerful performance tools.

Thus we see that the Baldrige criteria for performance excellence and the ISO 9001 standard with ISO 9004 enhancements differ fundamentally in their focus, purpose, and content. Let's look at this difference in more depth.

THE BNQP CRITERIA FOR EXCELLENCE

Note: Much of the following is excerpted or adapted from National Institute of Standards and Technology publications.

The BNQP now comes in three flavors:

■ Criteria applicable to all businesses, large or small and government entities
■ Educational institutions, at all levels
■ Organizations in health care

The criteria for all three essentially are the same but expressed in language familiar to the targeted users. (Because of space limitations, only the language of the business criteria will be used.)

The criteria's purpose is to:

■ Help improve organizational performance practices, capabilities, and results
■ Serve (internally) as a working tool for understanding and managing performance and for guiding planning and opportunities for learning

■ Facilitate communications and sharing of best-practices information among U.S. organizations. (Award-winners are obligated to furnish general information about their organizations and the practices that enabled them to qualify for the award.)

BNQP goals include helping an organization use an integrated approach to organizational performance management that results in:

■ Delivering ever-improving value to customers and contributing to marketplace success
■ Improving overall organizational effectiveness and capabilities
■ Learning on the part of the organization and its personnel

The core values and concepts upon which the Baldrige criteria are built include visionary leadership. For top management, this means:

■ Setting direction, creating a customer focus, communicating clear values and high expectations, and balancing all stakeholders' needs (similar, but broader and more future-oriented than ISO 9004)
■ Ensuring the creation of strategies, systems, and methods for achieving excellence, stimulating innovation, and building knowledge and capabilities
■ Inspiring and motivating the entire workforce and encouraging all employees to contribute (greater emphasis on employee participation than ISO 9004)
■ Serving as role models through ethical behavior and personal involvement in planning, communicating with, coaching, and developing future leaders

Customer-driven excellence is:

■ More than reducing defects and errors, meeting specifications, or reducing complaints
■ Based on addressing those features and characteristics that differentiate products and services from competing offerings, and on meeting basic customer requirements
■ A strategic concept directed toward customer retention, market share gain, and growth—which involves anticipating changes in the marketplace

BNQP criteria for organizational and personal learning:

■ ISO 9004 addresses the use of information (clause 6.5), whereas the BNQP focuses on "embedded" learning in organizational operations (e.g., part of daily work, applies at all levels, solving problems at their source, sharing knowledge, driven by intent to change and do better).
■ Organizational learning is seen as enhancing value to customers through new and improved products and services, developing new business opportunities, reducing waste and costs, improving cycle time, increasing productivity and effective use of resources, and enhancing performance relative to public responsibility.
■ Employee learning and development is seen as an investment, a means for retaining employees, encouraging cross-functional learning, and improving the environment for innovation.

Valuing employees and partners:

■ BNQP criteria focus on the organization's commitment to employee success, recognition beyond regular compensation, development and progression within the organiza-

tion, sharing organizational knowledge so that employees can better serve customers and contribute to achieving the organization's objectives, and creating an environment that encourages risk-taking.
■ BNQP fosters building internal and external partnerships.

Agility:
■ To successfully compete in the global marketplace requires a capacity for rapid change and flexibility.
■ Cross-trained and empowered employees are vital in this demanding environment.
■ Time performance is critical, and cycle time is a key process measure.

Focus on the future:
■ Pursuing sustainable growth and market leadership requires a strong future orientation and a willingness to make long-term commitments to key stakeholders (e.g., customers, employees, suppliers and partners, stockholders, the public, and the community).
■ A strategic planning process is emphasized.

Managing for innovation: BNQP encourages the integration of innovation as part of the organizational culture and daily work.
Management by fact:
■ BNQP expects the same data collection, analysis, and informed decision making as ISO 9004 but with a broader perspective.
■ BNQP calls for selecting and using performance indicators to affect performance improvement and change management.

Social responsibility:
■ The practice of good citizenship is emphasized.
■ BNQP delineates areas of responsibility, such as business ethics and the protection of public health, safety, and the environment. It extends to the lifecycle of products and services, resource conservation and waste reduction at the source, planning to reduce adverse effects from production, distribution, transportation processes, and product disposal.
■ Care must be taken to meet all local, state, and federal laws and regulatory requirements, as well as treating these as opportunities for improvement beyond simple compliance.
■ Stress is placed on ethical behavior in all stakeholder transactions and interactions.
■ BNQP fosters partnerships with other organizations for the above purposes.
■ Support of publicly important purposes is encouraged.

Focus on results and creating value:
■ BNQP calls for a balanced use of leading and lagging performance measures.
■ Results should be balanced in creating value for the key stakeholders.

Systems perspective:
■ The BNQP core values and seven BNQP categories form the building blocks and integrating mechanism for the system.

Figure 10.1

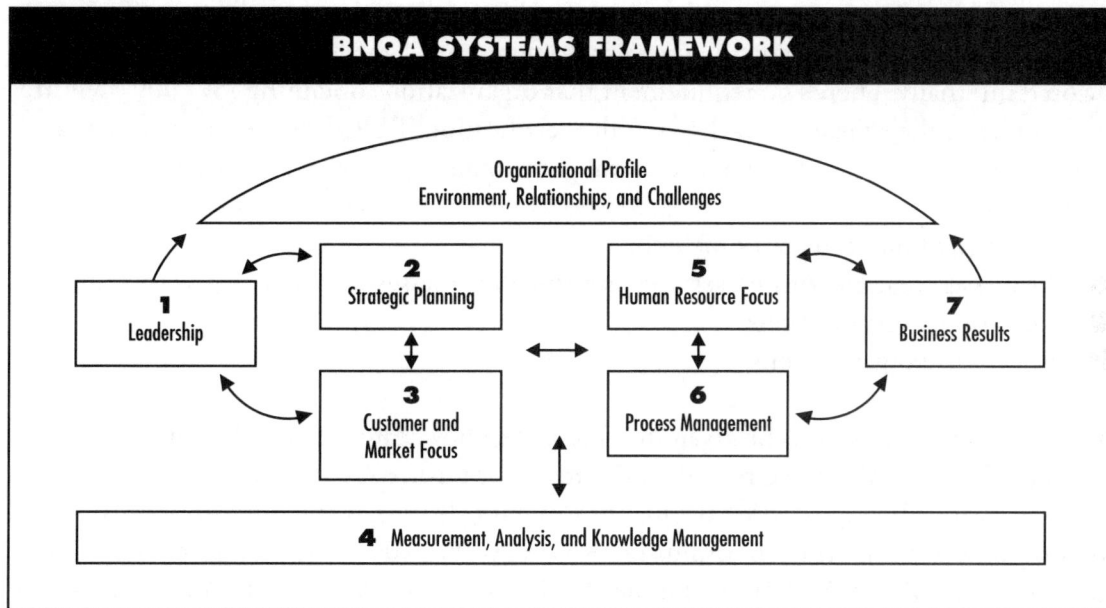

BNQA SYSTEMS FRAMEWORK

Organizational Profile
Environment, Relationships, and Challenges

1 Leadership

2 Strategic Planning

3 Customer and Market Focus

5 Human Resource Focus

6 Process Management

7 Business Results

4 Measurement, Analysis, and Knowledge Management

■ Aligning measures and strategy indicators to key processes and resources for overall performance improvement and customer satisfaction is stressed. The BNQP is depicted as a system shown in figure 10.1.

BNQP assessments—the term "audit" isn't used because it implies compliance to a standard—determine the presence and effectiveness of systems, processes, practices, and policies that embody the criteria's intent. Categories one through six are evaluated on the basis of approach used and how well the practices and policies are deployed throughout the organization. The seventh category, business results, is assessed based on the quantifiable achievements gained from the six other categories. Category seven offers proof that the systems, processes, practices, and policies integral to categories one through six are producing positive results.

BNQP award applicants prepare a comprehensive summary of their achievements in an application package. Generally, the material presented is in direct proportion to the relative importance of the category, as indicated by the maximum point values assigned to each, and by items within each category. Using tables and graphics is encouraged.

Applications are reviewed and evaluated by volunteer members of the board of examiners. The board adheres to strict rules regarding conflict of interest and confidentiality. The review is a four-stage process:
■ Independent review and evaluation by at least six members of the board
■ Consensus review and evaluation for applications that score well during stage one
■ Site visits to applicants that score well in stage two
■ Judges' review and recommendations of award recipients

Feedback reports are sent to applicants at various times during the award cycle, based on the stage of the review an applicant reaches in the evaluation process. These feedback reports are vital to the applicant and are considered to be worth far more than the costs of applying.

Keep in mind that a key purpose of the BNQP is to facilitate communications and sharing of best practices information among U.S. organizations of all types. Therefore, BNQP has both an internal and an external orientation, whereas ISO 9001/ISO 9004 is focused internally. There's no requirement that organizations obtaining ISO 9001 registration publicize their means for achieving the certification. BNQP, however, expects that all award-winners make public their successful performance strategies with other U.S. organizations.

Award eligibility categories include:

- Businesses: manufacturing, service, and small businesses
- Educational organizations
- Health-care organizations

Up to three awards can be given in each of the above categories each year.

A booklet describing the BNQP and criteria for business, education and health care is available from: Baldrige National Quality Program, National Institute of Standards and Technology, Administration Building, Room A600, 100 Bureau Drive, Stop 1020, Gaithersburg, MD 20899-1020. Phone: (301) 975-2036, fax: (301) 948-3716, e-mail: *nqp@nist.gov*, Web site: *www.quality.nist.gov*. One copy of the booklet is free.

ISO 9001'S AND ISO 9004'S STRENGTHS AND LIMITATIONS

ISO 9001 focuses on compliance to requirements, as evidenced by the quality management system and its effectiveness. ISO 9004 addresses efficiency and moving beyond the minimum requirements of ISO 9001. BNQP focuses on overall organizational excellence.

There are areas not specifically addressed by ISO 9001 or ISO 9004, some of which are:

- Developing business strategy for the future
- Means for enhancing organizational profitability
- Practices that foster continual innovation
- Concern for organization's effect on the environment
- Concern for management's and employees' personal and organizational ethical behavior
- Concern about the effect on employees, suppliers, and the community of workforce reductions, facility closings, reorganizations, mergers, and acquisitions
- Practices that foster organizational "citizenship"

An organization usually undergoes a big behavioral shift when moving from a focus on product and service quality to a broader concern for the organization's responsibility in society.

An ISO 9001/ISO 9004-based QMS typically is viewed as just one of several systems employed by an organization. The BNQP criteria, on the other hand, are promoted as the model of how an entire organization should function. That's why, when an organization is striving for or has achieved both ISO 9001 registration and qualified under the BNQP criteria, the certified QMS is subsumed within the BNQP criteria.

The framers of ISO 9004 intended it to be a companion to ISO 9001 (referred to as a "consistent pair"). Unfortunately, ISO 9004 hasn't been as widely used as predicted. ISO 9004 is a guideline, not a requirement, and an organization can't be registered to ISO 9004. Hence, no overt pressure exists to apply ISO 9004, even though by doing so organizations could expect very large returns.

Proof that this is the case can be obtained from the more extensive Baldrige Award winners. The trends of winners' business results have shown significant positive gains over organizations not working to the BNQP criteria. Thus, if their gains are realized from the Baldrige approach, it follows that gains will also be realized from applying the ISO 9004 guidelines, which have many of the same attributes, although not of the same magnitude.

Granted, it takes a "leap of faith" initially to step up to ISO 9004 and, ultimately, to the Baldrige criteria. As the time-tested adage goes, "Sometimes you have to spend money to make money." For example, an organization will commit $750,000 for a new piece of machinery that won't pay back the investment in fewer than six or seven years. Yet the same organization will balk at spending a few thousand dollars to make process and system improvements that can often pay back in a year or less—and usually with substantially more return on investment than for equipment and facility expenditures.

Lately, critics have expressed concern about the shift in emphasis noted in the Baldrige criteria. It appears to be veering away from mostly quality-related issues toward a focus on business results. If the criticism is correctly directed, it could mean the criteria-drafters are bowing to pressures from the "profit is paramount" constituency.

Meanwhile, the change in focus of the ISO 9001:2000 standard is considered to be shifting toward the application of quality principles within the whole organization. This controversy underscores the importance of focusing on the balanced best interests of *all* stakeholders—and stockholders are but one of the possible stakeholders.

To convey the message that the ISO 9000:2000 series (i.e., ISO 9000, ISO 9001, and ISO 9004) should be viewed as an integrated approach, the three documents have been marketed as a discounted package (although they also can be purchased individually). After purchasing the package, and an initial look-see, chances are that for many organizations the ISO 9004 document will become lost or reside in some bottom drawer. Unfortunately, this pattern repeats itself: The ISO 9004:1994 version was largely ignored, partly because of its format and apparent incompatibility with ISO 9001, ISO 9002, and ISO 9003.

Organizations wonder why they should bother with ISO 9004:2000 if it's not required. This thinking occurs despite the fact that the real key to increased profitability, improved customer satisfaction, greater employee involvement and competence, better supplier relations, and more effective and efficient operations lies in applying the ISO 9004 guidelines. ISO 9001 opens the door, but ISO 9004 offers the means to benefit from what you find on the other side of the door.

ISO 9001 is a beginning. Applying ISO 9004 guidelines represents a significant step up. Together, ISO 9001 and ISO 9004 expand management's perspective beyond the QMS to encompass the entire organization and the environment in which your organization operates. The Baldrige criteria represent a major step upward on the journey toward world-class status.

GOT A WORLD-CLASS PROCESS?

The next step up is to reach the point where your external organizational peers recognize one or more of your specific processes as being of world-class status. What does this mean?

A world-class process means you perform that process better or as well as any other world-class-recognized organization performing a similar process. It also means that orga-

Figure 10.2

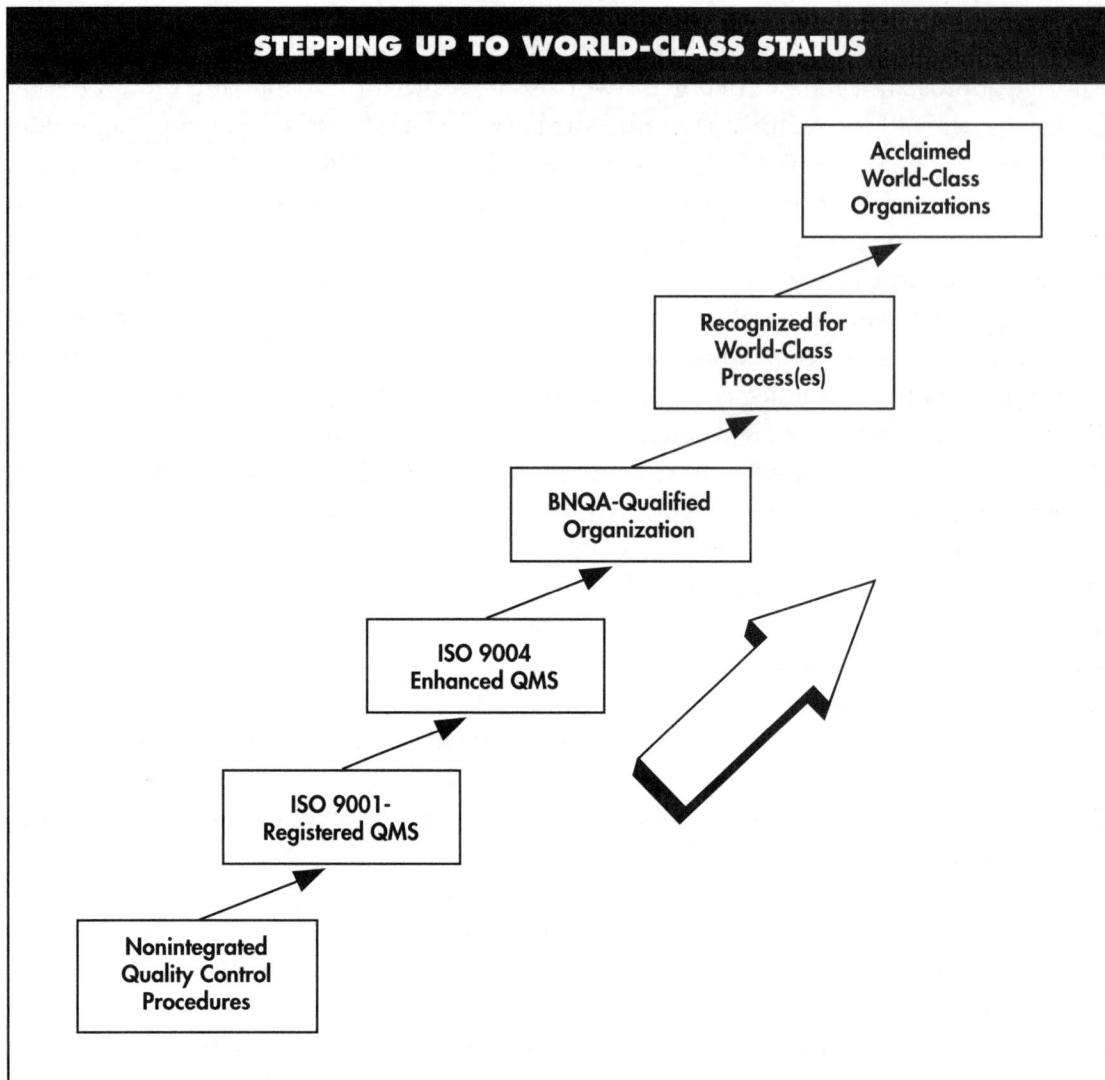

STEPPING UP TO WORLD-CLASS STATUS

nizations striving to meet your level of performance will seek you out for your guidance. Your organization has become a model for that process.

Achieving this level doesn't mean that everything your organization does is of world-class status. However, what you do well is widely recognized as an exemplary performance. For example, most of us are well acquainted with mail-order retailer L.L. Bean's highly regarded customer service policies and practices.

Have any organizations reached the pinnacle where everything they do, without exception, is world-class? Probably not. But by no means does this imply that such a goal is unattainable or unrealistic. Let's look at some of the actions and results that can lead to world-class status, as shown in figure 10.2. Then we'll ask (and attempt to answer) why your organization should consider this long-term goal. Finally, we'll explore some of the negative effects of pursuing it.

There's no single award given for achieving world-class status. You'll know it when you see and experience it—as will many others. Positive outcomes could include an increase in market share, fiscally sound and continually improving financial position, an enviable public image, and the personal satisfaction of every member of the organization in having made those possible.

ACTIONS THAT LEAD TO WORLD-CLASS STATUS

- Top management states the vision for the organization (for example, President Kennedy's declaration, "Put a man on the moon in ten years").
- Top management focuses its mission and goals to achieve the vision.
- Strategic plans structure the goals, objectives, and action plans that will ultimately achieve the goals.
- Authority and accountability are deployed downward and laterally to involve every employee and all suppliers in ensuring the objectives are met or exceeded.
- Actions taken are in the balanced best interests of all stakeholders.
- Communication channels are established and maintained to ensure every employee and every supplier is kept informed of the progress being made, and their contribution to it and the achieved outcome.
- Employees share in the successes.
- Personal growth and professional development is stressed.
- The organization plays a significant role in the communities in which it operates.
- Ethical behavior on the part of every employee is stressed and recognized.
- Continual learning, innovation, and improvement are inherent in the organization's culture.
- Emphasis shifts from "quality management" to "quality of management" and finally to "excellence in everything we do."

CHARACTERISTICS OF A WORLD-CLASS ORGANIZATION[1]

- Organizational performance is sustained at a high level over an extended period of time (e.g., ten to fifteen years).
- People want to work for the organization even if it means changing their career or profession.
- The organization is both efficient and effective in processes and continuously innovative in products.
- The organization pays less attention to profit margin and stock price than to what it contributes to society.
- Every employee sets and manages unit and/or process strategy. (Everyone is a manager, a process manager; there are no associates.)
- Every employee has ownership of the organization, and there's little difference between pay at the top and bottom of the organization. (Actually, it's hard to see who's at top and bottom because it's more a peer organization.)
- The organizational record is virtually zero: for landfill, accidents, labor disputes, legal and regulatory compliance problems, and product recalls.
- The organization is committed to long-term development and support of its employees.
- The organization fully understands the link between a highly motivated and trained workforce and its customers' extraordinary level of satisfaction.

SET A GOAL TO ACHIEVE WORLD-CLASS STATUS

There are many good reasons for doing so. Such a goal:

- Adds credibility to quality claims (e.g., "Awarded the best medium-size car for four consecutive years")
- Enhances brand recognition
- Could be a basis for premium pricing
- Increases profitability
- Can be positioned as both the organization's goal as well as each individual's goal
- Can ease attainment of funds for capital improvements or expansion (i.e., credit rating)
- Can aid in attracting and retaining talented people
- Can aid in developing both supplier and customer partnerships and alliances

CHANGING MANAGEMENT THINKING

Our managers' and political leaders' thinking processes must undergo a paradigm shift. They must shift away from primarily managing actions to managing interactions. The quality movement's direction has been, and mostly still is, toward improving processes. The step up to becoming a world-class organization calls for thinking about interactions between internal functions and activities as well as between the organization and its external environment. This also requires looking beyond outputs (i.e., the product of processes) to outcomes (the results of the interactions). For example, your organization produces the most reliable and cost-effective product of its kind in the world. The outcomes include increased profits and organizational growth. However, outcomes from producing that product might also result in economic instability (e.g., loss of jobs, polluting the environment, or political unrest).

There's a growing concern to consider a product's lifecycle, i.e., its life not only throughout its period of use but also to its ultimate disposal.

For example, we're presently experiencing as outcomes of some products:

- Overflowing landfills due to the residue of disposable but not biodegradable packaging
- Insufficient answers as to what to do with nuclear waste
- Shrinking fish populations due to highly efficient fishing practices
- Decreasing oxygen due to logging and farming that deplete rainforests

The list goes on. Management thinking must extend beyond the financial results of the next quarter (or the manger's personal financial agendas). The truly world-class organization must shift its focus to the outcomes it affects by the outputs it produces. No world-class organization has yet emerged to resolve world hunger, yet the products exist, the technologies exist, and the funds exist to do so. No organization, corporate or political, has overcome its constrained thinking sufficiently to enable reallocating those resources to solve the problem. We've been philosophizing about "systems thinking" for a few decades, but we still haven't adequately reached the stage of interacting within the world as a "system."

One of the largest, if not the largest resource in the world remains largely untapped. It's a resource that requires less extraction and transportation costs than mining ores. It requires less financial risk-taking than designing and launching a new product. It's relatively inexpensive and readily available. That resource is people. In isolated situations it's been proven that, given proper nurturing, training, education, opportunity, recognition, and rewards, people can far exceed other types of resources in creating cost-effective and environmentally effective outcomes. The growing field of knowledge management recognizes the innate capability of the human brain to acquire, make sense of, store, retrieve, and use enormous amounts of data and information. True, computers might surpass the human brain in some types of data manipulation. However, they're far outclassed by the brain's ability to develop meaningful links, to transform information into a knowledge base and develop wisdom that can be applied to new and challenging situations.

As a hypothetical experiment, go to an underdeveloped country. Pick a young, inexperienced man or woman. Give him or her a pointed stick, a handful of seeds, access to a piece of land, and a source of water. Give that person a modicum of knowledge (i.e., the relationship between planting a seed and the growth of a vegetable) and limited training (e.g., how to make a hole with the stick, how far apart to plant a seed, how much water to apply, and how to harvest), and that person will begin to produce an output. Do that for twenty villagers, and you produce outcomes such as relief from hunger, knowledge and skill that can be transferred to others, less dependence upon charity, better health for the families, and longer lives.

Now deliver the latest and greatest piece of farm machinery to the same village. That piece of machinery can do nothing without human intervention. It might be a world-class product but unused, or improperly used, it creates no world-class outcome.

To achieve world-class status, an organization's systems must be optimized; the product or service produced must have relevance and add value to meet human needs. Relevance goes beyond just satisfying customers. It means anticipating new customer expectations and even phasing out a presently profitable product to launch a new, more environmentally friendly and beneficial product.

WHAT COULD POSSIBLY GO WRONG?

Your organization is reaching the top of its game, but many things could still go wrong. For example, perhaps your organization:

- Has becomes more visible to the competition ("So that's their strategy...")
- Is more visible to its customers ("If they're so great, why doesn't my can opener work?")
- Finds it difficult to make any significant changes in top management or to reorganize itself ("What will we do without Jack?")
- Might become stuck with doing what made it famous and neglect to stay ahead of competition (e.g., the former leader in photocopiers)
- Could be a target for legal actions (e.g., a well-known pharmaceutical company)
- Might be affected by economic downturn (When you're at the top, it's tough to stay there.)
- Finds that success breeds complacency (a major retail chain)
- Could easily be inundated by other organizations seeking to learn from and replicate its practices (L.L. Bean)
- Is criticized for its compensation policies and practices, especially as the gap between workers' pay and executive compensation widens (e.g., a top-ranked, multinational company)
- Might be more susceptible to events that could tarnish its status, such as a product recall, environmental catastrophe, management scandal (e.g., a highly respected chemical products company)

The world-class organization must have world-class leaders. They in turn must have a vision that embodies the thinking discussed above. Above all, they must combat complacency not only throughout the organization but also and most importantly, among the top decision makers. To use the analogy of a lighthouse, these leaders:

- Have a unique view of the world around them
- Serve as a guiding "beacon" for those below and in front of them
- Sustain their light through the darkness that periodically surrounds them
- Offer hope and comfort to those laboring under their influence
- Periodically must undergo maintenance and upgrading
- Are held to high standards of integrity and performance
- Are in it for the long term

CONCLUSION

These ten chapters addressed many, but far from all, of the principles, policies, and practices that can be employed to make your organization the best it can be. It's hoped that some of what's been written here stimulates action within your organization and encourages discourse among organizations as they move toward world-class status. If you haven't already done so, start your organization's journey by stepping up to ISO 9004. Remember author Michael Hammer's observation:

"Only companies that strive to be the best and to outperform all others have a hope of surviving in a world where everyone else is trying to do the same."[2]

ENDNOTES

1. Insights adapted from Duke Okes, president of APLOMET in a private e-mail.
2. Hammer, Michael. *The Agenda: What Every Business Must Do to Dominate the Decade.* New York: Crown Business, 2001.

APPENDIX A

Next Operation as Customer: Concepts and Application

CONCEPTS

Every function and work group in an organization is both a receiver of product—including services, data, and information—from internal and/or external sources as well as a provider of products to internal and/or external customers. These interfaces between provider and receiver might be one to one, one to many, many to one, or many to many. Each receiver has needs and requirements. The manner in which delivered product meets these affects the receivers' effectiveness and the product quality passed on to their receivers. Examples include:

- *A* delivers part *X* to *B* one hour late; *B* might have to apply extra effort and cost to make up the time or risk perpetuating the lateness in delivering to the next receiver.

- Engineering designs a product, based on the salesperson's understanding of the external customer's need. Production produces the product, expending material, personnel, and other costs. The external customer rejects the product because it fails to meet the customer's needs. The provider reengineers the product, and production makes a new one that the customer accepts, late. Possibly the last order from this customer.

- Computer services delivers copies of a production cost report (averaging fifty pages of fine print per week) to six internal customers. Computer services has established elaborate quality control of the accuracy, timeliness, and physical quality of the report. However, of the six report receivers, only two need information of this type. Neither of these find the report directly usable for their current needs. Each has assigned clerical people to extract pertinent data manually for their specific use. All six report receivers diligently store the reports for the prescribed retention period.

- Production tickets, computer-printed on light card stock, are attached by removable tape to each module during assembly. When the module reaches the paint shop, it's given an acid bath, a rinse, high-temperature drying, painting, and high-temperature baking. Very few tickets survive intact. The operation following the paint shop requires attaching other parts to the painted modules, depending on information from the ticket. Operators have to depend on their experience to guess which goes with what. Ninety-five percent emerge from this process correctly, but this figure falls when unique specifications are needed or when an experienced operator is absent.

OBJECTIVES

- To identify internal provider/receiver interfaces
- To establish receivers' product needs and requirements
- To document service agreements between provider and receiver
- To establish improvement goals and measurements
- To implement systems for tracking and reporting performance and for supporting the continual improvement of the process

THREE TIMELY TENETS

- The only valid requirements for the product delivered to the external customers are the requirements they've provided.
- The only truly valid measurement of the product's quality is the external customer's level of the satisfaction.
- All internal provider/receiver requirements must be consistent with the external customers' requirements.

ASSUMPTIONS

- A quality improvement steering committee is in place.
- The committee has focused on NOAC as integral to its overall quality initiative.
- Cross-functional quality improvement process teams (QIPTs) have been formed specifically to implement NOAC.
- Requisite management support for NOAC is present.

CRITICAL STEPS

- Prepare a mission statement (e.g., achieve customer enthusiasm)
- Identify and prioritize areas for controlled rollout
- Train NOAC QIPT (i.e., implementers)
- Design procedures and forms for collecting data and documenting receivers' needs and requirements
- Design/adapt systems to track, measure, report, and improve receivers' satisfaction
- Design/adapt appropriate incentives for improvements in receivers' satisfaction
- Provide just-in-time training for all affected employees
- Monitor and evaluate implementation rollout progress
- Continually improve the NOAC process itself
- Positively reinforce all interim progress and celebrate all major successes

QUALITY IMPROVEMENT PROCESS TEAMS RESPONSIBILITIES

For each organizational area scheduled for NOAC rollout:

- Map the current process to identify each process or function that has discreet input and output; pinpoint important gaps.
- Identify the hierarchy of providers and receivers by name and title
- Collect and document all inputs and outputs. Specify one person responsible for each.
- Document receivers' overall needs and requirements for each output
- Survey the level of satisfaction each receiver has with each group of products they receive

- Map a potentially improved process flow; compare with current process map
- Pinpoint areas for improvement and prioritize
- Estimate potential payoff for improved quality for top five to ten areas.
- Select an area for which early success can occur, one that might produce a significant payoff
- Establish formal agreement between provider and customer on the level of product quality needed or required.
- Analyze present level of performance, including receivers' satisfaction; determine root causes of shortfalls in meeting receivers' needs and requirements.
- Implement continual quality improvement
- Select the next most important area for improvement
- Periodically return to first step

APPENDIX B

Tapping the Customer's Many Voices[1]

SYNOPSIS

The voices of the customer are critical in our competitive environment. Most companies have no systematic way to listen actively to customers, record what's been heard, then analyze, distribute, and act upon the information. A process known as Listen, Capture, Analyze, Learn, and Improve (LCALI) allows an organization, regardless of size or type of product or service, to capture pertinent customer data for analysis and action.

LISTENING TO THE MANY VOICES OF THE CUSTOMER (VOC)

In *Moments of Truth*, Jan Carlzon, then president of Scandinavian Airlines, writes about the often-unrecognized opportunities all employees have for gathering customer information.[2] In *At America's Service*, Karl Albrecht[3] further defines the "moment of truth" (MOT) as "any episode in which the customer comes in contact with any aspect of the organization and gets an impression of the quality of its service. An MOT is typically neither positive nor negative in and of itself. It is the outcome that counts."

Without a system for training employees to listen to the voice of the customer for collecting, analyzing, disseminating the information, and taking action, the organization is flying blind. Without a measure, or at least a sense of how satisfied your customers are, your organization has left the door open to the competition.

IN MOMENTS OF TRUTH, LET THE SELLER BE AWARE

Be aware that investigating reasons for returned product is but a small part of the picture. A customer's offhand remark to your sales or delivery person can appear insignificant by itself. However, these comments—heard in an MOT—can sound an alert to a potential problem before it turns into a formal complaint.

When a customer's engineer calls your organization's engineer to ask a question of clarification, it can indicate present or potential shortcomings in clearly identifying or satisfying customer requirements. Scattered remarks from a variety of customer personnel to several different people in your organization, although not appearing important when looked at individually, can, when collected and analyzed, form a pattern pointing to needed preventive action.

In *Creating Customer Value*, Earl Naumann[4] noted, "A firm that has no customer satisfaction program and no interest in starting one should be the delight of the firm's competitors."

To capture these early-warning indicators, combine the concept of moments of truth with developing "listening posts." This involves taking the following steps:

- Through employee training, build awareness of the need to gather all tidbits of information received from external customers' personnel, either directly or indirectly (e.g., a third party passing on what he or she heard). Every employee becomes an informal "field listener" on the job and in the community.

- Develop a system to feed information to a central collecting place, analyze, correlate, and disseminate the analyzed information, and designate responsibilities for taking action and follow-up.

- Deputize personnel who have frequent direct customer contact to listen actively to the VOC and feed information back through the organization's system. *In Thriving on Chaos*, Tom Peters[5] stresses: "Use every listening post you can find... Too few people, at too few levels, in too few functions, listen too little and too late—and ignore what they hear too often, and act too late."

- Create incentives for employees to communicate customer complaints so that action can be taken to avoid them in the future. Be aware, however, that performance awards for decreasing the number of complaints can encourage complaint cover-ups. Provide incentives for increasing client satisfaction and instill the value that a complaint, although undesirable, does trigger opportunities for improvement. This will demonstrate a commitment to excellence.

- Make review of VOC data, including an analysis of the customer contact record (CCR), part of the management review process in assessing the effectiveness of your organization's quality management system.

CAPTURING THE VOICE OF THE CUSTOMER

Much more than a "complaint management system," the intent is to capture the voice of the customer regardless of whether that voice is expressing:

- Dissatisfaction with a product or service
- Perception of customer service and quality
- Suggestions
- Expectations for future products or services
- Complete satisfaction

In *Creating Customer Value*, Earl Naumann declares, "Corporate culture must evolve almost to the point where there is a pervasive fear of losing contact with customers." How can your organization not only prevent loss of client or customer contact but also strengthen the contacts? Several approaches can improve listening capabilities:

- *Create awareness among employees.* Make all employees aware of the value of listening for and reporting customer comments—regardless of the message—through orientation programs, training, unit meetings, and positive reinforcement. Employees are your organization's "field listeners."

- *Establish a frontline intelligence network.* Every employee, regardless of organizational level, is a frontline intelligence gatherer. A casual comment heard by the organization's truck driver when making a delivery, a discussion overheard in a restaurant or supermarket, or a caller's complaint received by a clerical staff member could all become

Figure B.1

CUSTOMER/CLIENT CONTACT RECORD

Customer No.: _____   CCR No.: _____

A. Identification

Contact Name:	Title:
Organization:	Phone:
Address:	Fax:
City: State: Zip:	E-mail:
Field Name:	Position:
Listener—Dept./Location Mail Stop:	Phone:
Supervisor's Name: Title:	

B. Context/Situation/Place of Contact

❑ Complaint   ❑ Compliment   ❑ General observation

❑ Letter (Date): __/__/__   ❑ Phone call (Date): __/__/__   ❑ Face-to-face (Date): __/__/__   ❑ Other (Date): __/__/__

Describe context in greater detail if "other" is checked:

C. Quote or best recollection of words from customer/client and nature of the contact

Related to specific order/product (No.):   Date: __/__/__   Product:

Related to specific representative of this organization (Whom):   Date: __/__/__

Record words used by customer/client contact; if a direct quote use quotation marks:

Include any details that will make the understanding of the customer/client's perspective clear to persons reading this CCR. Note if customer/client specifically requested notification of resolution or other feedback (use back of form if needed):

Field listener's commentary (viewpoint, opinion, interpretation) and why:

D. Action activity

❑ Action needed now (Corrective action)   ❑ Investigate (Preventive action?)   ❑ Put on "trend watch"

Action assigned to (Name):   Location: Phone: Date: __/__/__

Follow-up (How):   1st: 2nd: 3rd: 4th:

Status reports (How):   1st: 2nd: 3rd: 4th:

E. Resolution and closeout

State how problem/question was resolved:

Corrective action no.:   Preventive action no.:   RMA No.:   Other:

Procedure/Work Instruction affected: Date to be changed: __/__/__   By whom:

Forms/computer program affected: Date to be changed: __/__/__   By whom:

Status/feedback to be provided (How):   To whom: By: By date: __/__/__

Closeout code: By (Print name):   Signature: Date: __/__/__

valuable input to the customer information system. Listening post employees (LPEs) are employees who consistently have contact with customer personnel. They're the official deputies for funneling collected data—theirs and that from "field listeners"—into the system. Every employee must know how to contact a listening post employee.

Figure B.2

CUSTOMER CONTACT LOG													
Date logged	CCR no.	CCR date	Field listener's name and phone	LPE name and phone	Customer name, address, phone	Customer no.	Triage code*	Action assigned to:	Date assigned	Follow-up date	Follow-up date	Close-out code	Close-out date and initial

Triage Code   1 = Immediate Action Required, contact customer;   2 = Action required;   3 = No immediate action

- *Designate data collectors.* The system must facilitate ease in reporting these voices of the customers to designated "listening post employees." Request that employees report comments, opinions, suggestions, accolades, and/or complaints (without embellishment and quoted verbatim, if possible) to LPEs. Request customers' names and contact data, where possible, and the context or situation and where and when the VOC was heard.

    LPEs will be responsible for collecting and formally inputting data on a CCR (see figure B.1) regularly to a customer information system coordinator or team. LPEs also maintain a log of CCRs received (see figure B.2).

- *Analyze data and respond.* If a field listener or LPE receives data that requires immediate action, the LPE is authorized to initiate a corrective action, including the data in the CCR process as well. The corrective action report and CCR must be appropriately cross-referenced.

    The continual improvement steering committee (CISC) or a team analyzes accumulated CCRs to determine frequency of each type of comment and to uncover problem patterns. The CISC or a team member, prepares summary information for review at the next quality steering committee meeting and/or management review. This summary should display a rolling three- or six-month trend and the CISC's recommended actions.

- *Take preventive action.* If trend analysis indicates a problem pattern, the CISC initiates a preventive action request for improving the quality management system to eliminate potential problem areas. In addition to follow-up required by the preventive action process, the CISC is notified of the outcome of the preventive action. The CISC provides feedback and reinforcement to the LPEs, who do likewise to their "field listeners," the contributors. In certain cases, a customer should be informed of the action being taken.

- *Encourage continual improvement.* Procedures and processes often must be changed as a result of preventive actions. In addition, the customer data-gathering process itself must be reviewed continually, reinforced, and strengthened (e.g., simplify the CCR).

ONE ORGANIZATION'S EXPERIENCE

To gain a better sense of how an organization can listen to, and benefit from, the VOC, it will help to examine the case of a small engineering-consulting firm that markets both structural design services and field inspections of facilities. The firm is organized on a project basis, with multiple projects underway at any one time, each of which is managed by a project manager. The firm's engineering, legal, and administrative resources are allocated according to project needs. Nearly everyone in the firm is, at one time or another, in contact with personnel from the clients' organization, at all organizational levels.

Prior to implementing its ISO 9001-based quality management system, the firm had no formal process for gathering client data. Therefore, the staff had no formal way of correlating data from multiple sources to evaluate needs for preventive action. A loss of nearly $1 million dollars in revenue (due to data not reaching the firm's management in time for action) punctuated the need to use the "listening post" approach.

Now, each project manager serves as an LPE, accumulating and reporting data, positive and negative, received from personnel assigned to him or her (i.e., "field listeners"). Except when the data requires immediate action, the LPEs funnel their CCRs through a CISC, who is a vice president of the firm.

The CISC "trends" the data, reports on this information, and initiates preventive actions resulting from the quarterly management review. These preventive action requests result from presentations and discussions of the trend analysis in the management review meetings.

A number of positive reports have been funneled through the system that have allowed management to provide an increased level of positive reinforcement to the personnel and/or project teams responsible for ensuring positive experiences for the firm's clients.

BENEFITS OF LISTENING TO THE VOC

Clearly, actively listening to your customer involves additional work and might be viewed as little more than increased paperwork in the form of reports and data. However, there are many reasons why it benefits your organization to know what's on customer minds, including:

- *Customer retention*. Your organization needs to know of and fix a developing situation before it results in a lost customer.
- *Customer satisfaction*. Having a method for gathering and processing customer feedback will enable your organization to obtain—and retain—a leading position in the marketplace. Your organization will be better positioned to make decisions about what customers want and need—and whether your organization is meeting those wants and needs—if it has hard data about the customer rather than relying on low-response-rate surveys and non-data-based assumptions.
- *Employee satisfaction*. Your organization will find it useful to reinforce its customer focus through measurements, feedback, and positive reinforcement of its responsible employees. These employees could receive positive reinforcement for reporting customer data (regardless of whether it results in action), reporting customer data that contributes to a quality system improvement and/or contributing to the improvement of the LCALI process itself.
- *Quality management system requirements*. Implementing a customer data collection, analysis, measurement, and reporting process not only will help your organization hear the VOC but it will also help meet the preventive action requirement of ISO 9001:2000 and ensure your organization's continued conformance to the standard.

■ *Cost avoidance.* Failing to hear the voices of your organization's customers will likely result in costly business mistakes. Thus, having VOC processes in place has decided advantages.

IS AN ACSI SCORE OF 73 GOOD ENOUGH?

The American Customer Satisfaction Index (ACSI), initiated in 1994, is a cross-industry measure of the satisfaction of U.S. household customers with the quality of the goods and services available to them—both those goods and services produced within the United States and those provided as imports from foreign firms that have substantial market shares or dollar sales. The ACSI is produced by the National Quality Research Center at the University of Michigan Business School, in partnership with the American Society for Quality (ASQ) and the CFI Group of Ann Arbor, Michigan. About 16,000 customers of companies surveyed are contacted each quarter. Scores can be obtained online at *www.bus.umich.edu/acsi* or from ASQ at *www.asq.org.*

Although the index is a difficult measure by which to compare your organization's individual progress in continually improving customer satisfaction, it does signal an overall lack of exemplary customer satisfaction. The message clearly is: much can be done to improve an organization's capability to "hear" their customers. Be one of those organizations that heed the message.

ENDNOTES

1. Adapted from the original article in the June 2000 issue of *The Informed Outlook.*
2. Carlzon, Jan. *Moments of Truth.* New York: HarperBusiness. 1987.
3. Albrecht, Karl. *At America's Service.* New York: Warner Books. 1988.
4. Naumann, Earl. *Creating Customer Value: The Path to Sustainable Competitive Advantage.* New York: Van Nostrand Reinhold. 1994.
5. Peters, Tom. *Thriving on Chaos: Handbook for a Management Revolution.* New York: Knopf. 1987.

APPENDIX C

Quality-Level Agreements for Clarity of Expectations

Internal management of expectations generates improved results.

ANSI/ISO/ASQ Q9001-2000 (paragraphs. 5.2, 7.2.1, 7.2.2, and 7.2.3) is quite explicit regarding responsibility for determining and meeting customer requirements with the "aim of enhancing customer satisfaction." In addition to ensuring that your organization and its customer are reading from the same page, it's also vital that the same rigor apply to internal process and support providers and their internal receivers and customers.

In-company service level agreements (SLAs) have been used in the information technology field for years to clarify users' requirements and document the agreement between information technology (IT) and the user. SLAs were created when it became obvious the measures employed within the computer center didn't truly reflect the delivered service level or the unique needs of the end-user. For example, IT might consider a 98.5 percent online availability of the computer system acceptable. However, it would be totally unacceptable to the retail salesperson waiting to verify customers' credit availability during peak sales periods. Typical criteria measured for each of the user-specified services or products of the IT function included accuracy and completeness of data, on-time delivery performance, system response time, response time to users' problems, even attitude and cooperativeness of IT personnel.

This appendix proposes using a variation of the SLA, a quality level agreement (QLA). To establish a QLA with their internal customers (i.e., service receivers), internal service providers would document agreement as to the level of service required by the receiver. A QLA covering service or product outputs might contain specifications for quality characteristics such as quantity, accuracy, distribution, timeliness, quality and/or usability, product life, service availability, response time, service support, response to problems, and providers' attitudes and cooperativeness. For each significant service or product output, one or more performance targets are specified with appropriate units of measure. Two examples are:

- *The requirements are expressed from the receivers' perspective, not the providers'.* In a manufacturing plant, a product-finishing department might specify how it wants to receive in-process product from a processing department, e.g., twelve units of X, placed with nozzle-end facing upward, in standard fifteen-inch by ten-inch egg-boxes, twelve boxes per pallet, with traveler packet taped to pallet, all previous operations properly signed-off and inspected, any nonconforming product removed before delivery, and quantities adjusted.

■ *An order processing function might specify how an organization will receive the daily report of orders entered.* For example, a report of each day's orders entered into the MRP system will be delivered by 4 p.m. each work day, in two segments: orders sorted by product family and orders entered by part number. All entries will be legible, 100-percent accurate, and complete.

Generating the QLA establishes a baseline for measurement. Either a periodic performance audit is conducted or a system for ongoing tracking, measuring, evaluating, and reporting performance relative to the terms of the QLA is established. Typically, QLAs are reviewed and modified, on a rotation basis, at least once a year, more often if changes are required. Identifying deficient performance in quality levels triggers corrective action and quality improvement.

STEPS TO IMPLEMENT QLAS

■ Select key internal service or product outputs and the appropriate receivers or customers, based on:
 ☐ The most critical potential effect on external customers
 ☐ Representative samples of key internal receivers, customers, and end-users for each of the selected outputs

■ Document present level of performance, as the provider knows it to be, for each key service or product output identified
■ Meet with selected receivers or customers—and end-users within customers
 ☐ Negotiate a realistic set of quality level specifications and measurements for each selected service or product output
 ☐ Draft a QLA (see figure C.1)

■ Review QLA within provider's organization to:
 ☐ Ensure that performance targets are achievable
 ☐ Ensure that meeting the specifications of a given output doesn't negatively affect delivery of another output

■ Negotiate final agreement between provider and receiver or customer
■ Prepare final QLA and obtain sign-off
■ Distribute copies to appropriate provider and receiver or customer personnel as well as to any established control system function
■ Periodically review performance against the QLAs and take corrective or preventive action as needed

An example of a QLA form is shown in figure C.1. QLAs can be implemented on a gradual basis, starting with the most critical deliverables.

Figure C.1

QUALITY LEVEL AGREEMENT	
Service/Product Receiver: Dept./Function Contact name: _____ Title: _____ _____ Contact no. _____	SLA no.: _____ Original issue date: ___/___/___ Date last revision: ___/___/___ Current date: ___/___/___
Description of service/product: _____ _____ _____	Identifiers: _____ Part nos.: __ _____ External customer: _____
Specific requirements: 1 _____ 2 _____ 3 _____ _____ 4 _____	Measurements: 1 _____ 2 _____ 3 _____ 4 _____
Conditions that might affect achieving agreed quality level: _____ _____ _____	Relative to requirement no.: ___
Report quality level agreement failure to: _____ Name: _____ Title: _____ Contact no. _____	Comments: _____ _____
Agreed for receiver/customer: _____ Name: _____ Title: _____ Contact no. _____	Date: ___/___/___ Signature: _____
Agreed for provider: _____ Name: _____ Title: _____ Contact no. _____	Date: ___/___/___ Signature: _____
Approval (if required) for receiver/customer: _____ Name: _____ Title: _____ Contact no. _____	Date: ___/___/___ Signature: _____
Approval (if required) for provider: _____ Name: _____ Title: _____ Contact no. _____	Date: ___/___/___ Signature: _____
This agreement relates to: _____ _____	Procedure nos.: _____ Work instruction nos.: _____

BENEFITS

QLAs increase employees' understanding of internal service and/or product expectations and reaffirm the importance of internal customer or receiver requirements from the receivers' perspective. Employees also can gain insights into the potential effect of their contribution to the business process in which they play a part.

QLAs and the documented performance achieved give objective evidence that providers have complied with their receiver or customer requirements, thus linking internal product or service quality with the quality management system and, ultimately, with external customers' requirements. QLAs provide a natural expansion to documented quality management systems by providing the basis for working-level performance measurement and review, which in turn leads to continual improvement. QLA content data will vary according to the needs of the providers and receivers of the products or services.

Initiating QLAs increases understanding and collaboration between providers and receivers. A QLA should remove all doubt as to what a receiver expects from a service or product received from the provider. It should eliminate needless controversy and confusion if expectations aren't met. The QLA can offer a sound basis for performance measurement and continual improvement. It helps to deploy the voice of the customer throughout the organization.

Note: This appendix was adapted from the author's article by the same title, published in the December 1999 issue of The Informed Outlook.

APPENDIX D

Customer Visits

Visiting customers frequently should be a TQM process. But which customers should be visited, who should go, and what should be done during the visit? Ideally, you should visit all your customers at least once a year, depending on a number of factors. Choose to visit larger volume customers more frequently. Remember: A small sales contributor now could grow to a large-scale buyer if you build a relationship through frequent visits.

Many companies limit visits to and with top management. However, bringing lower-echelon people together with the customers' lower-level people can payoff in smoother contacts and in understanding each company's needs and problems. Operations people sometimes have a limited or distorted perception of how the product they make is used. Seeing how firsthand can be an eye-opening experience.

So, do you just schedule a day, pack eight randomly selected employees in a rented van, and descend upon the customer's site? Not a good idea. To make the venture cost-effective, you must have a plan. Consider the following:

- Who decides a customer visit could be productive? Why?
- Why do we want to arrange a visit? What needs are we addressing?
- What company do we want to visit? Why?
- What do we know about the company, and how can we find out more?
- Who or what department in the customer's company should we meet with?
- What do we want to get out of the visit? Any measurable outcome?
- Whom and how many of our people should we send?
- Which specific areas, topics, or processes do we want to see and discuss? Why?
- What problems can we anticipate and what will our responses be?
- What questions do we expect to ask? Why?
- What information about our own operations are we prepared to share?
- Do we have authorization to offer a reciprocal visit to our plant?
- Is the date and time we selected OK with the customer? If not, what other dates and times are open?
- Have we prepared an agenda for our people? Sent a copy to the customer?
- What are the travel instructions, transportation, parking, security (e.g., clearances, cameras, recording devices), safety, and dress code issues?
- What about our company should our people be briefed on before the visit (e.g., sensitive issues, pending litigation, proprietary information)?

■ Have we allowed sufficient time to plan the visit? Have we allowed time to debrief immediately after the visit?

■ Have we planned for our people to prepare a summary of observations, what they learned, and any customer's questions remaining unanswered?

■ Have we planned how the information gathered from the visit will be summarized and disseminated? Might action items result and, if so, how will they be assigned and followed up?

■ Have we a plan to evaluate the effectiveness and efficiency of the visit and identify how future visits can be improved?

■ What post-visit communication will be made with the customer? What medium will be used? Who will make the contact? Should the communication be more than just a "Thank you?"

Note: If the objective of a visit is benchmarking, additional preparation is required. Benchmarking is more highly structured and focused.

APPENDIX E

Improving Workplace Competence

What is competence?

Competence = Knowledge + Skills + Experience + Aptitude + Attitude

Can competence be further categorized? Yes, competencies can be further defined as followed:

- Task competence—the task-specific skills needed to perform the job
- Interpersonal competence—the social skills and attitude needed to perform within the context of a work group or a team
- Pre-job competence—the basics needed to perform at a minimally acceptable level (e.g., work habits, literacy, numeracy)
- Cultural competence—learning about how things get done in the organization, the unwritten "rules" of the organizational culture
- Self-managing competence—needed if one is to become a self-starter, competencies that might not be present but are needed if empowerment is to succeed

WHY DO WE HAVE A COMPETENCE GAP?

The gap between the competence level we expect workers to have and what they do results from at least three conditions:

- Competitive pressures in a global market coupled with increased demand for quality products, delivered faster and at lower cost
- Meeting the first condition requires investment in expensive and complex equipment and processes.
- Conditions one and two occur at a time when entry-level workers lack the basics: reading, writing, arithmetic, and good work habits.

WHAT HAPPENS AS A RESULT OF THE GAP?

With costs spiraling upward and profit margins down, organizations tend to spend less on developing their employees. Further, the decline of worker competence forces management to spend substantially more time fixing problems and trying to control rising costs. Management in turn becomes less competent. This overall malaise results in poor quality, loss of business, and, if not halted early on, the organization's demise.

CAN WE GET OUT OF THE TRAP?

Yes, but it isn't easy. There are two routes:

1. The "sticky bandage" route, which require organizations to:

■ Set up a "school" to train new hires in the basics (costly)

■ Wherever possible, aggressively "steal" experienced people from other employers (expensive and bad for the image)

■ Purposely set higher-than-competition hiring dollars to entice more people to enter your workforce (creates a long-term compensation problem)

■ As a last resort, break down tasks to their simplest elements (so that even a trained monkey could do them—so much for job enrichment and empowerment)

2. The "bite the bullet" route, which requires organizations to:

■ Analyze all jobs, at the task level, and determine the competencies required (setting standards is an investment). Be careful to validate these requirements (absolutely needed to do the job)

■ Assess job incumbents to determine their competency levels relative to the competencies required (essentially a training needs analysis)

■ Develop individual training plans and training programs to bring all workers up to the established competence level for their job (focused training effort)

■ Establish a development plan to cross-train and reward individual workers for acquiring new competencies (optional but desirable to address the forces affecting the business)

■ Include an analysis of competencies required when designing new products, upgrading equipment, and/or improving processes and procedures (add people to your formula for evaluating process capability)

■ Make your minimum acceptable hiring standards known to your sources for new hires, in advance of your need to fill jobs

■ Verify that potential new hires meet your minimum acceptable standards

■ Work with local educational institutions to develop curriculum that will produce graduates who can meet your standards

WHAT ELSE CAN WE DO TO IMPROVE WORKER COMPETENCE?

■ Collaboratively set performance objectives. People must know what's expected of them.

■ Provide substantive performance feedback frequently. People must know how they are doing against the established criteria.

■ Understand and use positive methods to manage behavior. People must experience positive consequences from doing what's expected.

■ Be a coach, not an overseer. People must feel their bosses want to help, not hurt, them.

■ Put support systems in place to ensure people have the opportunity to change and improve, even to make mistakes as they master their jobs.

■ Especially be sure your reward/pay systems support competency and performance improvement, not inhibit, as do the majority of traditional systems.

WHAT IS THE ROOT CAUSE OF WORKER INCOMPETENCE?

W. Edwards Deming, as well as many others, acknowledged that the heart of the problem lies mainly with the system, and the system is management's responsibility. No amount of "quality" talk, statistical process control training, team meetings, or attempts to "fix" the workers will improve workplace competence. Management must overhaul the inhibiting systems or install new supportive systems.

WHAT COULD WORKPLACE COMPETENCY IMPROVEMENT MEAN IN DOLLARS?

Provided you have good performance measures in place, it's easy to compute:

- Total output data for a group of performers (i.e., a department or shift), expressed in dollars = baseline dollar value
- Output data for highest producer in the group (i.e., the exemplar) in dollars
- Exemplar's performance value multiplied by the total employees in the group, including the exemplar = target output value
- Target output - baseline = potential for improvement in dollars

WHAT'S THE DIFFERENCE BETWEEN A JOB TASK ANALYSIS AND A JOB COMPETENCE ASSESSMENT?

A job task analysis describes all who perform the job minimally well. A job competence assessment is focused on the differences between exemplary performers and less effective performers. For example: One employee performs each step in setting up a machine for a new operation, correctly following the procedure. The exemplary performer follows the same procedure but, in addition, examines the tools and fixtures for possible wear and replaces those that could cause an out-of-tolerance run.

A typical task analysis could overlook this type of extra initiative. If employee empowerment is the aim, training efforts should be structured to stress competency level, not just fulfilling the task steps.

APPENDIX F

Assessing Supplier Relations

QUESTIONS TO ASK

- What percentage of your final product or service cost is represented by purchased raw material, parts, and services?
- How many suppliers do you have?
- How many suppliers do you have for a specific material, part, or service?
- Is the number of suppliers increasing or decreasing?
- How often do you change suppliers?
- To what extent do you include your suppliers in planning for quality?
- What kind of support and communication do you provide your suppliers?
- What types of contracts do you have with your suppliers?
- What criteria determine when you purchase rather than make it in-house?
- How do you select a supplier?
- How do you measure the quality of purchased material and services?
- How do you determine your suppliers' process capabilities?
- How do you rate your present suppliers?
- What kinds of problems do you have with suppliers?
- Are the number and/or severity of problems increasing or decreasing?
- What goals do you have for improving supplier quality and relationships?
- How often and for what reasons do you visit each of your suppliers?
- What is your policy and/or practice for paying suppliers?
- What do you see as the major roadblocks to improving supplier quality and relationships?
- Who are some of your major customers?
- What quality requirements do your customers expect of you?
- Who are the people in your company who deal directly with your suppliers?
- What is your present cost of poor supplier quality?
- How do you keep track of partial shipments?
- How do you keep track of rejects and rework?
- If asked, what would your suppliers say about your company?
- How do you communicate post-order changes in requirements to your suppliers?
- How do you communicate your satisfaction (or lack thereof) to your suppliers?
- What is your present cycle time for your principal products or services?
- Is this cycle time longer or shorter for less critical products or services?

- How do you document nonconformance of purchased material, parts, and services?
- How much money did you spend (last month/last year) on purchased material, parts, and services?
- How much is it worth to you to improve supplier quality by 10 percent? By 50 percent?
- Describe your present relationship with your primary suppliers (adversarial, arm's length, limited trust, partnership)?
- Are your relationships with any/all suppliers such that you would consider a partnering relationship?
- Are your relationships with your key customers and your key suppliers such that you might consider a mutually beneficial alliance?
- Do you embrace supply chain management concepts (e.g., value stream mapping for improving supplier collaboration and interaction)?

SUPPLIER AUDIT DIMENSIONS

- *Organization and management*—culture, philosophy, policies and procedures, organization structure, communication, commitment to quality
- *Design*—organization, systems employed, level of specifications, focus on reliability, engineering change control, degree to which modern techniques are employed, percentage of organization's resources dedicated to applied research and development
- *Manufacturing*—facilities, equipment, maintenance, process capability, level of planning, lot identification and traceability
- *Purchasing*—specifications, supplier relations, procedures, types of contracts
- *Quality*—organization for, quality planning, quality assurance/control, reliability control, audits of conformance to plans, continuous quality improvement process
- *Inspection and test*—labs, instruments, measurement control, calibration, locus of inspection activities
- *Quality coordination*—communication, order analysis, control of subcontractors, quality cost analysis, corrective action loop, disposition of nonconforming product
- *Data systems*—procedures and programs (e.g., SPC, EDI, MRP, ship-to-stock capability, just-in-time capability), facilities, report content, report usefulness and timeliness
- *People*—orientation, competency, training provided, support of, involvement of, empowerment of
- *Quality results*—performance level attained, meets/exceeds your requirements and expectations, cost to quality relationship

APPENDIX G

How to Demonstrate a Return on Investment for Quality Improvements

CONCEPT

By integrating the return on quality investment (ROQI) or return on training investment (ROTI) model with quality improvement projects and/or training programs, an individual, team, or other organizational entity can plan for and demonstrate a return on investment. ROQI/ROTI assumes a partnering relationship between the entity initiating the intervention and the persons or organizations affected by it. The purpose of the ROQI/ROTI is not to attempt to identify "pure" benefits derived solely from the efforts of the initiator. Rather, it's measured by the payoff the affected person or group achieves in partnership with the initiator.

ROQI/ROTI OBJECTIVES

■ To enable the initiator of a quality improvement project and/or a training program project to demonstrate a measurable outcome and dollar payoff from implementing the project. Such a project can be derived from strategic or tactical plans or, in the case of training, from an employee competency assessment

■ To provide the basis, through project tracking and measurement, for each project initiator, and the partnering organization, to receive substantive performance feedback and positive reinforcement for work done well

■ To provide a monetary basis for both the initiator and the affected organization to evaluate the effectiveness of the quality improvement or training

■ To develop an increased awareness of the bottom-line effect of both stand-alone quality initiatives and training and, when aggregated, the net benefits of an entire initiative consisting of more than one project

USES FOR ROQI/ROTI

■ Augment needs assessment (i.e., is a project feasible?)
■ Substantiate requests for resources (e.g., people, facilities, equipment, tools, material, services)
■ Demonstrate the dollar effect of a strategy or approach
■ Justify decisions made
■ Provide a knowledge base for justifying future initiatives

BASIC PREMISES

■ If it appears the project can't be measured and derive a potential dollar payoff, it won't be worth doing.

■ Every action has a measurable outcome. Some actions are just harder to measure than others, but ways can be found.

■ It's more important to measure outcomes from the perspective of the person or organization the project affects than strive to sort out exactly what the initiator's "pure" contribution was. Cross-functional teams are the accepted norm for implementing improvements. In this case it's the team's effect on the affected organization(s)' outcome, not the individuals' or team's outcome that's measured.

TYPES OF OUTCOMES

■ Quality improvements in products, services, and systems

■ Productivity improvement (e.g., personnel, processes, facility changes, equipment replacement/acquisition), including cycle-time reduction

■ Cost reduction

■ Cost avoidance, including mandated actions

OUTLINE OF STEPS TO FOLLOW

1. Define the desired outcome (not activities)
2. Select and/or establish the standard by which the outcome will be measured
3. Determine the present baseline (i.e., present level of performance)
4. Compute the value of the potential improvement (i.e., difference between baseline and standard)
5. Identify the cause of the present level of performance, problem, or deficiency and select an appropriate action or solution
6. Determine the cost of the solution
7. Compute the net payoff (i.e., item four minus item six, annualized)
8. Determine if improvement is worth implementing
9. If worth doing, identify when and by whom
10. If approved, implement, track, measure, report progress, correct process, or stop as necessary
11. Identify measurable outcomes derived from project
12. Compute ROQI/ROTI
13. Evaluate effectiveness of results
14. Complete project documentation
15. Use documented project as a:
    ■ Demonstration of the payoff that can be obtained from the initiative
    ■ Learning opportunity
    ■ Case study to train future project initiators
    ■ Basis for positive reinforcement for work done well
    ■ Basis for justifying future projects

CONCLUSION

The concept discussed above emphasizes the value of the improvement initiator partnering with the organization(s) affected by the initiative. This eliminates much of the traditional friction that can develop between a quality improvement or training person, department or team, and the organization targeted for the improvement. This approach also recognizes (and perhaps even rewards) the joint effort of the initiator and the organization showing the improvement.

For example, in past times training departments measured their "success" on numbers of trainings offered, number of attendees, and number of new trainings designed and offered. Until recently, the focus has been on justifying the training departments existence through its activities and outputs, not the organizational outcomes it affected. With no objective evidence of outcomes affected readily available, is it any wonder why training departments have often been the first sacrificed in a downturn?

REFERENCES

R.T. Westcott & Associates (Russ Westcott) has published the following material relating to return on training investment (ROTI) or return on quality investment (ROQI):

"ROI: An Often Overlooked Quality Tool," *Quality Advocate* (online publication), American Society for Quality: May 9, 2003.

"Has Your Quality Initiative Overlooked ROQI?" (chapter), *Essence of Quality Management Anthology Series, Vol. 3*. American Society for Quality: 1999.

"A Quality System Needs Assessment," (case study of Formations In Metal Inc.), *In Action: Conducting Needs Assessment*, American Society for Training and Development: 1995.

"ROQI: Overlooked Quality Tool," *The Total Quality Review*: Nov/Dec 1994.

"Behavior Management Training," (chapter incorporates ROTI) in *Human Resources Management & Development Handbook, Second Edition*, AMACOM: 1994.

"Applied Behavior Management Training," (case study of North County Electric & Gas incorporates ROTI*), *In Action: Measuring Return On Investment*, American Society for Training and Development: 1994.

"Return-On-Quality-Investment: The Overlooked Quality Tool," *The Quality Management Forum*, Quality Management Division, American Society for Quality: Fall 1993.

"Behavior Management Training," (chapter incorporates ROTI) in *Human Resources Management & Development Handbook*, AMACOM: 1985.

*This case is referenced in *Return on Investment in Training and Performance Improvement Programs*, by Jack J. Phillips. Houston: Gulf Publishing Co., 1997.

APPENDIX H

Additional Reading

ASSESSING, BENCHMARKING, MEASURING

Brown, Mark Graham. *Keeping Score: Using the Right Metrics to Drive World-Class Performance*. Portland: Productivity Press, 1996.

Camp, Robert C. *Business Process Benchmarking: Finding and Implementing Best Practices*. Milwaukee: ASQ Quality Press, 1995.

Chang, Richard Y. and Mark W. Morgan. *Performance Scorecards: Measuring the Right Things in the Real World*. San Francisco: Jossey-Bass, 2000.

Czarnecki, Mark T. *Managing by Measuring: How To Improve Your Organization's Performance Through Effective Benchmarking*. New York: AMACOM, 1999.

Fitz-enz, Jac. *Benchmarking Staff Performance: How Staff Departments Can Enhance Their Value to the Customer*. San Francisco: Jossey-Bass Publishers, 1993.

Hutton, David W. *From Baldrige to the Bottom Line: A Road Map for Organizational Change and Improvement*. Milwaukee: ASQ Quality Press, 2000.

Kaplan, Robert S. and David P. Norton. *The Balanced Scorecard: Translating Strategy Into Action*. Boston: Harvard Business School Press, 1996.

McNair, C.J., CMA and Kathleen H.J. Leibfried. *Benchmarking: A Tool for Continuous Improvement*. New York: John Wiley & Sons, Inc., 1992.

Provonost, Denis. *Internal Quality Auditing*. Milwaukee: ASQ Quality Press, 2000.

Rust, Roland T., Anthony J. Zahorik and Timothy L. Keiningham. *Return on Quality: Measuring the Financial Impact of Your Company's Quest for Quality*. Chicago: Probus Publishing Co., 1994.

Shank, John K. and Vijay Govindarajan. *Strategic Cost Management: The New Tool for Competitive Advantage*. New York: The Free Press, 1993.

Spendolini, Michael J. *The Benchmarking Book*. New York: AMACOM, 1992.

Trischler, William E. *Understanding and Applying Value-Added Assessment: Eliminating Business Process Waste*. Milwaukee: ASQ Quality Press, 1996.

Vavra, Terry G., Ph.D. *Customer Satisfaction Measurement Simplified: A Step-by-Step Guide for ISO 9001:2000 Certification*. Milwaukee: ASQ Quality Press, 2002.

Wilson, Paul F. and Richard D. Pearson. *Performance-Based Assessments: External, Internal, and Self-Assessment Tools for Total Quality Management*. Milwaukee: ASQ Quality Press, 1995.

CONTINUAL QUALITY IMPROVEMENT

Andersen, Bjorn. *Business Process Improvement Toolbox*. Milwaukee: ASQ Quality Press, 1999.

Andersen, Bjorn and Tom Fagerhaug. *Root Cause Analysis: Simplified Tools and Techniques*. Milwaukee: ASQ Quality Press, 2000.

Bauer, John E., Grace L. Duffy and Russell T. Westcott, editors. *The Quality Improvement Handbook*. Milwaukee: ASQ Quality Press, 2002.

Berk, Joseph and Susan Berk. *Quality Management for the Technology Sector*. Boston: Newnes (Butterworth-Heinemann), 2000.

Campanella, Jack, editor. *Principles of Quality Costs: Principles, Implementation and Use, Third Edition*. Milwaukee: ASQ Quality Press, 1999.

Cartin, T.J. *Principles and Practices of Organizational Excellence*. Milwaukee: ASQ Quality Press, 1999.

Deming, W. Edwards. *The New Economics: For Industry, Government, Education, Second Edition*. Cambridge: Massachusetts Institute of Technology, Center for Advance Engineering Study, 1994.

_____. *Out of the Crisis*. Cambridge: Massachusetts Institute of Technology, Center for Advance Engineering Study, 1986.

Dettmer, H. William. *Goldratt's Theory of Constraints: A Systems Approach to Continuous Improvement*. Milwaukee: ASQ Quality Press, 1997.

_____. *Breaking the Constraints to World-Class Performance*. Milwaukee: ASQ Quality Press, 1998.

Evans, James R. and William M. Lindsay. *The Management and Control of Quality, Fifth Edition*. Cincinnati: South-Western (Thompson Learning), 2002.

Hinckley, C. Martin. *Make No Mistake! An Outcome-Based Approach to Mistake-Proofing*. Portland: Productivity Press, 2001.

Juran, Joseph M. and A. Blanton Godfrey, co-editors-in-chief. *Juran's Quality Handbook, Fifth Edition*. New York: McGraw-Hill, 1999.

Kobayashi, Iwao. *20 Keys To Workplace Improvement, Revised Edition*. Portland: Productivity Press, 1995.

MacInnes, Richard L. *The Lean Enterprise Memory Jogger: Create Value and Eliminate Waste Throughout Your Company*. Salem: GOAL/QPC, 2002.

Phillips, Jack J. *Return on Investment in Training and Performance Improvement Programs*. Houston: Gulf Publishing Co., 1997.

Robitaille, Denise E. *The Corrective Action Handbook*. Chico: Paton Press LLC, 2001.

_____. *The Management Review Handbook*. Chico: Paton Press LLC, 2003.

Rossett, Allison. *First Things Fast: A Handbook for Performance Analysis*. San Francisco: Jossey-Bass Pfeiffer, 1999.

Shearer, Clive. *Practical Continuous Improvement for Professional Services*. Milwaukee: ASQ Quality Press, 1994.

Stamatis, D.H. *The Nuts & Bolts of Reengineering*. Chico: Paton Press LLC, 1997.

Womack, James P. and Daniel T. Jones. *Lean Thinking: Banish Waste and Create Wealth in Your Corporation*. New York: Simon & Schuster, 1996.

CUSTOMER RELATIONS

Barlow, Janelle and Claus Moller. *A Complaint Is a Gift: Using Customer Feedback as a Strategic Tool.* San Francisco: Berrett-Koehler Publishers, 1996.

Carlzon, Jan, *Moments of Truth.* New York: HarperBusiness, 1987.

Guinta, Lawrence R. and Nancy C. Praizler. *The QFD Book: The Team Approach to Solving Problems and Satisfying Customers Through Quality Function Deployment.* New York: AMACOM, 1993.

McQuarrie, Edward F. *Customer Visits: Building a Better Market Focus.* Newbury Park: Sage Publications, 1993.

Nykamp, Melinda. *The Customer Differential: The Complete Guide to Implementing Customer Relationship Management.* New York: AMACOM. 2001.

Reichheld, Frederick F. *The Loyalty Effect: The Hidden Force Behind Growth, Profits, and Lasting Value.* Boston: Harvard Business School Press. 1996.

Simmons, John. "For effective site visits… follow the Z." *Journal for Quality and Participation*, Oct./Nov. 1994.

Timm, Ph.D., Paul R. *Seven Power Strategies for Building Customer Loyalty.* New York: AMACOM, 2001.

Whiteley, Richard and Diane Hessan. *Customer Centered Growth: Five Proven Strategies for Building Competitive Advantage.* Reading: Addison-Wesley Publishing Co., 1996.

KNOWLEDGE

O'Dell, Carla and C. Jackson Grayson, Jr. with Nilly Essaides. *If Only We Knew What We Know: The Transfer of Internal Knowledge and Best Practice.* New York: The Free Press, 1998.

Ruggles, Rudy and Dan Holtshouse. *The Knowledge Advantage: 14 Visionaries Define Marketplace Success in the New Economy.* Dover: Capstone US, 1999.

Stewart, Thomas A. *Intellectual Capital: The Wealth of Organizations.* New York: Doubleday/Currency, 1997.

LEADING

Belasco, James A. and Ralph C. Stayer. *Flight of the Buffalo: Soaring to Excellence, Learning To Let Employees Lead.* New York: Warner Books, 1993.

Hesselbein, Frances and Marshall Goldsmith, Richard Beckhard, editors. *The Leader of the Future.* San Francisco: Jossey-Bass Publishers, 1996

Hesselbein, Frances and Paul M. Cohen, editors. *Leader to Leader.* San Francisco: Jossey-Bass Publishers, 1999.

Hesselbein, Frances, Marshall Goldsmith, and Ian Somerville. *Leading for Innovation and Organizing for Results.* San Francisco: Jossey-Bass Publishers, 2002.

MANUFACTURING

Liker, Jeffrey K., editor. *Becoming Lean: Inside Stories of U.S. Manufacturers.* Portland: Productivity Press, 1998.

Montgomery, Joseph C. and Lawrence O. Levine, editors. *The Transition to Agile Manufacturing: Staying Flexible for Competitive Advantage.* Milwaukee: ASQ Quality Press, 1996.

Peppard, Joe & Philip Rowland. *The Essence of Business Process Re-Engineering.* New York: Prentice Hall, 1995.

ReVelle, Ph.D., Jack B. *Manufacturing Handbook of Best Practices: An Innovation, Productivity, and Quality Focus.* Boca Raton: St. Lucie Press, 2002.

Rother, Mike and Rick Harris. *Creating Continuous Flow: An Action Guide for Manager, Engineers and Production Associates.* Brookline: The Lean Enterprise Institute, 2001.

Schonberger, Richard J., *Let's Fix It! Overcoming the Crisis in Manufacturing.* New York: The Free Press, 2001.

ORGANIZATIONAL CHANGE/IMPROVEMENT

Ashkenas, Ron and Dave Ulrich, Todd Jick, Steve Kerr. *The Boundaryless Organization: Breaking the Chains of Organizational Structure.* San Francisco: Jossey-Bass Publishers, 1995.

Boone, Tonya, Ph.D., and Ram Ganeshan, Ph.D. *New Direction in Supply-Chain Management: Technology, Strategy and Implementation.* New York: AMACOM, 2002.

Cooper, Robin. *When Lean Enterprises Collide: Competing Through Confrontation.* Boston: Harvard Business School Press, 1995.

Goldman, Steven L., Roger N. Hangel and Kenneth Preiss. *Agile Competitors and Virtual Organizations: Strategies for Enriching the Customer.* New York: Van Nostrand Reinhold, 1995.

Hammer, Michael. *The Agenda: What Every Business Must Do To Dominate the Decade.* New York: Crown Business, 2001.

Henderson, Bruce A. and Jorge L. Larco. *Lean Transformation: How To Change Your Business into a Lean Enterprise.* Richmond: The Oaklea Press, 2000.

Hesselbein, Frances and Marshall Goldsmith, Richard Beckhard, editors. *The Organization of the Future.* San Francisco: Jossey-Bass Publishers, 1997.

Kanter, Rosabeth Moss. *World Class: Thriving Locally in the Global Economy.* New York: Touchstone (Simon & Schuster), 1997.

Rackham, Neil, Lawrence Friedman and Richard Ruff. *Getting Partnering Right: How Market Leaders Are Creating Long-Term Competitive Advantage.* New York: McGraw-Hill, 1996.

Schein, Edgar H. *The Corporate Culture Survival Guide: Sense and Nonsense About Culture Change.* San Francisco: Jossey-Bass Publishers, 1999.

Senge, Peter M. *The Fifth Discipline: The Art & Practice of The Learning Organization.* New York: Currency-Doubleday, 1990.

Silverman, Lori L. Critical Shift: *The Future of Quality in Organizational Performance.* Milwaukee: ASQ Quality Press, 1999.

PROJECT MANAGEMENT

Barkley, Bruce T. and James H. Saylor. *Customer-Driven Project Management: Building Quality Into Project Processes.* New York: McGraw-Hill, 2001.

Devaux, Stephen A. *Total Project Control: A Manager's Guide to Integrated Project Planning, Measuring, and Tracking.* New York: John Wiley & Sons Inc., 1999.

Greer, Michael. *The Manager's Pocket Guide to Project Management.* Amherst: HRD Press, 1999.

Kezsbom, Ph.D., and Katherine A. Edward. *The New Dynamic Project Management: Winning Through the Competitive Advantage, Second Edition.* New York: John Wiley & Sons Inc., 2001.

Levine, Harvey A. *Practical Project Management: Tips, Tactics, and Tools.* New York: John Wiley & Sons Inc., 2002.

Lewis, James P. *Mastering Project Management: Applying Advanced Concepts of Systems Thinking, Control and Evaluation, Resource Allocation.* New York: McGraw-Hill, 1998.

_____. *Project Planning Scheduling & Control: A Hands-On Guide to Bringing Projects in on Time and on Budget, Third Edition.* New York: McGraw-Hill, 2001.

Lowenthal, Ph.D., Jeffrey N. *Six Sigma Project Management: A Pocket Guide.* Milwaukee: ASQ Quality Press, 2002.

Martin, Paula and Karen Tate. *Project Management Memory Jogger: A Pocket Guide for Project Teams.* Methuen: GOAL/QPC, 1997.

Verzuh, Eric. *The Fast Forward MBA in Project Management: Quick Tips, Speedy Solutions, Cutting-Edge Ideas.* New York: John Wiley & Sons Inc., 1999.

Wysocki, Robert K. and James P. Lewis. *The World Class Project Manager: A Professional Development Guide.* Cambridge: Perseus Publishing, 2001.

PUBLICATIONS

Industry Week—www.industryweek.com (Penton Media)

Informed Outlook, The—www.informintl.com (co-published by ASQ & INFORM)

Quality Digest—www.qualitydigest.com (QCI International)

Quality Progress—www.asq.org (American Society for Quality)

Six Sigma Forum Magazine—www.asq.org (American Society for Quality)

Target Magazine—www.ame.org (Association of Manufacturing Excellence)

QUALITY MANAGEMENT: GENERAL

Okes, Duke and Russell T. Westcott, co-editors. *The Certified Quality Management Handbook, Second Edition.* Milwaukee: ASQ Quality Press, 2000.

STANDARDS, AWARD CRITERIA, AND IMPLEMENTATION

American Society for Quality, *American National Standard: Quality Management Systems—Guidelines for performance improvements. ANSI/ISO/ASQ Q9004-2000.*

_____. *ISO/TS 16949:2002 Quality Management Systems—Particular requirements for the application of ISO 9001:2000 for automotive production and relevant service part organizations.*

Blazey, Mark L. *Insight to Performance Excellence: An Inside Look at the 2003 Baldrige Award Criteria.* Milwaukee: ASQ Quality Press, 2003.

Cianfrani, Charles A., Joseph J. Tsiakais and John E. West, editors. *The ASQ ISO 9000:2000 Handbook.* Milwaukee: ASQ Quality Press, 2002.

Ketola, Jeanne and Kathy Roberts. *ISO 9000:2000 In a Nutshell, Second Edition.* Chico: Paton Press LLC, 2001.

Monnich Jr., Herbert C. *ISO 9001:2000 for Small- and Medium-Sized Businesses.* Milwaukee: ASQ Quality Press, 2001.

National Institute of Standards and Technology. *2003 Baldrige National Quality Program: Criteria for Performance Excellence* (Business Criteria, Education Criteria, Health Care Criteria). Gaithersburg: NIST. Phone: (301-975-2036), fax: (301-948-3716), e-mail *nqp@nist.gov*, Web *www.quality.nist.gov*.

Peach, Robert W., Bill Peach and Diane S. Ritter. *The Memory Jogger 9000/2000: A Pocket Guide to Implementing the ISO 9001 Quality Systems Standard.* Salem: GOAL/QPC, 2000.

STRATEGIC PLANNING

Cowley, Michael and Ellen Domb. *Beyond Strategic Vision: Effective Corporate Action with Hoshin Planning.* Boston: Butterworth-Heinemann, 1997.

DeFeo, Joseph A. 1999. "Strategic Deployment" in *Juran's Quality Handbook, Fifth Edition* (Joseph M. Juran and A. Blanton Godfrey, co-editors). New York: McGraw-Hill. pp. 13.1-13.23.

Goodstein, Leonard D., Timothy M. Nolan and J. William Pfeiffer. *Applied Strategic Planning: A Comprehensive Guide.* New York: McGraw-Hill, 1993.

Haines, Stephen G. *Strategic and Business Planning: The Systems Thinking Approach.* Amherst: HRD Press, 1999.

Mintzberg, Henry. *The Rise and Fall of Strategic Planning.* New York: The Free Press, 1994.

APPENDIX I

Glossary

A

Action plan—specific plans that respond to short- and long-term strategic objectives. Actions plans typically include persons responsible, steps to be taken, time lines, resources required, and the measurement criteria. An action plan is a simpler type of project plan.

Affinity diagram—a technique/tool for organizing ideas into natural clusters in order to stimulate new and creative ideas.

AIAG—Automotive Industry Action Group

AND—Activity Network Diagram. A type of arrow diagram showing the link between activities.

ANSI—American National Standards Institute

ASQ—American Society for Quality

B

Balanced scorecard—a set of comprehensive performance measures providing a balanced view of an organization, e.g., financial, customers, internal business processes, and learning and growth.

Baldrige criteria—the seven categories that constitute the criteria for performance excellence used for assessing an organization planning to qualify under the Baldrige National Quality Program.

Batch processing—the processing large batches of a single product through the process at one time, usually creating queues awaiting the next step in the process.

Benchmarking—a process for locating, studying, and adapting best practices to improve organizational performance.

Benefit-cost analysis—the ratio or dollar value derived from comparing the cost of implementing an improvement to the value of the benefits received from the improvement.

BNQP—Baldrige National Quality Program

Brainstorming—a technique/tool used to generate a volume of ideas about a particular subject.

C

Calibration—the act of comparing the accuracy of an organization's measuring instrument or system to the known accuracy of an officially certified standard to detect any variation from true value. This can include adjustment of the measured instrument to meet the true value.

Cell—the physical layout of work units and machinery to facilitate operator multitasking and the sequential performance of steps enabling single-piece flow of product.

Chain reaction—W. Edwards Deming's concept that if quality is improved, costs decrease, productivity improves, and more of the market is captured with better quality and lower price, allowing the organization to stay in business and to provide more jobs.

Competence—refers to a person's ability to learn and perform a particular activity. Components of competence include knowledge, experience, skills, aptitude, and attitude (KESAA).

Concurrent engineering—a preventive approach to collaboratively designing a product or service with the various functions that will ultimately produce and deliver the product or service in order to anticipate and deal with potential problems and balance the needs of all functions. Customers and suppliers can sometimes be included.

Constraint—tangible or intangible objects or factors blocking or impeding performance of an activity.

Core competency—the set of capabilities and characteristics that define an organization's uniqueness.

Corrective action—action taken to eliminate the root cause(s) and symptom(s) of a known deviation or nonconformity to prevent recurrence.

Cost of quality—four types of costs pertaining to product or service quality: internal failure costs, external failure costs, appraisal costs, and prevention costs.

Critical path method (CPM)—the use of an arrow diagram tool to show the interrelationships of project or process activities and the time and cost to completion. CPM uses a single estimate.

Culture (organizational)—the values, beliefs, and behaviors inherent within an organization.

Customer relationship management (CRM)—an organizationwide process for acquiring and employing the knowledge of customers' unique requirements, needs, and expectations to build customer loyalty and market share.

Customer segmentation—a process for differentiating customers based on one or more characteristics or dimensions in order to develop marketing strategies specific to each segment.

Cycle time—the time it takes to complete a process from beginning to end.

D

Data—facts presented in descriptive, numeric, or graphic form.

Data mining—a process for examining and analyzing (via a computer program) large databases in search of synergistic relationships, the outputs becoming information for decision making, e.g., targeting markets for new promotions based on purchasing behaviors and demographics.

E

Education—the process of building a person's knowledge base over time. (Contrast with "training.")

Effectiveness—a measure of the achievement of planned activities to planned results.

Efficiency—a measure of the relationship between results achieved and resources used. The ratio of the output to the total input in a process.

Environmental scanning and analysis—the process of monitoring factors from both inside and outside the organization that could affect the long-term viability of the organization.

F

Failure mode and effects analysis (FMEA)—a tool to identify and analyze potential product, service, or process failures, in the design and/or production stages, in order to determine actions to prevent occurrence of failure.

Five S's—five practices for maintaining a clean and efficient workplace (Japanese concept).

Flowchart—a graphical representation of the steps in a process.

Focus group—a group of eight to ten persons invited from a segment of the customer base to discuss an existing or planned product or service and lead by a trained facilitator (usually with predetermined questions). Focus groups can be convened for other purposes as well, e.g., employee opinion or supplier concerns.

G

Gantt chart—a bar-type chart used to depict timelines for process or project steps. (Also see "milestone chart.")

Goal—a higher-level statement of a desired intent or aim, the direction designated by strategic planning. Usually goals are nonquantitative. Goals are supported by quantifiable objectives.

H

House of quality—another name for the quality function deployment chart (see "QFD").

I

Indicator—See "key indicator."

Information—data transformed into an ordered format, making it usable for drawing conclusions and making decisions.

Input—the data, physical object, or activity that is provided to enable a process to occur.

IRR—the discount rate that causes net present value to equal zero.

ISO—a prefix (based on the Greek word "isos") for a series of standards published by the International Organization for Standardization.

J

Just in time (JIT)—the planning for and delivery of a product or service to the place of use at or near the time of use.

K

Kaizen—a Japanese term referring to the continual and gradual improvement of small things. Equivalent to the term "incremental improvement."

Kaizen **blitz/event**—an intense, short time frame, team approach to reduce cycle time and increase throughput.

Kanban—the method whereby a downstream operation or location signals an upstream operation it needs more material, product, or a service to continue a process (also called a "pull" system). The intent is to process only what is needed, when it is needed, thus reducing or eliminating inventory or buffer stock.

KESAA—acronym for knowledge, experience, skills, aptitude and attitude, the components of competency.

Key indicators—those selected factors that when measured and analyzed enable management to make informed decisions to direct the organization in achieving its goals. Key indicators may be leading or lagging indicators.

Knowledge—the meaning derived from examining information. The retention of accumulated and interpreted related information.

Knowledge management—the processes and technology involved in transforming data into knowledge, as well as the processes of acquiring knowledge and the management of the knowledge base. The intent is to make critical knowledge available to those who can best use it to make meaningful decisions and plans.

L

LCALI—acronym for listen, collect, analyze, learn, and improve. A method for capturing, trending, deploying, and utilizing the hidden voices of the customer in order to improve processes and prevent problems.

Lean thinking—the development of plans and approaches for an organization to reduce cycle time and eliminate waste.

Learning organization—an organization whose vision, values, and policies foster among its employees the desire to continue to learn and improve its products, services, processes, and outcomes to create a better future.

LOQSI—acronym for log of quality system improvements. The log in which the return on investment from improvements derived from implementing ISO 9001 or ISO 9004 are documented.

M

Management review—the formal action (meeting) whereby top management reviews and evaluates the status, adequacy, effectiveness, and efficiency of the quality management system in relation to the organization's quality policy, objectives, and requirements of the ISO 9001 standard.

Market segment—a category of a total market comprising customers having similar characteristics and demographics.

Milestone—a point in time when a critical event is to occur; a symbol placed on a Gantt chart to locate the point when a critical event is to occur. A "milestone chart" is a Gantt chart with milestones added, and usually with symbols depicting actual times when events or activities took place superimposed on the planned timelines.

Mission statement—an explanation of the purpose or reasons for existing as an organization; a definition of the scope of the business.

Monument—the point of time, object, or place within a process which necessitates that a product must wait in a queue before further processing; a barrier to continuous flow.

N

NIST—National Institute of Standards and Technology

NOAC—Next operation as customer (internal provider-receiver relationship)

Nonconformance—an item, action, or condition that fails to conform to a requirement (also "defect" or "nonconformity").

Nonvalue added—tasks or activities that can be eliminated with no effect on product or service functionality, performance, or quality as perceived by the customer.

NPV—net present value; the discounted cash flow technique for finding the present value of each future year's cash flow.

O

Objective—a quantitative statement of future expectations with indication of when the expectations should be achieved; an objective flows from goals and serves to clarify what people must accomplish.

Outcome—the quantitative statement of the result of organizational activities and outputs.

Output—the result of an activity or process completion.

P

Pareto chart—a tool used to rank causes from most frequent/significant to least frequent/ significant. Vertical bars represent the magnitude of the frequency or significance.

Payback period—the number of years required for the project or capital investment to recover the investment from net cash flows.

PDCA—plan-do-check-act (also referred to as the "Shewhart cycle," for Walter A. Shewhart, the concept's originator, and also the "Deming cycle," named for W. Edwards Deming because he introduced the concept in Japan).

PDSA cycle—plan-do-study-act (a variation of PDCA)

PERT—program evaluation and review technique; an arrow-diagramming technique used to identify project events and compute the critical path needed to complete the project. The tool provides three time estimates: optimistic, most likely, and pessimistic.

Poka-yoke—the Japanese term for mistake/error-proofing a process by building in safe-guards to prevent errors or immediately find errors.

Preventive action—an action taken to eliminate potential causes of a nonconformance, defect, or other undesirable situation in order to prevent its occurrence.

Process—the set of interrelated activities that transforms inputs into outputs.

Process map—a tool used to flowchart a work process in detail, including key measurements and responsibilities.

Process reengineering—a breakthrough strategy used to rethink and restructure a process (the "clean sheet of paper approach").

Product—the tangible or intangible output of a process (usually includes "services").

Q

QFD—quality function deployment is a structured methodology in which customer requirements are translated into appropriate technical requirements for each stage of product development and production. "Deployment" refers to the cascading of these requirements downward through the organization, through a series of interrelated matrices. QFD is also referred to as listening to the voice of the customer and also called "house of quality."

QLA—a quality level agreement is a tool for identifying key outputs/deliverables from an internal provider to an internal receiver/customer. A QLA documents the requirements of the receiver, the metrics by which delivery will be measured, and those responsible for the quality level. The use of the tool follows the concept of NOAC and assumes fulfillment of the agreements will be monitored and corrective action taken as needed. (Also called SLAs—service level agreements.)

Quality principles—rules or concepts that an organization believes in collectively. The principles are formulated by senior management with input from others and are communicated and understood at every level of the organization.

R

Reengineering—(see process reengineering)

Resource requirements matrix (RRM)—a tool to relate the resources required to the project tasks requiring them (e.g., resources such as number and types of individuals needed, material needed, subcontractors needed).

Risk assessment and management—the process of identifying what risks might be present in a situation, determining the potential impact of such risks, and what actions would be necessary to mediate or eliminate the risks.

ROA/RONA—a measurement of the return on assets (or net assets) to determine the earning power of the organization's investment in assets.

ROI—a measurement of the return on investment when an organization invests in new equipment, improvement projects, or other activities (e.g., training). Variations include: ROQ (quality) I, ROT (training) I, ROP (project) I.

S

SIPOC—acronym standing for supplier, input, process, output, customer; a macro-level model used to analyze processes.

Six Sigma—a measure relating to the standard deviation of a process; a quality philosophy; a collection of techniques and tools used in reducing variation in a process; or a program of improvement.

Stakeholder—people, departments, work units, and organizations that have an investment or interest in the success or actions taken by the organization (e.g., employees, customers, supplier, investors, owners, community).

Strategic planning—a process to establish an organization's long-range direction and goals, objectives to achieve the goals and actions needed to reach the goals.

Supplier—a provider of goods and services that may be used at any stage in design, production, and delivery of an organization's product and services (e.g., raw material producers, distributors, dealers, repair services, transportation contractors, or subcontractors of outsourced processing services).

Supply chain—the identified series of processes and organizations that are involved in producing and delivering a product to an end-user.

SWOT analysis—an assessment of an organization's strengths, weaknesses, opportunities, and threats.

T

Takt time—the available production time divided by the rate of customer demand. The measure for setting the pace of production to customer demand.

Theory of constraints (TOC)—Eliyahu Goldratt's theory deals with techniques and tools for identifying and eliminating the constraints (i.e., bottlenecks or barriers) in a process.

Total productive maintenance (TPM)—a process for reducing and eliminating equipment failure, setup and adjustment, minor stops, reduced speed, product rework, and scrap.

Total quality management (TQM)—A process for applying quality principles to integrate all functions and processes of an organization to achieve the goal of customer satisfaction through continual improvement. The term "TQM" has been misused to represent a fragmented, poorly planned, and nonintegrated approach.

Training—the measurable skills employees require to perform or improve the performances of their present tasks or jobs, or the process of providing those skills. Contrast with "education."

V

Variation—a change in data, a characteristic, or a function that is caused by common causes, special causes, tampering, or structured variation.

Vision—a statement that briefly outlines what an organization wants to become and what it hopes to achieve.

Voice of the customer—the needs, wants, and perceptions of customers heard and acted upon by the organization. See "QFD" and "LCALI."

W

Waste—activities that consume resources but add no value.

Wisdom—the culmination of the continuum from data to information to knowledge to wisdom.

Work breakdown structure (WBS)—a project planning tool by which a project is divided into task, subtasks, and units of work to be performed.

Work environment—the context and conditions in which a worker performs his or her assigned tasks; the factors affecting a worker (e.g., organizational culture, processes and systems, supervisory practices and style of management, union-management relations, organizational structure, polices, rules, regulations, workmanship standards, equipment, facilities, supplies and materials, tools, budgets, compensation and benefits, peer pressure, and external pressures).

World-class—a term used to indicate the highest standard of excellence; the best of the best.

APPENDIX J

About the Author

Russell T. Westcott is president of R.T. Westcott & Associates, a consulting firm headquartered in Old Saybrook, Connecticut, that assists clients with strategic planning, the ISO 9001/ISO 9004 quality management system implementation and registration process, the application of lean manufacturing and benchmarking as well as qualifying under Baldrige-type criteria. He's a Fellow of the American Society for Quality (ASQ) and an ASQ-Certified Quality Auditor and Certified Quality Manager and serves on several committees of ASQ's Quality Management Division. A frequent speaker on quality topics and a Certified Quality Manager refresher course instructor; Westcott is also co-author of the *ASQ Certified Quality Manager Section Refresher Course* and co-editor of both the *Certified Quality Manager Handbook* and the *Quality Improvement Handbook*. He serves on the ISO 9004 Subteam No. 6 (under the U.S. TAG's ISO 9001/4 Product Support Initiative). He can be contacted by e-mail at *russwest@snet.net*.

INDEX